# Murder, the Media, and the Politics of Public Feelings

# Murder, the Media, and the Politics of Public Feelings

*Remembering Matthew Shepard and James Byrd Jr.*

Jennifer Petersen

INDIANA UNIVERSITY PRESS

*Bloomington & Indianapolis*

This book is a publication of
Indiana University Press
601 North Morton Street
Bloomington, Indiana 47404-3797

iupress.indiana.edu

*Telephone orders*    800-842-6796
*Fax orders*          812-855-7931
*Orders by e-mail*    iuporder@indiana.edu

© 2011 by Jennifer Petersen

MANUFACTURED IN THE UNITED STATES OF AMERICA

**Library of Congress Cataloging-in-Publication Data**

Peterson, Jennifer, [date]-
Murder, the media, and the politics of public feelings : remembering Matthew Shepard and James Byrd Jr. / Jennifer Petersen.
p. cm.
  Includes bibliographical references and index.
  ISBN 978-0-253-35659-8 (cloth : alk. paper)—ISBN 978-0-253-22339-5 (pbk. : alk. paper)  1.  Hate crimes—United States—Public opinion. 2. Shepard, Matthew, d. 1998 3. Byrd, James, d. 1998 4. Gays—United States—Crimes against. 5. African Americans—Crimes against. 6. Mass media and public opinion—United States. 7. Mass media and gays—United States. 8. Mass media and race relations—United States. 9. Mass media—United States—Influence. I. Title.
  HV6773.52.P48 2011
  070.4'493641523—dc22
                                2011004521
        1 2 3 4 5 16 15 14 13 12 11

# Contents

# Acknowledgments

I could not have completed this project without the assistance, support, and wisdom of many people. First I want to thank all of the individuals who were willing to be interviewed. Their time and willingness to speak to me about the activism, politics, and history of the passage of the Laramie Bias Crimes ordinance and the James Byrd Jr. Hate Crimes Act made this project possible. To Jeanne Hurd, I extend extra thanks for her generosity and trust in loaning me her records of the Laramie Coalition's efforts to get the city council to first consider and then pass a city bias crimes ordinance. This help was invaluable in putting together the history of both the activism around the law and the passage of the Laramie Bias Crimes Ordinance. In addition to the participation and assistance of those I interviewed, I want to thank the institutions that have supported this project. The University of Texas at Austin's Continuing Fellowship supported a year of research and writing. At the University of Virginia, the Professors as Writers fellowship and research grants have supported additional research, writing, and editing.

Many readers have offered assistance and direction along the way in this project. I am indebted to Laura Stein, John Downing, Dana Cloud, Michael Kackman, and David Philips. They gave me the tools and guidance I needed to complete the project as well as suggestions on making it a stronger book. I hope I have done justice to their input and that I live up to their examples as scholars. I also want to thank my editor and the reviewers at Indiana University Press, whose comments and suggestions helped me situate the project and clarify my contributions.

In addition, two wonderful writing groups have given me sustenance along the way. In Austin, Kyle Barnett, Chris Lucas, Afsheen Nomai, Allison Perlman, and Avi Santo read early drafts of multiple chapters. Their support, comments, and keen eye for compelling detail helped give shape to the project; they often helped me to see and focus on what was best in the project. From structural advice to literary detail, their reading has improved the project. They also gave me a regular appointment for outstanding conversation and dinners to look forward to throughout the writing process. Thanks to Allison as well for rereading and commenting on later drafts of several of these chapters. I deeply appreciate her unflagging support for the project, and I continue to benefit from her intellectual community and friendship. In Charlottesville, Yarimar Bonilla and Simone Polillo have been generous readers and friends. Their questions and comments have helped me to hone my argument and clarify chapters. Their company has made me feel at home in Charlottesville. I want to thank my family for all their support over the years, and their continuing interest in my work. In particular, I am grateful to my parents for providing examples and encouragement to pursue a vocation that provides challenge and passion. And finally, to Hector Amaya, who has been my most tireless reader and my closest companion, my deepest thank you for everything you have given me.

**Murder, the Media,
and the Politics
of Public Feelings**

# **[ *Introduction* ]**

## **Media, Emotion, and the Public Sphere**

IN THE LATE EVENING of Saturday, June 6, 1998, in Jasper, Texas, three young white men in a pickup truck offered a ride to James Byrd Jr., a middle-aged black man who was walking home from his niece's bridal shower. The men shared beers and cigarettes with Byrd as they drove, before stopping along a remote stretch of road. There, they beat Byrd before tying him by the feet to the back of the pickup truck and dragging him for 2 ½ miles and then leaving his decapitated body by the side of the road near a predominantly black church. According to forensic evidence that would become important to officials seeking capital punishment for his killers, Byrd was alive and conscious for part of this ride. The manner of Byrd's death and the placement of his body in a black neighborhood, so near the church, led the police to treat the murder as a hate crime.

Just four months later, Matthew Shepard, a college student at the University of Wyoming, was horribly beaten and left to die. Shepard met his killers, Russell Henderson and Aaron McKinney, in a downtown bar on Tuesday, October 6. They left together. Henderson and McKinney drove Shepard to the outskirts of town. They took his wallet and shoes and tied him to a fence, where they kicked him, taunted him, and beat him unconscious with the butt of a pistol. Then they left him tied to the fence in the cold, though not yet freezing, night. He was found 18 hours later by a mountain biker who said he initially thought Shepard's seemingly lifeless form, crumpled on the ground, was a scarecrow—a comparison that would be much cited in the coverage and cultural imagery of Shepard's murder. Shepard was airlifted to a hospital in Colorado, where he lingered in a coma for five days before passing away.

Both murders clearly marked the failure of liberal political ideals. They also spurred highly mediated national outrage, mourning, and discussion. Both murders were covered extensively in the national news. This coverage frequently conveyed expressions of shock, indignation, and grief, which became the basis for vigils and demonstrations, focusing public interest on the murders and the issues of homophobia and racism. It was arguably the passionate tenor of the media coverage that garnered such interest and pulled people into discussion and action. The particulars of this passionate discourse illuminate the politics of public feelings: the ways that expressions of feeling become political, shaping political action.

The immediate responses were varied, ranging from local demonstrations to national vigils. In each community, expressions of shock, dismay, and disbelief took a similar form: "We don't raise children like that here." Yet in each case the killers were young local men, a fact that challenged the communities' civic identities. These expressions of shock were joined by political demonstrations. In Jasper, a local chapter of the KKK marched through the streets, to be met by a black militia from Houston calling themselves the "New Black Panthers." Locals tried to emphasize racial cooperation, forming a committee to address racial tensions exacerbated by the murder. In Laramie, the homecoming parade turned into a vigil and protest march, with residents marching behind a banner for Matthew Shepard. The football team, along with other university sports teams, donned the green and yellow symbols of peace offered by the campus multicultural and lesbian, gay, bisexual, and transgender organizations. People from across the country and beyond sent flowers, money, and e-mail to the hospital where Shepard lay dying. Nationally, he was memorialized in a star-studded service that brought thousands to the National Mall in Washington, D.C. Smaller vigils took place in communities around the country. As is the case with many moments of public violence, the responses to these murders were full of feeling. This feeling was apparent in the fact that people gathered in the streets and in the energy that went into the various ways the murders were documented, explained, and reimagined in multiple places.

This outpouring of feeling cannot be explained solely by the brutality of the attacks. Sadly, these murders were not the only, or even the most brutal, crimes committed against gay and black men and women in 1998. The murders of Byrd and Shepard, however, were the most mediated, circulated, and condensed into various media narratives. As highly mediated events, reactions to and ramifications from the murders have echoed for years in national and local social life. Each man's death has echoed through popular culture texts, from music to visual art to commercial media texts. This uptake in popular texts was not equal, however. Several books document the aftermath of the murder of James Byrd Jr. in Jasper. Showtime and PBS dramatized and documented the murder and its aftermath. Shepard's figure took on even greater visibility in popular culture. He was memorialized in more than 50 songs; Melissa Etheridge and Elton John were some of the most famous musicians to compose songs protesting his death.[1] The play *The Laramie Project* dramatized the murder and its implications for many before HBO brought a televised version to 30 million viewers. There are too many memorial websites to count. Byrd's death, while it certainly has not receded from public memory, has not been so visibly memorialized, taken up, circulated, and remembered in the media. This fact alone asks us to think about the politics of who we remember, who we are asked to feel for, and how.

There were also ramifications within institutional politics, from the Byrd family's dissatisfaction with Texas governor George W. Bush, publicized during his first run for president, to efforts to include violence based on sexuality in federal hate crime law. Bush went on to become president, and the federal hate crime law was not amended at the time, but three years after the murders, hate crimes laws were passed in Texas at the state level and in Laramie as a city ordinance. Eleven years later, federal legislation carrying the names of both Shepard and Byrd amended federal hate crimes laws to include violence based in sexual orientation and gender identity. The passage of the local measures in Laramie and Texas, arguably socially conservative locales, forms an interesting story of cultural politics, publicity, and the political productivity of emotion. This story and the details of how these two murders came to matter so intensely to so many are the subject of this book. The particularities of the national mourning of each man and the political and legislative responses to the murders offer insights into the politics and power, both cultural and institutional, of public expressions of emotion.

The plethora of political and activist responses to these murders inspires this project. I focus here on the mobilizing impact of the feelings deployed in response to the murders. Other scholars have pointed out the de-politicizing elements of the public discourse surrounding the murders of these two men. This scholarship has noted the way that individualizing and scapegoating rhetorics in the national media coverage absolved individuals and national institutions (such as the law) from responsibility for the crimes or implications in the larger social problems of racism and homophobia.[2] Likewise, cultural critics were concerned that the attack on Byrd might overshadow other, more common examples of racial inequity and oppression. Others have noted that the national attention to Matthew Shepard's death worked against more radical queer politics, for example, by focusing on violence rather than other forms of oppression. Some have suggested that by creating such a white, middle-class, middle-American face for gay rights claims, the public focus on Shepard worked to entwine gay and lesbian rights politics with exclusionary discourses of whiteness and bourgeois respectability.[3] These are compelling critiques of the national fascination with the violence visited upon these men. These critiques, however, do not capture the full range of implications of this fascination. For one, they are all limited to the ideological impact of media at the level of the nation. And the impact of media discourse is not uniform. A closer look at how this media discourse was taken up on the ground in local settings shows quite different responses. The national media discourse hailed locals (those living in Jasper and Laramie) differently than the national audience. This different address led to different emotional politics and to mobilization; often what at the national level looked like a rhetoric of absolution and avoidance became at the local level mobilizing, the source of political urgency. Performing only a textual, top-down analysis will not shed light on all the various impacts or emotional politics of media texts. Here, I use interviews and analysis of local media (both letters to the editor and articles in local newspapers) to demonstrate not only the divergent meanings of national news at the local level but also the divergent emotional, ethical, and political impact, the way that media texts helped to construct relations between people and distant events and others.

Through these relationships, strangers came together to form publics; that is, they came to see themselves as part of a larger group of people united by a common interest in the murders through these texts. The fact that such publics formed and even demanded political–legal changes from various levels of government provides the central concern of this book. In each case, publics formed around expressions of feeling. These publics, in fact, were the active and legislatively minded publics prized by political and media scholars as signs of a functioning democracy. In the media coverage of these murders, emotional discourse performed the various functions typically associated with rational dialogue. For this reason, these cases compel a closer attention to how media communication actually functions within democratic politics. The cases demonstrate that emotion in media is not necessarily privatizing (turning structural and political issues into personal, moral concerns) or the opposite of politically oriented action, as many fear.

It is common in academic as well as popular discourse to assume that expressions of emotion in politics take attention away from matters of policy, diverting them into issues of personality, character, and morality, and directs energy toward the self rather than toward action in the social world.[4] It is true that emotional discourse can recast structural issues as issues of morality and private character.[5] However, in the mediation of the murders of Byrd and Shepard, emotion can be seen to do something quite different. It worked to articulate the murders as matters of public discussion, mobilizing and endorsing action aimed at policy issues. What might have been moments of private feeling became glaring examples of structural inequity and, at least for some, the failures of justice and political institutions. This impact was particularly striking at the local level, where the emotional tenor of media texts provided the grounds for the formation of lobby groups and arguments for legislative action. The public reactions to these murders make a strong case for recognizing the emotional work done by media and attempting to rethink models of democratic communication and the public sphere to account for this work.[6]

In this book, I offer an analysis of the deployment and productivity of feelings in the wake of these murders that acknowledges feelings as investments in and ties to exclusionary discourses without reducing the political productivity of feelings to these investments. I trace the affective politics of the media coverage of each murder, with a particular focus on how specific feelings and imagined relations between the men and media audiences were constructed, offering an analysis of the structural reasons for the deployment of specific feelings in each case. I also show how this emotional discourse made its way into the text of the law, the institution that acts as the legitimating foundation for liberal democracies. Feelings became the basis for public formation and provided the discursive grounds of necessity for legislative action. In detailing this work, I hope to do several things: demonstrate that affect and emotion are central to political speech and decision making; provide critical tools for evaluating public deployments of feelings; and supplement contemporary theories of the public sphere and the norms of democratic communication that are supposed to take place within it.

My analysis of the emotional mediation of these murders engages with longstanding conversations about the role of media on democracy and political communication more generally. The book moves beyond attention to the cultural politics of emotion to highlight the impact of emotion (through media) on formal, institutional politics. My study traces this impact in the political bodies that passed hate crimes laws in Laramie and in Texas. I focus on these cases in part because of the way each linked affect to political-legal action and in part because they were each deeply enmeshed in discussions of racism and homophobia, two ongoing sites of inequality and social contradiction within contemporary political and social life. The media texts covering these cases encouraged emotion; this emotion was taken up by publics across the nation, though most clearly and effectively by local publics. The way that emotion was encouraged both tells about the social structure and concerns of a particular historical moment and directs political and ethical responses. The political actions that this emotional discourse authorized are instructive sites for exploring the relations between mediated expressions of feeling and legislative institutions. Both murders raised questions about the equality in life and law in the contemporary United States. And both gave rise to emotive publics, some of which directed their energies to policy change.

The public discussions surrounding both murders provide examples of how deeply bonds of affiliation and need enter into public discourse and policymaking. In the circulation of images, narratives, and explanations for the murders, emotions and affiliations were particularly visible—and ultimately politically productive, in that they played so central a role in the passage of laws. The productivity of these cases challenge instrumental conceptions of the role of public communication in political and legal processes and suggest that more affective sides of communication should be taken into account in prescriptions about political communication, which are largely steeped in the language of proceduralism, rationality, neutrality, and disinterest. In order to do so, this book brings together work on media and the public sphere and work on the cultural politics of emotion and the expressive and poetic aspects of communication. The former investigate the institutions, norms, and practices that structure the ability of individuals to speak and listen to one another, engage in political discussion, and make demands on the political institutions of the state. They offer a sustained analysis of how well the infrastructure and norms of communication in public life mesh with the ideals and needs of democracy. The latter offer a compelling argument on the aesthetics of communication and the various impacts of feeling, sensation, and sentiment in cultural life and politics. The book brings together these two sets of work to investigate the deployment of feeling as political discourse. In doing so, the book demonstrates that the politics of feeling extend beyond the cultural, into sites of institutional politics; it also shows the importance and consequences of the emotional work of the media—what I call *emotional mediation*—and the important contributions that media studies and communication scholarship can make in unpacking the structure and implications of this mediation.

## Public Feelings and Political Institutions

The language of proceduralism and disinterest has been influential in scholarship on media and formal, institutional politics and discussions of media as an organ of the public sphere. Democratic communication, or the processes of communication required in order to have a well-functioning and inclusive democracy, is often characterized normatively as a process of consensus building via informed, rational dialogue.[7] Good politics are judged by their adherence to this norm of rational, critical, and dispassionate debate. It is taken for granted in much media scholarship, policy, and reform movements that good democratic communication should be defined in terms of rationality, education, and engagement. The majority of policy proposals and media reform efforts follow this line of thinking, focusing on different strategies for improving the reasoning capacity and informational resources of citizens. For instance, many activist programs aimed at more democratic media focus on either filling the media with better information or providing better citizen access to media.[8] This is, in part, based upon the liberal interest in rational, civil ideals of citizenship and democracy: the deliberating public over the rowdy crowd. Many of the current debates about infotainment, the translation of serious events into talk show format or docudrama, are at heart concerns about the loss of sober, rational discourse. They are concerns that this translation inherently trivializes issues, turns matters of public concern into spectacle and/or issues of personality, taste, or morals, decreasing the possibilities for reasoned self-governance.[9]

These debates are based on the assumption of a dichotomous divide between reason and emotion or, more broadly, affect (a term that encompasses not only the nameable emotions but also more amorphous dispositions and sensations). Emotion and affect are often considered problems in political theory and practice.[10] If rational deliberation is the heart of democratic politics and emotion is its opposite, it follows that emotion is either outside the realm of political deliberation or something to be suppressed as antithetical to rational critique. Within liberal political theory, reason and impartiality have been seen as the route to universality and equality: bodies, needs, and emotions are the location of particularity, which pulls us apart, whereas reason (as the opposite of all of these) can bring divergent people together.[11] Rationality and impartiality allow for critical distance and reciprocal turn taking. Too much emotion, or too much attachment, gets in the way of deliberation as the proper mode of communication and reasoning among citizens: with too much emotion, we are immersed in subjectivity and our own interests (attachments) or act as an irrational crowd.[12]

The cases I examine—the public discussion of James Byrd Jr. and Matthew Shepard—however, trouble a uniform dismissal of affect as antidemocratic, irrational, or even always conservative. Affective discourse may sometimes get in the way of critical reflection, but this is far from always true. It may at times be immobilizing, obscuring politics and quashing critique, but that is not always the case. The murders of these two men became, through the form and magnitude of public attention, moments of intense public discussion and scrutiny, the genesis for formation of active publics, in addition to moments of personal loss. The ways in which the murders of these two men entered into public discourse had much to do with how they were connected to larger issues of race, sexuality, and liberal ideals. In this, the discussion engaged analyses of political principles. I do not want to suggest that the discussions or outcomes of these discussions were utopian moments or exemplars of good politics. They were, however, expressly political and concerned with questions of equity and social justice; as such they were not examples of privatization or of purely conservative politics. I also do not intend to valorize affective discourse as a privileged mode of political discussion. Rather, I wish to suggest ways of analyzing and critically evaluating affective discourse—understanding it as a component of political communication and making room for it in our normative models of democratic communication in the public sphere. I also want to suggest that rationality alone (that is, defined in opposition to emotion) is not a sufficient measure by which to judge the contemporary highly mediated public sphere.

There are, of course, good reasons for the focus on rationality as a discursive norm for politics. The impetus behind critical and activist desires to promote more sober and educational media discourse, and more rational publics, is nicely encapsulated by Jürgen Habermas's critical articulation of the public sphere. The concept of the public sphere defines the way that media, and public communication in general, are expected to work within liberal democratic societies. It is the virtual social "space" where ideas are exchanged, public opinion is formed, and from which citizens can make demands on the state. As such, a functioning public sphere is a basic requirement for the legitimacy of Western liberal democracies. As articulated by Habermas, the public sphere is ideally a venue (or, in later works, multiple overlapping venues) for rational-critical dialogue and the formation of informed public opinion necessary for democratic self-governance.[13] Habermas's articulation is not an invention but a distillation of the communicative norms underlying the foundation of liberal democracies in Western Europe and North America beginning in the eighteenth century. Nor is the Habermasian vision the only articulation of the public sphere. It is, however, the most influential. Despite years of critique, this model retains a deep hold on discussions of media and politics.[14] No doubt one of the reasons that his articulation has had greater influence and a deeper hold in Western European and American debates than other conceptions of the public sphere (for example, Hannah Arendt's more dramaturgical public sphere) is the fact that Habermas's version is so deeply embedded in the liberal political philosophy that dominates much of these countries' political discourse.

One reason the public sphere has been influential in media studies is that the public sphere, particularly the liberal-Habermasian articulation, provides a model for the intersection of media and politics. The model of the public sphere highlights the importance of media for formal, institutional politics, and it provides normative criteria for evaluating the politics of media communication. The liberal-Habermasian definition has been an important tool for media scholars to analyze the content of media and the political economy of media institutions, and it has been a tool for political theorists to think about communication and media. The public sphere, as a normative vision, valorizes rational discourse as the best venue for self-governance; it prizes the turn-taking and deliberative rules (proceduralism) of rational talk, the promise of the universal capability of reason as a tool for evaluating arguments and political rhetoric.[15] For Habermas, this very rationality is what makes the public sphere open (anyone may use reason) and what gives the discursive content of the public sphere its political potential: namely, rational discourse allows for the transcendence of personal interests in the name of critical evaluation.[16] The norm of rationality offers a sort of level playing field. Not everyone has the money, power, and access to put forth beautiful messages in commercially driven media, but everyone has the ability to reason and critique. When the critical evaluation of political claims via reason recedes, the legitimacy of democratic governance becomes more difficult to assess: it becomes harder to discern whether we are actually self-governing or merely assenting to the private interests of those who have access to commercially driven media.

This norm of rationality offers, in many ways, an important ideal. However, a narrow focus on rationality also vastly limits what may be considered legitimate political discourse—and in doing so, it misses out on some key sites and workings of political communication. Quite simply and empirically, the rationalist focus, dictated by the rationalist focus of most liberal political theory,[17] does not and cannot account for many of the things that we do when we communicate, either interpersonally or on a mass scale via media. It cannot account for many of the elements of communication that drive politics, for good and for bad. Conceptually, it separates rationality from aesthetics, sensation, and affect, losing sight of the fact that we can reason and feel at the same time. In practice, it tends to reduce the function of mass communication to that of information sharing, ignoring the more poetic and constructive elements of communication (and their political implications). My project seeks to go beyond this instrumental conception of communication, yet to remain engaged with the institutional workings of politics.

My analysis of the news coverage of the murders of Byrd and Shepard focuses more on issues of identification, community formation, and references to feelings than on the who, what, when, where, and why. These five pillars of journalism are important aspects of news, but I seek to highlight the ethical and emotional work performed by news coverage. This builds upon communication scholarship and feminist political theory that has pointed out communication is never only about information exchange but also about recognition, the construction of "imagined community," and the projection of a shared world.[18] Such attention to the poetic and performative aspects of communication acknowledges media as not only conduits of information but also as creative forces, projecting and mapping the world and constructing (imagined) relationships among strangers, as well as the more intimate sensations and feelings associated with those relationships. In analyzing the news coverage of the murders of Byrd and Shepard, I track the way news texts constructed imagined relationships to the men (and their communities), presented and invited feelings for and about the men, and placed the murders within broader cultural and emotional contexts. I ask how these more affective elements of communication encourage or discourage the formation of publics and produce or disable political will and mobilization. In its concern with the way media produces social relations and political will, the project falls within discussions of the ethics of mediation as well as within discussions of the public sphere and public feelings.[19]

## WHY EMOTION?

Understanding the way that mediation structures relationships among strangers sheds light on the conditions of possibility for politics and public formation. These relationships define who is imaginable as "one of us" in the reflexive moment of public subjectivity that constitutes public formation.[20] The formation of publics, or the ability of strangers to organize and form what is known as "public opinion" and make demands on the state (or, increasingly, non-state institutions), is always a question of how people are able to see themselves as simultaneously private individuals and public, mass subjects—to experience themselves and their engagement as part of an imagined social collectivity or body. The experience of these relationships exceeds the language of rational-critical debate; it is richer and more affective than this model will allow. The insufficiency of this language is particularly compelling and evident when applied to the persistent inequalities that surround the discursive formations of race, gender, and sexuality. The language of rationality is simply insufficient to describe the experiences of identity and of raced, gendered, and classed exclusions, much less the manifestations of community and violence in political life in the United States.[21] In order to understand these failures, we need to better understand how relationships, especially those imagined relationships with others that define the possibility of public formation, are structured and lived, how the boundaries of who we can imagine to be close to, who is conceivable as lovable and mournable, are formed and maintained. Projects of social justice must take into account the way that affective relations draw boundaries and direct action. And the circulation of images and narratives in media texts goes far toward sketching these boundaries.

In employing the language of affect and emotion, a few definitions are in order. By *affect* I mean to include these feelings and the more tenuous and less nameable sensations and attachments (desires, aversions, felt proximities and distances) that orient us toward others and objects in our world. *Emotions* refer to categorizable sentiments with labels such as happy, sad, and frutrated. I use the term *feelings* interchangeably with affect.[22] Whereas some scholars draw a strong line between emotions (as cognitive) and affect (as physical and precognitive), I am not invested in whether feelings are cognitive or not. Whether or not a feeling is driven by deep drives or by cognitive processes and judgments, its direction and expression will be shaped by culture and discourse. It is the social and discursive character of affects and emotions that interests me here; my level of analysis is, after all, the social and not the individual.[23]

Understanding affect as a part of politics, and the way that the circulation of media texts asks us to feel relationships to others is a necessary component to understanding the political role and impact of media. Roger Silverstone suggests that within a highly geographically dispersed and mediated world, the media provide the only "public" or shared space: a space of appearance.[24] The conditions of appearance in the media provide our orientations toward the world and the others in it. The media provide both a phenomenological and an ethical map of the world, especially of the world beyond our doorsteps. The media may provide a space of appearance, but the import and ethical character of this appearance cannot be described without affect. Sara Ahmed uses the term *orientation* to describe how affect directs and motivates;[25] the media, rather than offering us windows on the world, can be seen as orienting us toward and within the world. Per Ahmed, affect or emotion is always relational: it is produced by and defines our interactions with others. The lived reality and political effects of these imagined relationships must be described with a rich critical language that takes into account the affective dimensions of relationships. The affective dimensions of such relationships are often associated with the private realm of personal experience and interpersonal interaction, although our imagined relationships with strangers are never derived only from immediate experience—they are always also highly mass mediated, informed by texts, images, and narratives emanating from the many mass-produced pages and screens that surround us. As such, these relationships and feelings are public issues, not private ones. It is a key tenet of this book that one of the most important political functions of the media is not the capacity of media texts to convey information but the way these texts and their circulation project or invite felt proximities, distances, desires, disgust, and disconnections.

## The Politics and Productivity of Feelings

Models of politics and the public sphere that favor critical distance over proximity, immersion, and emotion have a particularly gendered genealogy. While I do not doubt the benefits of reflection and critical distance, I am suspicious of the wholesale denigration of proximity and feeling (as the opposite of critical reflection). The bifurcation of rationality and emotionality is deeply entwined with that of masculine and feminine. The contributions of feminist political and moral theory and those strains of queer theory and politics that place sexuality, the body, and feeling as ways of being publicly political in particular suggest the importance of thinking through public feelings as a valid part of political action and communication. The privileging of distance favors masculine and heteronormative ways of performing publicity and also is at odds with the ethical and political project of establishing connections between people.[26]

The very definition of what constitutes reasoned dialogue is based upon gendered dichotomies between public and private and reason and emotion. There is a strong cultural construction of communication in gendered terms, as numerous pop-cultural discussions and publications attest (think *Men Are From Mars, Women Are From Venus* and its ilk). Within this construction, reasoned deliberation is a masculine practice, whereas feminine communication takes on empathetic or melodramatic form. Thus impartiality and political reasoning are defined in terms of rhetorics and performances associated with modern notions of masculinity, while femininity is associated with what Michael Warner has called "a language of private feeling."[27] Hence the avoidance of emotion, or its dismissal as "bad thinking," in discussions of institutional politics and the media is a result of the stigmatization of emotion as gendered and private, personal, even frivolous. This dichotomy is, of course, also steeped in histories of race. The performance of impartiality and reason is defined in terms of Eurocentric whiteness (and the ability to seem neutral or disinterested is more available to white men than to black and other minority men). The symbolic association of whiteness with mastery of feelings and abstraction and blackness with passions, particularity, and physicality (within the Cartesian mind-body dualism) constructs reason and impartiality within the terms that define whiteness.[28]

It is important to note that in all of this, disinterest is a performance as much as any theatrical display of emotion—a highly racialized and gendered one at that—yet we are less likely to see it as such, due to cultural constructions of emotion and reason as binary. The fact that displays of disinterest articulated through masculinity and whiteness are not legible as performance or as a type of political emotion is symptomatic of the politics of embodiment. The ability of white men of certain class positions to represent a broad public has to do with the invisibility of the particularity of their bodies, an effect of power and social hierarchies.[29] This has meant that speakers in positions of greater social status (namely, white, middle to upper class, masculine) have been more able than others to convince us that they are able to divorce their arguments from their particular ideological and material interests as well as from their bodies. Not only the bodies but also the very forms of speech and participation associated with people of lower social status (for example, women, ethnic minorities, immigrants, sexual minorities, the poor) become "marked" as particular. These modes of speech and participation become devalued, as outside of the ideal of rational and disinterested discourse. In this way, as Nancy Fraser famously points out, the content and forms of speech valued in the public sphere mirror the hierarchies found in the material social organization of any given society.[30] Hence cultural definitions of race, gender, and sexuality in terms of particularity have effectively sidelined women and people of color, and queer and classed modes of speech, from full participation in the public sphere.

The above distinctions and marginalizations rest on the dichotomous opposition of reason and emotion. Yet the notion that there is a strong divide between reason and emotion is currently being eroded by scholarship in the humanities, social sciences, and biological sciences, as well as in interdisciplinary work on public feelings and the social history of emotions.[31] Indeed, the reason-emotion divide is a relatively recent idea, a historical and ideological remnant, based in the mind-body split of Descartes and in the rise of a new notion of politics and political action rooted in modern ideas of manly activity and the suppression of passion in the seventeenth through nineteenth centuries.[32] Increasingly, academic scholarship, if not popular discourse, recognizes that affect/emotion is culturally specific, learned, and historical; that decision making (rational or otherwise), commitment, and action require feeling.

The case studies at the heart of this project illustrate this entanglement of reason and emotion, within one of the most formally reasonable institutions of democratic society: the institution and letter of the law. I focus here on the presence of emotion in mainstream media, whose texts have the widest and most symbolically powerful circulation, and in the formation of law, as one of the most formally rational and procedural sites of institutional politics. In focusing on the presence of emotion in public discourse, I want to be careful not to replicate this thinking/feeling divide. The entrenchment of the reason/emotion dichotomy in common language makes this difficult. In highlighting feeling, I do not mean to suggest that emotion exists independently from other mental processes or that focusing on feeling should come at the expense of rationality, but to heuristically isolate and explore the social functions of emotion and, more broadly, affect.

Looking at the discursive side of feelings and refusing a stark reason/emotion divide allows us to see expressions of feeling not as the psychic property of individuals but as social goods, structured by power, history, and social relations. Unmooring emotion from individual psychology allows us to look at questions of feeling as ones of structure. If feelings are not private matters of individual psychology, then they can be seen as part of the public life of power, formed by and reconstituting social relations. Investments in certain markers of identity (for example, whiteness) or political publics (that is, publics defined in terms of abstract political maps) help define whom we relate to as proximate and as distant—in other words, which strangers we care for. As described above, affect describes relationships between individuals and institutions, ideas or ideology, and social structures. These relationships are not given but political; they must be learned and can be contested. Some feelings are more "normal" or legitimate than others, learning the right emotions and affects is a process of politics and rhetoric.[33] In keeping with this definition, texts can teach or invite emotions and affective orientations in how they structure relationships among social actors (including their readers/viewers) as well as in explicit references to emotions and feelings. In the contemporary political and social context, questions of whom we valorize, commemorate, and/or mourn in public are clearly political ones.[34]

Attention to affective relations, or the ways in which connection is enabled or disabled via public discourse, supplements attention to the messages or formal structures (processes, ownership, access) of media communication. Analyses of the meanings of (and ideologies promoted by) media texts are necessary, but they do not describe the full range of ingredients in democratic communication.[35] The productive, politically, and ethically charged work of affect needs to be accounted for in order to better describe the actual uses or abuses of communication, much less make normative prescriptions. If communication and communication systems are key to achieving democracy, as any articulation of the public sphere and many constitutions assume, the evaluation of affective communication in terms of justice is a key political project. The varied and impassioned public responses to the murders of Byrd and Shepard are the cases through which I undertake this project.

CRITICAL ANALYSIS AND EMOTION

Of course, evaluating the politics and ethics of affect is notoriously difficult. This is in part because emotions are frequently treated as amorphous and as subject to the vagaries of individual psychology. Analysis of emotions as discursive, and even structural, makes critical analysis of emotions somewhat easier. It also means that the politics of emotion do not necessarily hinge on whether the emotions circulating in public are "positive" (love, empathy, compassion) or "negative" (despair, mourning, even hate). Such a focus would end up emphasizing the intent of the discreet "feelers" of emotion. Rather, the central political issue is how public articulations of feeling mediate access to material and political goods. Whose feelings may be deployed in public, and who may be the object of these feelings, as Lauren Berlant has argued, has "[powerful] material and personal consequences" for, among other things, shaping access to informal and formal social safety nets and the ability to make claims on justice.[36] Hence my analysis focuses on what, and whose, feelings were circulated via media and how some feelings came to provide the grounds for justice claims. I explore which feelings were able to act as the basis for claims on justice, and why, and which emotions are recognized within political structures—or even incorporated into those political structures, as is the case in the examples of lawmaking I examine here. In this analysis, the circulation and varying legibility, legitimacy, and discursive force of different emotions are more important axes of analysis than quality of feeling, authenticity, or intent. It is necessary not only to note whose emotions are visible/legible in public, and how these emotions are selectively associated with/attached to some bodies and not to others, but also to look for the outcomes of these emotions and attachments—in a word, their productivity.

In the cases I examine here, this productivity can be seen in the crafting of legislation. The media publicity around each case had a number of outcomes, among them changes in local (city and state) law. These were not the only responses to the murder. The memorials to Matthew Shepard in popular media are abundant, and James Byrd Jr.'s name still evokes the horror of lynching in the United States. Foundations dedicated to reconciliatory (cultural) projects of education and understanding survive each man. The Byrd Foundation for Racial Healing oversees the James Byrd Jr. Racism Oral History Project, which archives interviews on race and racism in order to instigate dialogue about race in the United States and provide an archive on racism. The Matthew Shepard Foundation is likewise dedicated to documentation of and education about discrimination based on sexuality. The Rainbow Connection Network instituted a scholarship for gay, lesbian, bisexual, and transgender students and their allies to attend the University of Wyoming (UW) in the wake of Shepard's murder. UW holds the Shepard Symposium on Social Justice each year in Shepard's memory. On a more individual level, family members and friends of each man have gone on to become activists in gay rights, anti-racism, and anti–death penalty campaigns, and the lives of many individuals in Laramie and Jasper were touched by the murders. The changes in local and national hate crimes law, however, are particularly institutional and material responses. These measures also demonstrate the impact of the mediation, in particular, the emotional mediation, of the murders.

In each case, a focus on the law was perhaps presaged by the media coverage. "Hate crime" was a primary lens through which these men's deaths were articulated, responded to, and mourned. From early on in the investigation of Byrd's death, local authorities focused on the racial motivation of the murder and the potential jurisdiction of the federal government in prosecution. Media outlets picked up on this as a primary frame for news coverage. The attack on Shepard was also covered from the beginning under the banner of "hate crime." The term provided the headline that announced the story throughout its coverage on the big three networks' nightly news reports. In all media, the attack was covered as the result of homophobia, albeit often simplistically defined in terms of individual pathology, animosity, and physical violence. The purchase that these attacks took on national discourse and popular culture, as well as the legislative direction the responses took, must be located at their particular historical moment. Both took place in the waning years of Bill Clinton's second term as president, at a time when neoliberalism had emerged as the predominant political and policy philosophy in national politics, and at the beginnings of what would become a rising conjunction of neoliberal and social conservative agendas.

In focusing in the legislative responses to these murders as markers of the expansion of legal markers of national personhood, I am not trying to suggest that the law is the best, or even a particularly good, barometer of social change. Rather, I recognize that law is often engaged in protecting the interests of the powerful and in maintaining hegemonic relations of power and property. At the same time, it is a key sociopolitical institution that does register various social changes. The laws that were enacted after the murders of Shepard and Byrd are not necessarily the best laws that could have been passed or fully progressive political outcomes. Hate crimes laws have been critiqued in critical scholarship for reaffirming the very social inequalities that they seek to remedy, for furthering the repressive politics of criminal justice, for treating the law as a solution to problems of inequality created in part by the law, and for detracting from other, more pervasive forms of discrimination and oppression than physical violence.[37]

While the latter set of objections are important cautions, my own position is that they are not grounds to dismiss hate crimes laws as simply bad politics. They are much more complicated than this. I want to acknowledge the critiques of hate crime law, often embedded in a valuable appraisal of the paradoxes and oppressions of liberal legal structures. In particular, I want to acknowledge critiques that hate crimes laws are often steeped in a reactionary rhetoric of penalties and criminality that creates strong divisions between the perpetrators and the rest of society, often within a reductive, individualist model of motive that does not account for the ways in which racism and homophobia are outcomes of dominant political discourses and institutions. These problems, however, are not specific to hate crime legislation but are deeply engrained in criminal law-making. Such laws are not necessarily the most effective legislative avenue for decreasing discrimination;[38] however, they do mark an important recognition of structural violence and inequality within liberal legal structures—a difficult task. While my main aim here is to point out the mere fact of legal change, the difficulty of simply dismissing hate crime law is important. The laws, and efforts to pass them, seek an ambivalent and pragmatic end: for the law to recognize and treat with seriousness violence and threats of violence that draw their power from broad social hierarchies.[39] They do so only within the limited scope of physical violence. Physical violence is only one mechanism via which social hierarchies and disenfranchisement of minority populations are maintained within liberal democratic societies; it is, of course, the most recognizable as oppression within liberalism.[40] These laws attempt to recognize and respond to widespread, structural discrimination and oppression, notably providing a mandate to investigate hate crimes, and resources to do so, in places where local authorities may be otherwise reticent. While the punitive aspect of these laws is often the most publicized, in the cases I examined, often other aspects of the laws were considered more important to their supporters. Supporters of the measures in Laramie and Texas emphasized that these measures would provide avenues for treating hate-related acts of vandalism as intimidation (and not just property damage), provide civil remedies for targets of violence (such as injunctions and the ability to sue to recover costs involved in hate-related property crime), and mandate police training in recognizing hate-related crimes and processing them.[41]

The focus of my analysis is on the process by which these laws were discussed and enacted. In each case, the violence visited upon these men provoked response and recognition within the law. The necessity of this legislative action was articulated through public feeling. The ways this necessity was (successfully) articulated as a matter of justice tells much about the political and ethical climate of the nation as well as about the power of emotional discourse. The discussion of each murder drew upon rich repositories of cultural memory and geography that illuminate the structuring of public sentiment about gender, sexuality, and race at a particular historical juncture. This structuring is vital to efforts to understand the continuing grip of gendered, sexual, and racial hierarchies in U.S. life and politics. The public responses to each man's murder demonstrate the construction proximities and distances, affinities and disgust across distance, with absent others, in mediated publics. These responses were projects of defining and redefining the way we draw the boundaries of national membership in cultural and legal texts.

The public response, and in particular the emotive/affective component of this response, was structured by many historical, geographic, and political contexts. In the chapters that follow, I outline this response and its effects. I begin with the responses to the murder of Matthew Shepard, as the case that is in many ways closest to me. The local response, confined to a city, and a small one at that, is also a much simpler starting point to discuss the ways that emotional discourses mobilized publics and enabled, if not forced, lawmaking. The legislative response at the state level in Texas offers a much more complicated case. The James Byrd Hate Crimes Act was the culmination of close to a decade of work to add substance to the state's existing hate crime statute. The passage of the law was deeply entwined within the ongoing debates and rivalries of professional politics, a shifting political culture, and regional relationships with the state's troubled racial history. It was also at the crux of a growing local gay rights movement as well as, at the opposite pole of the political spectrum, the growing power of socially conservative political rhetoric within Texas politics.

I begin then by looking at the public discourse and imagery that circulated in the news of the attack on Shepard. I show how affective discourse was deployed in the newspapers, magazines, and movies documenting his death. In the first chapter, I discuss the politics of mourning and how Shepard became iconic, a national body. The sets of identifications deployed around his death provided a distinct form of mourning that was structured by notions of cultural geography, modernity, class norms, and white masculinity. The forms of feeling that defined this mourning highlight the normative power of public feelings, a power that is highlighted and complicated by a closer analysis of the role of shame in the local response to the national discourse in Laramie, Wyoming.

The next chapter continues this discussion; I use interviews, letters to the local paper, and transcripts of city council meetings to look at local political and discursive responses to the murder and its articulation in the national press. The responses, especially those consolidated around expressions of shame, show

how emotional discourse worked in this case as a mobilizing factor, one that articulated a new definition of social justice for activist citizens and that demanded an institutional response from others. The debates surrounding the passage of the law manifested a discussion about community norms and boundaries, as well as the official memory of both the murder and civic values. The law itself was a compromise between those activists who wished to deeply change definitions of the community and justice and those residents who wished to forget the whole thing.

The third chapter turns to the public responses to the murder of James Byrd Jr. In this chapter, I trace how newspaper, magazines, and movies discussed the murder in terms of melodrama and the past. The news coverage fell into a well-worn tradition of presenting racial violence in terms of melodrama, borrowing from cinema and other texts. The melodramatic structure of the news discourse invited pity and a desire for redress as a form of resolution. The encouragement of pity, as well as the temporal framing of the murder, distanced both Byrd and the implications of modern racism and exclusion from the reading public. The media coverage and melodramatic narration emphasized the law as the site of redress, reinforcing the idea that current political systems and institutions are not only capable of but the best venue for achieving racial justice.

The fourth chapter follows the language of repetition and melodrama that explained and contained Byrd's murder through the lobbying efforts and legislative debates that culminated in the passage of the James Byrd Jr. Hate Crimes Act. The figure of Byrd became, like other victims of violence against minority populations before him, a rallying figure for a coalition of gay and lesbian, Latino and black activists, lobbyists, and politicians. The framework of melodrama in the media coverage transferred to the political debate in the Texas legislature, where demands for justice were articulated through the visibility of the suffering of victims of hate crimes. In particular, the sympathetic figure of Byrd as a victim demanded redress. The force of this appeal convinced many politicians who had refused for years to sign onto legislation that recognized sexuality as an axis of discrimination (and recognized state protection for gay and lesbian citizens) to finally do so, in the name of James Byrd Jr.

The book concludes with a consideration of the different affective politics exemplified in each case and a consideration of how scholars of media, communication, and culture might critically evaluate the implications and politics of public feelings. I argue for the consideration of feelings as social goods; analyzing the political economy of these goods expands normative approaches to the public sphere and democratic communication This expansion offers greater promise in attempting to understand the continuing purchase of cultures of inequality and injustice than traditional approaches to communication and the public sphere.

### Ethical Positions

Choosing to look at the public mediation of the murders of Shepard and Byrd has brought with it some ethical obligations to which I hope I have done justice. The publicity surrounding their deaths perhaps inevitably flattened the memories of Byrd and Shepard as people into iconic images and short-cut descriptions: Byrd was described as a 49-year-old black man (or often a disabled 49-year-old black man) and Shepard as a gay college student. These descriptions took away the specificity of each man and his life, allowing them to stand for larger groups of people. This process, while it reduced the complexity of the men and often facilitated memories of them more as icons than as human beings, also was part of what allowed for the public mourning, outrage, and mobilizations that I trace as affective politics in this project.

Academic writing about the dead may inevitably participate in their "textualization." While the deaths of these men are central to my project, they themselves are mainly absent. In the public discourse on their deaths, even the family testimony, we do not get to know these men. My analysis does not attempt to build knowledge about the men. It does build knowledge about the public response to their deaths and the very processes and discourses by which the men were made symbolic. The claims on justice in each case were made to a public that was often implicitly defined in terms of heteronormativity, whiteness, and class privilege.[42] The project examines how this public formed and mobilized around the murders of these two men, as examples of anti-gay and racist violence. In writing about the murders, I have tried to find language that gives voice to their details and violence without tipping into hyperbole and cliché.

This project began tightly focused around the theoretical and political questions about the role of emotion in forming publics and in social change, for good or ill. Over the course of my project, the details of the media texts I examined and the sometimes surprising commentaries and interpretations of my interviewees have broadened the lens of my analysis to encompass more discussion of the intersection of notions of modernity, cultural geography, and the vicissitudes of national memory. The local interpretations of the news coverage of each murder coalesced around a deep desire to be included in the category of the modern, which in turn pointed to a very interesting way in which the public discussion of each murder illuminated the intersections of current notions of modernity and normative visions of the nation with gender, sexuality, geography, history, race, and class. The history in these pages also sheds light on a particular moment in the rise of gay rights politics within the "mainstream" press and politics—and the rise of an opposing, socially conservative politics linked with the religious right.

As this is a project focused on the proximities and distances we construct with distant others, it seems only fitting that I mention my own. The proximities that pulled me into this project focused initially around the death of Matthew Shepard and my own relationship to home. I lived in Laramie as a teenager, so it was with more than passing interest that I read about the attack on the front page of the *New York Times* in October 1998. My own feelings and understanding of the horrible story that unfolded beneath that dateline were wrapped up in my memories and feelings about Laramie. Like many of the former Laramie residents who wrote to the local paper after his death, I have ambivalent feelings about Laramie as "home." I was not fully at home there when I lived there, and I have since distanced myself in many ways. The news of the attack on Shepard asked me to revisit and reflect on Laramie and my own relationship to the place and community. My relationship to the murder of James Byrd Jr. was more geographical when I took on this project. I had just moved to Texas when Byrd was killed. The murder, and its media coverage, in many ways provided my introduction to the state. Yet this introduction took place from the physical and cultural location of Austin, which as I learned through this project is always eager to distance itself from rural East Texas. This distancing, a form of cultural mapping and struggle over regional memory, was an active feature of the legal debates over the James Byrd Jr. Hate Crimes Act that I observed.

Despite my geographic proximities, as a relatively urban, upper-middle-class, white, heterosexual woman, I am also in each case a member of the national publics hailed by the dominant discourses utilized in both news and political-legal debate. While I write in an analytical mode that demands some separation from the object of my analysis, I do not hold myself outside or above the discourses I critique in these pages. There are, finally, another set of proximities that matter: the politics and intentions that shape this book are feminist, queer, and anti-racist. All of these factors influence the conception, shape, and tenor of the analysis contained in these pages.

# [ *1* ]

## Mourning Matthew Shepard
*Grief, Shame, and the Public Sphere*

> Something about the attack on young Matthew Shepard—his head bashed in, his cherubic face mutilated, his body strung up like a dead coyote on a split-rail fence on the cold, desolate plain outside Laramie, Wyo.—has cut through the nation's impulse to turn away.
> —Justin Gillis and Patrice Gaines, "Pattern of Hate Emerges on a Fence in Laramie," *Washington Post,* October 18, 1998

> We have to mourn this and we have to be sad we live in a town, a state, a country where shit like this happens. And I'm not going to step away from that and say, "We need to show the world this didn't happen." I mean these people are trying to distance themselves from this crime. And we need to own this crime. I feel. Everyone needs to own it. We are like this. We ARE like this. WE are LIKE this.
> —Zubaida, a Laramie resident quoted in *The Laramie Project*

MATTHEW SHEPARD DIED on October 12, 1998, almost a week after he was beaten and left tied to a fence. His death was noted and mourned by thousands. It was also headline news, with correspondents from national papers and news crews from the major broadcast networks and CNN on-site to cover the event within days of the attack. Correspondents from regional papers as well as most of the national papers (*New York Times, Washington Post,* and AP) were in Laramie by October 8.[1]

In the weeks after the attack, the question of what had happened to Shepard was soon followed by why. The details of the murder, the murderers' rationales for the attack, and their implications were featured TV segments on *20/20* and *Nightline.* In the months that followed, the murder was analyzed in depth in news magazines such as *Time, Newsweek,* and *U.S. News & World Report* and featured in general interest magazines such as *People* and *Vanity Fair.* In these venues, a very public and mediated story about what happened that night slowly emerged.

Shepard, an openly gay, white college student, was having a drink by himself at the Fireside Lounge on the evening of October 6, when he met two young
white men, Russell Henderson and Aaron McKinney. The three left together
some time later, at which point Henderson and McKinney drove Shepard down
a dirt road on the edge of town. There they stole Shepard's wallet and shoes and
then tied him to a fence and pistol-whipped him, beating him so badly that he
was difficult to recognize. After Henderson and McKinney left Shepard, they
got into a fight with two young Mexican American men, which sent them to
the hospital and would help the police identify them as Shepard's attackers. A
mountain biker found Shepard 18 hours later, after initially mistaking his body
for a scarecrow, seemingly lifeless and collapsed on the ground. The comparison
to a scarecrow, and the (erroneous) image of Shepard tied in spread-eagle fashion that this called to mind, would be much cited in the coverage and cultural
imagery of his murder. He was transported to a hospital in nearby Ft. Collins,
Colorado, where he died five days later.

Any moment of violence takes on its particular meaning and tenor (the
way in which it is terrifying or troubling or even heroic) through the narratives
in which it is embedded and through its sites of circulation. The framework
through which the mainstream media publicized the attack was not purely as an
isolated incident but rather as an example of anti-gay violence, under the rubric
of hate crime. This framing took on a particularly authoritative and pervasive
mantle through the repetition of the story as a national event across different
media. It was publicized in multiple channels and markets. The TV news reports
ran the story under the headline of "hate crime." One-third of these reports were
used as lead-ins to stories about state hate crime laws. *Time* magazine ran a special issue, "The War over Gays," alluding to both the anti-gay social conservative
politics that were beginning to gain ground in public discourse in the late 1990s
and the growing political visibility of gay rights movements. *Newsweek* and *U.S.
News & World Report* focused on the conditions that might have led to the crime
and the debates over hate crime laws. Newspapers followed a similar pattern.
The broad outlines of this coverage included positing the primacy of homophobia as a motivating factor, outlining the explicit and complicit homophobia of
small-town life, and tying the attack to larger trends in anti-gay violence and
politics.

Outside of media institutions, national attention manifested itself in the
many e-mails, flowers, and monetary donations strangers sent to Shepard's family and to the hospital that was caring for him. Individuals and groups around
the nation organized memorial services. In Laramie, the local university's
homecoming parade, held the weekend after the attack on Shepard, doubled

as a protest against anti-gay violence. The University of Wyoming sports teams adopted in their uniforms the green and yellow protest banners being hung by the campus lesbian, gay, bisexual, and transgender (LGBT) and multicultural groups.[2] In New York, more than 4,000 people attended the "political funeral" organized by activists. In Washington, Ellen DeGeneres and Barbara Streisand addressed crowds of thousands rallying on the Capitol steps in favor of national hate crime legislation.

A different type of sentiment was evidenced in other places. In Ft. Collins, an hour and a half south of Laramie, a fraternity float in the homecoming parade featured a giant scarecrow with the words "I'm gay" spray-painted across its head (reminiscent of a New York incident in which a police officer in blackface appeared to reenact James Byrd's dragging death) and a local LGBT resource center received electronic hate mail cheering the attack on Shepard. And at vigils/memorials for him in Madison, Wisconsin, and St. Cloud, Minnesota, a cross-dressing man and a gay student were attacked and beaten. At Shepard's funeral, anti-gay activist Fred Phelps led picketers carrying signs suggesting that Shepard had been damned. The homecoming float was the subject of much national concern and spurred a flurry of stories in national and local news investigating homophobia on college and high school campuses as a serious social issue. Histories of homophobia show that illiberal expressions such as the homecoming float are all too common and rarely censured. The fact that these expressions were strongly condemned has much to do with the affective politics of mourning and national iconicity. The process by which Matthew Shepard became a mournable body, his death articulated in terms of national loss, is instructive in understanding both affective politics and the role of media in circulating affect.

### A National Victim

The murder became a national story, and Shepard a nationally iconic victim. This is particularly striking given that this national symbolism coalesced within a fragmented media environment. The story was covered across broadcast and cable TV, to varying degrees in leading newspapers, and in news and cultural magazines. There were televised dramatizations prepared for multiple demographics: NBC, HBO, and MTV all crafted dramatizations aimed at their target audiences. While the murder was discussed in terms of national politics and character, the (always less centralized and more regional) print coverage reveals interesting variations in circulation. Newspapers in Boston, New York, Washington, Cleveland, St. Louis, and Minneapolis carried the most coverage.[3]

It was less well covered in the South: the *Atlanta Journal-Constitution*, one of the largest daily papers in the South, ran only one story on the murder, in contrast to eight news stories and four editorials in the *New York Times* during October. The story had less purchase on the West Coast as well. While it was highly covered in Seattle, the *San Francisco Chronicle* never sent a correspondent, and the *Los Angeles Times* only sent a correspondent after Shepard's death (by which time the attack was already a major story).[4] There was a coastal division within left-leaning media outlets as well. The *Nation* ran several articles on the attack, but the West Coast publications *Mother Jones* and *Utne Reader* did not.

The centralization of network broadcasts flattens the local, sending the same stories to all, telegraphing the same vision of what is nationally significant. Local papers, in the other hand, make judgments about what is of interest or significance to the local market, creating more varied projections of the nation. So, while Shepard's murder was a national story, the distribution of its coverage and its significance (as imagined by local print gatekeepers) varied. It was deemed important as something readers should and would care about, more in the Northeast and in pockets of the Midwest. This unevenness in the circulation of the story within regional print media constructs an uneven distribution of feeling: literally, some regions were presumed to care, or to need to be encouraged to care, more than others. People in the latter locales often did care and respond with public vigils and protests, even without local newspaper coverage. In Atlanta, for example, the paper covered the local protests against anti-gay violence but not the murder itself. In contrast, television and news magazines hailed the nation as caring about the murder, effectively making it a national event and instigating a conversation about how it spoke to national identity, politics, and policy.

The national media coverage focused on and encouraged expressions of grief and mourning. These expressions in many ways function as political discourse. There is a tie between public displays of grief, social values, and politics, whether it is the reinforcement of the power of the nation on display at state funerals or the construction of museums and memorials to mark the dead.[5] The logics by which some lives become mournable and some people and events are publicly memorialized are not arbitrary but the work of political and media institutions. This is the work of defining the terms of inclusion.[6] An inventory of who is mourned as a national loss is telling of contemporaneous ideals of citizenship and their exclusions. For example, citizens lost in war or in attacks upon the nation are memorialized by the state in various forms: dedicated spaces, holidays and rituals of remembrance, museums, and the repetition of official narratives. These losses are mourned as ideals of sacrifice. While these examples of grief are tied to state power and arguably exemplify preexisting norms, other examples are less predicable in their politics and more amenable to consideration as part of the bottom-up politics of the public sphere.[7] Some losses make the national stage through media coverage rather than public ceremony. Every once in a while, a local tragedy becomes a national one; one community's loss becomes iconic for national narratives or debates. From Emmett Till to Lacey Peterson, these disparate moments of national mourning are part of the circulation of emotion, a debate and process of cultivation of feelings. These feelings are part of the constitution of who we are and who we are not as a nation; who and what we must care about become technologies of belonging and citizenship. It is not an accident that Shepard's murder was compared to those of Emmett Till and James Byrd Jr. by activists and others framing LGBT rights as civil rights. In comparing Shepard's death to famous casualties of racism, especially those associated with the civil rights struggle, these comparisons argue for a particular set of public feelings and dispositions that include a sense of responsibility linked to ideals of citizenship and the jurisdiction of the state.

In this light, mediated moments of mourning become lessons on how media institutions perform the political work of defining proper emotional dispositions for their "publics." Such moments provide flesh-and-blood descriptions of who may be considered a full member of the national "political community" and also provide telling details of the terms of this membership. The media coverage of Shepard's murder is an example of public mourning as symbolic national inclusion.

This coverage performed what others have termed a drama of inclusion and exclusion: much of the ink and airtime was filled with defining and displaying a vision of the center or norm of national identity. The murder, as a crisis, called into question the treasured ideals of tolerance and equality. The repetition of the story of the murder within and across media, as a national event, made a demand for audiences to attend to the murder, calling for a collective watching and reading. In contrast to most examples of crisis or heightened events as moments of celebration of existing national narratives and values, the mediation of Shepard's murder was a drama of inclusion within the national body—here, a drama that expanded the repertoire of who may represent the nation.[8]

This is not to say that the coverage was uniformly "positive" or that it aligned with gay and lesbian advocacy or queer politics. (There are ways in which the coverage worked against queer politics.) It did not make national discourse less normative; what it did was to alter the terms of these norms. Within the mediation of his murder, it is possible to see not the reestablishment of previous norms but a negotiation and shift in norms. Shepard was the first victim of anti-gay violence to be so publicly mourned as a national loss in the mainstream media.[9] The quantity of coverage was an aberration; in general, even sensational murders targeting LGBT people go without much media coverage.[10] These losses are often not afforded public space for grief, falling into the categories of those bodies and individuals that matter less in dominant public spheres.[11] However, Shepard's life and death were narrativized, mediated, and textualized in ways that made him a compelling victim, one that many people felt for. Politicians and the cultural institutions of media (both entertainment and news media) deemed him a proper (and bankable) object of public sympathy and identification. He was aligned with the public, if not made an icon of that public. Speaking after Shepard's death, President Clinton said that the attack struck "at the very heart of what it means to be an American and at the values that define us as a nation."[12] In this, his life was marked not only as valuable but also as representative of national values.

## Mourning the Boy Next Door:
## Media Narration and Public Identification

Following Shepard's death, strangers in cities across the nation took to the streets, attending vigils, writing to newspapers, composing poems, and sending money, flowers, and letters to the family. In this outpouring of emotion, a public was formed: strangers related to one another (in solidarity and in antagonism) through a common relation to the texts that described Shepard. Publics are particularly discursive social collectivities, linked to the hailing powers of mass media, whether it is the reading public instantiated by the printing press or the imagined communities formed by the circulation of national media. They are differentiated from audiences and other collectivities by virtue of activity and reflexivity: publics do more than merely watch, becoming part of a social collective through engagement with media.[13] The circulation of media texts both constructs a public in speaking to an imagined audience and convenes one by providing the medium through which audience members respond self-reflexively, recognizing themselves for a moment not as isolated readers but as part of a larger mass. This reflexive recognition is distilled, as Benjamin Lee points out, in the foundational political phrase "we the people": the move from first person to third in this passage exemplifies the subjective identification with an abstract mass (the people) at the heart of public formation. As this example makes clear, publics are always both abstractions (or "fictions") and realities. This is to say that media texts do not address already formed publics in waiting but cumulatively form a productive discourse which shapes the contours and experience of that public: this testifies to the ability of communication to form shared experiences and conceptions of the world.[14] It follows that the terms in which publics are addressed shape the tenor and self-identity of these publics; the idiom, aesthetics, style, and central metaphors of this address form the abstraction that people do or do not respond to. The ways that people are invited to form publics, then, are important. They are also traceable in the idiom and aesthetics of media texts. Examining the media texts surrounding Shepard's murder, it is possible to see the projection of a feeling public. These texts projected a particular relationship between materially and socially situated people and abstractions such as the reading/viewing public and the nation.

The repetition of public texts (news, memorials, dramatizations) and the proliferation of discourse on Shepard offered a cumulative address to a particular public. Such addresses (to a public) are only socially and politically meaningful if people experience themselves as both individual and mass (we and the people). A public must be populated. In the wake of the murder of Matthew Shepard—as well as that of James Byrd Jr.—people did indeed respond to this address to populate publics. The media texts that described both men and their deaths invited people to come together, to form imagined relationships with each other and the slain men. As evidenced by protests and bodies in the streets, as well as letters to the editor and echoes of each murder in popular culture, this was an effective address. People responded to the invitation to become part of a social collectivity.

What was it about the media coverage that provided such an effective invitation? While the crime itself was compelling in its brutality, the fact that there were at least 11 other murders of gay men and women in 1998 and several particularly sensational murders of gay men in previous years that did not galvanize publics so well suggests there was something particularly effective in the way the crime and Shepard were discussed that engaged people, making them actively mourn Shepard's loss.[15] These other murders were no less horrible or political. They were, however, less mediated. Media texts, and the narration of Shepard's life and death that they offered, were the vehicle by which Shepard became a representative of the national body, the subject of intense expressions of identification and intimacy. After all, most people only knew of the attack and could only form feelings about it through media texts, which not only relayed information but also offered emotional mediation between audience, victim, and killers.

This mediation invited people to forge strong (imaginary) relations to the figure of Shepard, for in the proliferation of discourses surrounding his death, Shepard the man receded and an iconic figure took shape. He was, according to the *Advocate,* "the lost brother of gay men and lesbians across the country who were suddenly united in a devastating grief for a man they had not heard of just a week before."[16] News reports on vigils in Minneapolis and New Orleans emphasized statements by members of lesbian and gay student groups that described a feeling of interchangeability (that such violence might have/might be visited upon them) that heightened feelings of vulnerability.[17] The construction of intimate ties extended beyond gay and lesbian communities. Gay and straight mourners used rhetorics of kinship to refer to Shepard, calling him Matthew or, even more intimately, Matt. Strangers talked about having "met" him (posthumously), expressing a felt association and identification with him.[18] The president of the University of Wyoming, speaking on the first anniversary of his death, urged those present to remember him as a brother and a son. News reports characterized him as an "all-American nice kid next door" whom you would trust to take care of your grandmother and as having an "open American sweetness." He could have been, as one friend noted, "any person's son."[19]

The above quotes show the intense identification that characterized the mourning of Matthew Shepard and how people came together through shared feelings and relationships to the deceased. They also point to the centrality of media texts. All of those cited above "met" Shepard through media texts. It was the texts that invited felt intimacy and in return the experience of this intimacy as shared that defined the public formed around the mediation of the murder. Descriptions and details in the mainstream media encouraged identification with Shepard; his body, as figured in images and descriptions, formed the center of a cumulative address to a public in media texts. This address was made not only through abstract textual relations and shared meanings but also through the ability of discourse to involve the bodies and feelings of the participants. These quotes foreground the visceral compulsions and repulsions, presences and absences, commitments and apathy, closeness and distance of material bodies that pervade and structure public life. Through these quotes and their grammar of substitution (him for me, him for my loved one), Shepard was imagined as kin, part of the family.

The mediation of the murder, in these instances, made Shepard, as the victim, and the crime, as a social issue more than as an individual act of violence, appear close to distant readers and viewers. This management of intimacy and distance has been discussed in media studies as a technological as well as rhetorical effect of mass media; the mediated intimacy with fictional and real others as they appear in texts is one of the key social features of media culture. While this relationship always, at least in nonfiction texts, has ethical implications, the ethics and politics of mediation are perhaps most pronounced in representations of violence and suffering.[20] Work on the ethics of mediating suffering suggests that (ethically and politically) effective representations demand action by making the suffering particular and real, even in some way proximate, and by linking this suffering to more general, abstract discourses of rights, humanitarian action, etc.[21] This work tends to be focused around the representation of crises in which intervention could alleviate suffering or alter the outcome. The case of Shepard was a bit different. The construction of intimacy and proximity with him was not, and could not be, directed toward alleviating his particular suffering. The feelings for Shepard, however, were linked to a larger political discourse and cause: how to respond to and prevent anti-gay violence. That is, it was directed toward alleviating the suffering of others not present (not represented) in the media coverage and toward condemnation of injustice.

This is not explained by the explicit arguments in the media coverage linking the crime to anti-gay violence, as these explanations varied in the way they understood this violence. On the one hand, network news outlets ran segments that demonstrated the ubiquity and "normalcy" of homophobia and anti-gay violence, explaining that hate crimes were frequent and more likely to be committed by the teenage boys down the block than by fringe neo-Nazi groups. These news segments aimed to bring homophobia and hate crimes into focus as violence that happens close to home, symptoms of pervasive homophobic discourse rather than aberrations. Local news outlets discussed incidents of anti-gay violence in their communities, often as a problem within schools, and revisited past incidents of anti-gay violence that were ignored, downplayed, or not adequately investigated at the time, pointing to the damaging normalization and invisibility of anti-gay violence as an outcome of homophobia.

On the other hand, some news coverage gave publicity to the "gay panic" defense, promoting the idea that hate crimes are motivated by a type of personal animosity. (This definition suggests that hate crimes can only be committed by those who have an agenda or history of anti-gay or overtly racist attitudes or behaviors and tend to locate the problem in aberrant individuals.) The purchase and use of such definitions were on display in the explanation for the attack given by Shepard's assailants and their girlfriends. Aaron McKinney's girlfriend, Kristen Price, appeared on ABC's *20/20* on October 11 to explain what happened: she said that Shepard had come on to her boyfriend, at which point McKinney and accomplice Russell Henderson decided to "teach him a lesson: not to come onto straight people and don't be aggressive about it anymore." This statement became a frequently cited explanation for the crime in other media reports. When Price offered this public explanation for her boyfriend's actions, she was doing more than just telling her version of what happened. In appearing on TV with an explanation (her boyfriend hadn't intended to kill Shepard, just beat him), she was also pleading for understanding and sympathy based on the idea of "gay panic." Her plea was based on the assumption that people would sympathize with a straight man who had reacted to an unwanted same-sex sexual advance. This "gay panic" defense did not, in the end, garner much sympathy, and in 2004, the three gave *20/20* reporters another explanation: the men had robbed and beat Shepard under the influence of crystal methamphetamine, explaining the violence as the side-effect of the drugs.[22] Each statement appeared to be an attempt to mitigate personal responsibility and guilt. These shifts (and particularly Price's contrasting statements) demonstrated attempts to position the actions of all three as more legitimate and more sympathetic. In this attempt, they were tapping into larger discourses about motive and crime. In particular, they drew upon a discourse of hate crimes as expressions of individual animosity rather than as violence based in pervasive anti-gay discourse and structural discrimination.

While the different treatments of anti-gay violence in the media texts reflect conflicting discourses on legitimate and illegitimate violence and the role of the law and state in defining this distinction, the portrayal of Matthew Shepard as a victim was remarkably uniform. The mainstream media discourse was organized around similarity (of the audience to Shepard). The public was positioned as proximate and similar to Shepard, often in the name of liberal tolerance. *Liberal tolerance*—liberalism as the political philosophy placing protection of individual rights, autonomy, and property as the primary end of politics rather than liberal as a left vs. right partisan label—is the term I use to define the ways in which assumed common grounds of decency, opinion, and ethics were expressed. Editorials across the board addressed a public outraged by the crime. The public addressed was defined by an assumed liberal tolerance opposed to violence. The invocation of a public unified in sympathy and identification with a young, gay man in the name of "liberal tolerance" was an important articulation of inclusion. At the same time, the media narratives describing Shepard called upon a complex mixture of discourses about class, race, masculinity, and cultural geography; inclusion was underwritten by these often oppressive discourses. These became the discursive axes around which media texts encouraged highly charged relations of proximity/identification and distance/dis-identification.

In pointing to these axes, I want to highlight the structures of affective discourse and identification. While these axes of identification were interwoven in complex ways, I offer snapshots of how each informed the texts that circulated and provided the basis for public discourse on the murder. Even though I treat them as separate, they are of course interconnected; this is particularly evident in analyzing the roles of masculinity and sexuality, as they were constructed in and through the recurring images and myths about the West and discourses on race and class that pervade these texts. While the discussion of the murder and its social implications was presented as universal, addressing a broad public under the rubric of liberal tolerance, it actually addressed that public through highly particular notions of modernity and cultural geography, whiteness, class norms, and masculinity (often over, and in place of, sexuality).

## THE ICONOGRAPHY OF INCLUSION AND EXCLUSION: GEOGRAPHY AND MODERNITY

The first image of Matthew Shepard within public discourse was not a photo but an image forged by the words used to describe his discovery. When the passing mountain-biker found Shepard on the evening of October 7, he initially mistook him for a scarecrow. The linguistic comparison evoked the first of many mediated images associated with the murder: of a man tied spread-eagle to a fence. This mental image was a powerful one, evoking crucifixion and lynching, both spectacular displays of the suffering body. The news, picking up on this imagery, told us that he had been tied to the fence, "strung up," "spread-eagled," "lynched," and "crucified." The *Vanity Fair* article that ran many months later was titled "The Crucifixion of Matthew Shepard," despite the fact that police had publicly noted that he had, in fact, been crumpled on the ground, his hands tied to a fence post.

The brutality of this image (mental or photographic) might seem enough to ignite concern and response, to convene an outraged public. Yet, as Barbie Zelizer reminds, we have seen an increasing parade of atrocity images in the twentieth century that fail to ignite action or concern. They may ignite a moment of horror or compassion, but she suggests that the very proliferation of photographic images has not meant greater action or responsibility in the face of the suffering of others. With the ubiquity of modern televisual media, few in industrialized nations can claim ignorance of the suffering of others; however, the audiovisual evidence of this suffering has not been met with a similar increase in the quality of witnessing or response.[23] So it is all the more remarkable that people responded to the image of Shepard tied to the fence: it was not even a photographic image but a mental one. In fact, the mental image, encouraged in wording that referenced lynching and headlines suggesting "crucifixion," was perhaps stronger than a photographic image could have been in its ability to morph to fit iconographies of Christianity, repudiated racial violence, and frontier mythology. The issue of distance (Wyoming being closer than images of suffering from abroad) is not sufficient to explain the effectiveness of these images and the texts within which they were embedded; there were, after all, close to a dozen other less noted murders of gay men in the United States (some of them geographically closer to the majority of readers addressed in the news coverage). It is not the level of atrocity itself that dictates response but rather the aesthetics of mediation. It is the way in which the institutions of media pick up and circulate images and narratives of events, within what aesthetic and ethical frameworks these events are placed, that invites or disinvites public response.[24] The aesthetics of the images through which Shepard's murder was publicized provided a rich set of associations and disassociations and affective politics that constituted an important part of the ethical work of mediation in this case. These aesthetics transferred and translated across texts and even across media. The "image" of the fence and crucifixion presented in the words of print media was referenced in the actual images as well as the narration of the television coverage. This convergence makes it difficult to draw strong lines of separation between different media. Coverage in any one medium was highly intertextual, building on words and images conveyed in others. It is worth noting that there were no actual visual spectacles of Shepard or his body. Shepard was visually represented by a single snapshot of him, standing in a kitchen, wearing a plaid shirt. This snapshot was repeated across channels and media. The image that came to convey his suffering was that of the site of the attack. Images of the fence itself, absent Shepard's body, circulated as emblems of the scene of violence.

Television news, magazines, and newspapers all displayed the lonely rustic buck-and-rail fence crossing a flat expanse of brown grass and sagebrush—an image that telegraphed isolation and exposure.[25] It was one of the most prominent visual images in the news coverage, calling upon many of the narratives and ideas of the West as a site of physical labor, rough masculinity, close communities, and America's both idealized and repudiated past. It was also an image that was carefully crafted. The lonely spot where his killers left him was not as isolated as it appeared in the images on the TV screen and the covers of magazines, as is evidenced in the earliest TV news footage. To the west, luxury homes were under construction, and to the south, roofs of the Sherman Hills subdivision dotted the horizon. The later images and footage excised these reminders of suburban development, finding the angle that maximized the impact of the southern Wyoming landscape as open and empty, emphasizing distance from suburban or urban experience. These images were the most arresting, no doubt, because they played upon the ambivalent mythic place that the frontier and the West have in U.S. culture and history, as outside of modernity. They were not images that demanded witnessing, involvement, or action. They did, however, engage the story (and viewers) in a compelling set of narratives and mythology, orienting them toward some interpretations and ethical responses over others.

The mythology of the West as developed in cinema, TV, literature, and popular culture is wrapped up in ideas of freedom, the "American dream," and exceptionalism. The West promises unfettered territorial expansion, prosperity, an excess of land (property), and rugged individualism. It is the site of one of the competing origin myths for the nation, in which the nation is not founded by aristocratic intellectuals but by hardworking, self-sufficient, and ultimately violent frontier men.[26] This mythology paints the West as a masculine space, despite the historical importance of women in frontier life. The masculinity encapsulated in this mythology of the West prizes physical endurance, stoicism, and plain language (an ethos of deeds over words) over the "effete" and too highly "civilized" urban intellectual traits and social manners.[27] Yet the masculinity idealized in this system has few places of power within the contemporary information economy; although this masculinity can be wielded symbolically for rhetorical power, the economic slots aligned with this masculinity are certainly disempowered today. Despite the fact that the West and the iconic frontiersmen associated with it are increasingly critiqued within a multicultural nation, it continues to be a powerful mythology in popular culture and political rhetoric.

In addition and perhaps most important, the West is emblematically premodern. It is evoked as a time as much as a place. This temporality holds an ambivalent place in U.S. culture. The vision of the premodern romanticized in Western iconography is a simpler, harsher time before modern conveniences and material goods and the smoothing influence of "civilization" but also before multiculturalism, women's rights, and the visibility of multiple genders and sexualities. It is also popularly imagined as a straight space. As Judith Halberstam points out, cultural geographies are overlaid with ideas of sexuality and temporality. This mapping aligns rural spaces, particularly in the West and South, with both the premodern and the heterosexual, figured as the "traditional" sexual and gender system.[28] Such mappings define urban spaces in terms of multiple sexualities, freedom of mobility, and a cosmopolitan modernity. This mapping underwrites narratives of queer migration from rural to urban spaces and articulates city spaces as safer (and more proper) zones for queer lives. Of course, it also obscures the many rural queer lives and spaces—and the many dangers to queer life that can be found in the city. This complex gendering and sexualization of the West in terms of a particular (hetero) masculinity, also connected to a fraught vision of the nation, provides an important context for the images and narratives through which the murder of Shepard and the vision of him as a victim were circulated.

The visual rhetoric of the media coverage of the murder, distilled in the oft-repeated image of the fence, placed the murder firmly within a particular geography and, as suggested above, temporality. The desolation of the landscape and primitive construction of the fence suggested images of the West stuck in the past. This had the effect of distancing the murder and the questions about homophobia (casual as well as violent) that it raised from the norm or the national body. The murder and the reasons for it were out of time, out of place.[29] The public addressed by the media was positioned as outsider and spectator to this place and, as such, was rhetorically absolved from implication and responsibility. The Western motif also had a different narrative function in pulling the reader closer to Shepard. He was presented as something of an outsider, like the journalists and their (imagined) readers. One of the first national articles on the crime, in the *New York Times,* described Shepard in this way:

> Six weeks after returning to Wyoming and enrolling as a freshman here, Mr. Shepard became depressed, said [a friend]. Accustomed to life in Europe and Denver, Mr. Shepard, a foreign language student who wanted to become a diplomat, found himself living in this isolated city of 27,000 people. Set in a treeless landscape defined by barbed-wire fences, grazing cattle, and a busy freight railroad line, Laramie is a town where pickup trucks outnumber sport utility vehicles, where fall entertainment revolves around this Saturday's homecoming football game and the start of the hunting season in the nearby mountains.[30]

While some news stories described Laramie as a college town and a lone liberal oasis in an otherwise conservative state, many more, like this example from the *Times,* emphasized an iconic Western landscape. Such descriptions are all the more notable because Shepard was a Wyoming native, who lived in Casper (an oil town, even more stereotypically Western) until high school. What made Shepard seem out of place within prevalent common sense and sexual geographies was his person, not his biography: his sexuality and masculinity, the way he seemed to embody a cosmopolitanism that is defined in part through whiteness and class privilege and that is at odds with the mythology of the West. The intellectual pursuits he was associated with (languages, debate, international relations) are at home in the white-collar information economy that predominates many (especially coastal) cities, whereas the manual labor McKinney and Henderson performed was associated with an industrial economy that, while it undergirds the very information economy, is often discursively tied to the past. These discursive alignments proved more compelling than Shepard's own biography and the statements of his friends, which emphasized that Shepard felt at home in Laramie. If the rhetorical alignment of place, premodern temporality, and violent masculinities (as always, inflected with class and race) distanced the public from the site of the murder (and by extension, from homophobia, as a thing that happens over there), then the descriptions of Shepard as out of place rhetorically aligned him with the reading public.

The designation of Matthew Shepard as part of an American "us" was accomplished in part through the definition of a threatening "them." This was alternately the killers and the Western or rural/small town environment; the distance between "us" and "them" hung crucially on masculinity. The differing masculinities used to characterize Shepard, his killers, and his location were evoked through the mythology of the premodern West/frontier but also through reference to race and class.

### CLEAN HANDS, DIRTY HANDS: CLASS AND RACE

Shepard was described repeatedly in terms of his small stature, education and intellectual pursuits, and gentle personality and demeanor. These descriptors, which came to characterize him in the many media texts detailing the murder, focused much attention on his masculinity. His body, at least its physical size, was a major focus. Only 5'2", it was easy to think of him as childlike and vulnerable. Many reports described him in terms that emphasized his youthful innocence and potential: "gentle," "cherubic," "fresh of face," and as having exceptional promise in life.[31] Childlike terms and references to his physical stature suggested that he was unthreatening and unable to fight back. This was particularly evident in a piece of misreporting that placed Shepard in stark contrast with his attackers. A report in *Time* said that Shepard had met two "tall, muscular men . . . both high school dropouts" who would murder him. In actuality, neither was particularly imposing: at the time of his arrest, McKinney was 5'6" and weighed 145 lbs.[32] Judging from photos, Henderson was of a similar build. This error of fact is telling in the assumptions made, assumptions about the differing masculinities of the men. The starkness of the contrasts assumed here and implicitly elsewhere in the coverage (tall vs. short, brutal vs. gentle, football vs. debate) suggest that popular discourses on masculinity determined the reporting, to the extent that this error of fact made it past the editorial desk unchecked. Size in this report is clearly linked to a whole system of masculinity: Shepard's small size referenced what might be termed a "soft" or "sensitive" masculinity and the description of his attackers in terms of manual labor, aggression, and lack of education (all traits associated with a "hard" or "tough" masculinity) triggered assumptions about physical size.

Ironically, while his sexual identity was central to the discussion of the crime, these depictions frequently vacated Shepard's sexuality from the discussion. Descriptions that emphasized his childlike or cherubic image downplayed his adult sexuality. He was, in a way, an example of gay masculinity without any reminders of sexual activity. The mainstream media discourse did not mention any potential sexual undertones to the attack, although some news outlets speculated that the three may have left the bar on sexual pretenses.[33] This avoidance was accompanied by an overall desexualization of Shepard's sexual identity, which meant that his physical size and "soft" personality traits (rather than sexuality) often operated as the significant differentiations between him and the straight "tough" masculinity he was contrasted with. This emphasis on attributes of his masculinity that fit some cultural expectations of both gay and straight masculinities constructed attachments along the lines of shared sexual identity but also along the lines of a shared "metrosexual" gender identity.[34] MTV in a sense relied on the idea that young straight men would identify with Shepard and his masculinity when they produced an anti–hate crimes drama focusing on Shepard; the producers said he was a powerful figure because he could have been a neighbor to their audience members.[35] In all of these examples, Shepard is marked as being similar or familiar to the public(s) addressed. He is part of an "us" constructed in this discourse—part of a group of people close to the public addressed, either in demographic terms or in terms of affinity and identification.

These lines of affinity were drawn, in part, through his masculinity, heavily inflected by constructions of race and class. That lines of inclusion and exclusion were drawn through masculinity is clear in the way that Shepard was contrasted to his killers and often to Laramie in general. Shepard was part of an "us" composed of well-off, tolerant citizens with cosmopolitan attitudes and masculinities defined more in terms of intellect, interest, and taste. This "us" was contrasted against a "them" characterized by the rigid excesses of alternately "tough" masculinity, defined in terms of physical strength, skill, and roughness, as well as a not-quite "modern" culture and economy. In drawing these lines of affiliation, the news coverage presumed the hegemonic status of certain aspects of Shepard's masculinity (disarticulated from his sexuality). These aspects of his masculinity, heavily inflected by race and class, were those of a masculinity fit for the white-collar economy. As Robert Connell has argued, the dominance, or hegemony, of some forms of masculinity over others hinges upon wider social and economic hegemonies.[36] Hence different masculinities vie for normative or dominant status in a way that parallels struggles for economic and political hegemony. This struggle can be seen in the depiction of Shepard, his killers, and their surroundings in the news coverage. Shepard's masculinity, as contrasted to that of his killers, placed him closer to economic power; the masculine characteristics assigned to him aligned with the dominant economy (in particular, dominant among the target audiences of the news outlets examined here), and which are rewarded with greater access to institutions and opportunities for economic success. In contrast, the portrayal of his killers' masculinities used terms and images that, while they wield symbolic and cultural power, are more fitted to increasingly struggling industrial, manufacturing, and agricultural sectors, which require greater physical labor.

The contrast of these different masculinities, and the lines of affiliation and distance they sketch out, spoke to a classed and racialized public. While some depictions tried to align him with black victims of white violence, most descriptions of Shepard's person and masculinity aligned him with bourgeois/ elite ideals of whiteness. Both the primary visual representation of Shepard and the emphasis placed on his education and travels highlighted his ability to embody ideals of middle-class whiteness. On the TV news and in newspapers and magazines, he was represented by a very youthful head shot, a clean-cut smiling boyish man with short blond hair, blue eyes, and a tidy button-up blue Oxford shirt. His image fit neatly within a long tradition of images of good, white college boys. In addition, as multiple news outlets reported, he went to boarding school in Switzerland and had traveled in Europe and the Middle East. His ability to speak multiple languages and his education overseas identified him as affluent and as having a particular worldly sensibility defined as desirable through discourses of whiteness and class.[37] In particular, his education in Switzerland (sometimes more generally described as in Europe) took on a prominent role in news reports, placing Shepard within various social and cultural categories and in the narration of his life.

> He was shy and gentle in a place where it wasn't common for a young man to be either: in Casper, a rough-and-tumble oil town, in Wyoming, a state that features a broncobuster on its license plate. When his family moved to Saudi Arabia for business, they plunked Matthew down at the American School in Lugarno, Switzerland. He learned Italian and German and to accept the truth about himself: he was gay. After graduation, he wandered in search of a life. This fall, at the age of 21, he finally found his way. He moved to Laramie and enrolled at the University of Wyoming—his father's alma mater. He'd chosen to study international politics, he told his friends, and to fight for human rights.[38]

This particular narration of Shepard's life draws distinct geographic lines around sexuality and masculinity. He is clearly marked as out of place in Casper, Laramie, and Wyoming in general (even while the fact that this was his first home is acknowledged). The narrative makes Europe a necessary stopping-off point in his ability to become the man he was, to develop an interest in international politics, to be openly gay. This link with Europe is a way of explaining his masculinity and sexuality. The geographic linkage took him away from the ideas of Western masculinity and culture, as linked to both "tough" masculinity and manual labor. The importance of his European education and intellectual pursuits also emphasized his whiteness and class. Not only his European education but also his preferred pastimes marked him as refined, as in the following passage:

> He was a freshman at the University of Wyoming in the Cowboy State, a campus where real men were supposed to love football and all-night parties. Shepard, barely 5-ft. 2-in. tall and on a good day 105 lbs., preferred political debate and languages (German and Arabic) to the stereotypical masculine pursuits of his father's alma mater.[39]

In contrast to the stereotypical masculine pursuits associated with the body and physical labor, Shepard preferred those of the mind: debate and languages. The way he is marked as different from his surroundings (and proximate to the readers of magazines such as *Newsweek*) is through a masculinity defined in terms of race and class. The way Shepard was described in relation to that of his killers emphasized his temperance, tidiness, contained physicality (he was more interested in debating than in football), refinement, and understated sexuality. While race was not an explicit category for discussing Shepard's life or death, the ways in which he was discursively connected to a broad public were shaped by cultural constructions that define whiteness (and upper-class status) in terms of tidiness, control, transcendence, restraint, and mastery of the body and sexuality. Indeed, the very fact that his race was not expressly remarked upon is one of the hallmarks of how whiteness works within culture and politics: whiteness is constructed as the absence of race in dominant discourse. Within dominant discourse, whiteness is not named but works to define "the normal."[40]

Class, however, was an explicit category for discussing the crime. And the way that Shepard was presented as upper class was implicitly racialized. That is, the descriptions of middle- to upper-class ideals of education, well-traveled worldliness, and smart appearance (Shepard's grooming as well as fashion sense) were at times also shaped by cultural definitions of whiteness. News reports and magazine features described Laramie in terms of class and culture clashes in which elite class comforts familiar to cosmopolitan city dwellers sat side by side with trailer parks and ranchers scraping out a living. An AP article on the economic context, and possible motivations, of Shepard's murder depicted Laramie as economically depressed and marked by clear class distinctions, contrasting the life of college students with those eking out a living in service jobs—and suggested that there were few of the latter among Shepard's local mourners, positing class divisions as a possible contributor to the murder. The article, reprinted in the local paper, enraged many residents for its depiction of Laramie as economically depressed. This outrage may well have been triggered by a sense that the reporter presented the economically depressed Laramie as distant from the economic and cultural world of national news readers. A report by Donna Minkowitz in the *Nation* made these lines of identification and affiliation through class explicit.

Minkowitz's article argued that there were two Laramies, one of the service jobs and unpaved streets and the other more upper-class, which she termed "Matthew's Laramie." She drew strong lines of identification and similarities between Matthew's Laramie and her home of Park Slope, Brooklyn:

> [Laramie] is full to bursting with scrumptious consumer goods. If I weren't here to write about an antigay torture-murder, I would be buying pottery at Earth, Wind and Fire, pricing silver at Green Gold, acquiring delicate, feathery pastries at Jeffrey's Too. Matthew did. He spent money for fun, the way I often do; he bought fabulous clothes; he shelled out money for delightful items to improve his physical appearance in a way that straight men rarely feel entitled to do.[41]

Here, class was combined with gender and sexuality through consumption as points of identification and proximity. The article invited readers to draw points of connection with Shepard through a gendered description of class privilege and taste. "Matthew's Laramie" is not the only Laramie; Minkowitz contrasted the Laramie she experienced with the Laramie of Henderson, McKinney, and other manual laborers, in which city services are scanty at best and where the city "doesn't even pave the streets."[42] While she is critical of the classed disparities in Laramie, her language constructs proximities among herself, her readers, and Shepard through class privilege. The points of presumed connection, between herself and Shepard, between her readers and herself, are detailed descriptions of luxury goods. Here, the author's identification (and her assumptions about her readership's identifications) relies on shopping, an activity described in terms of femininity and upper-class taste as well as income bracket. While Minkowitz may be making an explicit political point in claiming Shepard as one of her own, as a virtual member of queer New York, she does so through logics of consumption and class as much as gender and sexuality. She asks readers who were distant in geography and culture to feel connections to Shepard through similarities in consumption, taste, and gender identity.

Consumption and class also drew lines of distinction between Shepard and his killers. In retelling the story of Shepard's fateful encounter with his killers, the bartender who served all of them the night of the attack recounted to various journalists and commentators the contrast between Shepard, polite and clean and a good tipper, and his killers, counting out change with dirty fingers to pay for their pitcher. These details suggested a world of difference between Shepard and his attackers. As multiple media texts stressed and lamented the bright future that had been cut short, photo layouts in *Vanity Fair* displayed the killers' less bright present and prospects. The photo layout focused on the peeling paint and dilapidated furniture in Aaron McKinney's former trailer home. Similarly, *NBC Nightly News* interviewed his neighbor in a backyard filled with discarded machinery and other debris. The *New York Times,* in noting how Shepard and McKinney briefly lay near one another in the Laramie hospital, stressed the distance between them:

> In one room lay Matthew Shepard, a gay 21-year-old freshman at the University of Wyoming and a graduate of the American School in Switzerland, who had been robbed and severely beaten in an episode that the authorities say was at least partly linked to his sexual orientation. Four rooms away lay one of Mr. Shepard's accused assailants, Aaron J. McKinney, a 22-year-old roofer who dropped out of high school. Mr. McKinney, the father of a new baby, had suffered a hairline fracture of the skull in an attack on two Hispanic men after Mr. Shepard's beating, the police say.[43]

Similarly, an editorial in the *San Francisco Chronicle* contrasted the futures and capabilities of the men:

> Shepard was a college student. He had attended school in Europe. He spoke three languages. He had a bright future ahead of him.
> Not so, Henderson and McKinney, who met Shepard in a bar. McKinney has a record for burglarizing a Kentucky Fried Chicken. Both men are high school drop-outs. And stupid, so stupid they left one of Shepard's credit cards and a bloody .357 Magnum in their pickup.[44]

These descriptions served to create similarities between the economic opportunities and education of Shepard and readers and to highlight the distances between readers and the killers. This distance, in this context, invites readers to step back from the killers in dis-identification and condemnation. Such distance furthers the scapegoating rhetoric identified by Ott and Aoki, in which condemnation for the killers overshadows questions about the pervasive complicity in homophobic discourses or about the way that heteronormative practices and policies lend symbolic legitimacy to acts of anti-gay violence.[45]

Statements by the killers, their girlfriends, and families were used to vilify and distance them more than to raise questions about how and what the killers were thinking. For example, Aaron McKinney's father told the *Denver Post* that while there was "no excuse" for what his son had done, if Shepard had been straight, the murder would never have made the national news.[46] McKinney Sr.'s statement was taken up and reprinted by the *Times, Washington Post,* and *USA Today* (as well as by smaller papers) as an attention-catching quote, but also as evidence of local character and attitudes. In *Time* magazine, an article stated:

> Laramie, along with the rest of the nation, found itself wondering what dark hole this kind of ugliness bubbles up out of. But some of that mystery was cleared up when McKinney's father Bill opened his mouth. The media, he said in an interview with the *Denver Post,* "blew it totally out of proportion because it involved a homosexual."[47]

This quote was presented and circulated as a vehicle for distancing and despising: McKinney's father became an iconic representation of a backward culture of intolerance that well-meaning readers might define themselves against. Another news report, which described McKinney Sr. in tears, noting that he had raised his son better than that, did not find so much traction. There was scant information or encouragement of compassion or invitation for readers and viewers to reflect on potential lines of similarity with the McKinneys. He was an inappropriate subject for compassion, much less identification. The public addressed by these publications was defined to some extent by proper feeling: sympathy and attachment to Shepard and distance from the McKinneys and others like them in "backward" places. The training of proper feeling was a key part of being able to see oneself as a member of the tolerant public. This is not to celebrate or excuse but to note how feelings toward strangers became ways of publicly performing political membership and identity.

Russell Henderson, Aaron McKinney and his father, and the young men's girlfriends (in particular, Kristen Price, who spoke more publicly in defense of her boyfriend) seemed out of time, out of civilized norms. They seemed to be backward purveyors of masculinities and homophobias out of step with the rest of the liberal, modern nation. This is of course a self-congratulatory rhetoric, in which the onlookers can congratulate themselves for being more tolerant, more modern, than these "others." This allows those not directly aligned with the killers and their immediate community to appear tolerant and inclusive to themselves, often without actually being so. The distance between the killers and mainstream national culture, as depicted in the media coverage, made it easy to localize the reasons for the attack in bad individuals, in "backwards" masculinity and culture, and to disavow the extent to which the same homophobic logic pervades dominant U.S. culture and law.

National membership, as I suggested above, is articulated through the display of proper feelings for the proper bodies. The bodies of Russell Henderson and Aaron McKinney came to represent a dangerous illiberalism against which right-thinking observers might identify themselves. Their bodies, discursively cast as rough, dirty, and mean, stood in contrast to Shepard's body, representative as it became of the national body. Through racial, gender, and class identification, Shepard's body became a geographical location culturally uniting its members through the values of tolerance, right-thinking citizenship, and liberalism. Because feelings of proximity and similarity were structured by race, class, and masculinity, not all were invited in to claim national membership through these particular feelings. Because feelings of distance and disapproval were structured through geography (and its complex references to masculinity and class) and cultural memory, the map of the illiberal and uncivilized against which national membership was defined was expanded beyond the killers to Laramie, Wyoming, or even "the West." In the narration of the murder, Laramie (and/or Wyoming) came to stand outside the nation and represent everything that could go wrong with America. Laramie became a locale imagined through the actions of Russell Henderson and Aaron McKinney.

The way that Shepard was turned into an iconic and representative body had progressive and regressive elements. It was an important moment of incorporation in which a gay man was publicly mourned in many heteronormative places. Some people writing letters to national news magazines reported for the first time being moved to feel solidarity with a gay man. And Shepard is still a powerful mobilizing figure, his name attached to federal hate crime legislative efforts more than 10 years later. The coverage of Shepard's murder was the most widespread and sympathetic mainstream news coverage of anti-gay violence to date and became a hook for discussion of pervasive homophobia and harassment in schools and for coverage of local anti-gay violence in many cities, as well as more sociological analyses of hate crimes. Yet some of this inclusion was writ upon other exclusions, distancings, and disavowals.[48] In locating the cause of the murder in a specific masculinity and locale, presented as distant from and even menacing to distant readers/viewers (to the extent that they were aligned with the victim in rhetorics of kinship and substitution), opportunities for discussion of the very normalcy of homophobia across the nation and in more urban and urbane locations were foreclosed—and opportunities to invite introspection, feelings of responsibility, or mobilizations toward and within one's own community were lost. For distant readers, identifying with the national and affective politics invited proximity to Shepard at the expense of inviting critical evaluation of the structures of homophobia closer to home. For those in Laramie, on the other hand, the affective politics of this media coverage were very different.

## Normative Feelings:
## Shame before the National Public

The responses to the media coverage make evident the problems of our political language and division. I have been discussing the formation of publics around the mediation of the murder. The use of publics, of course, implies a political dimension; the legitimacy of democratic governance rests on the presence and activity of publics. As distinguished from audiences, publics are self-regulating political bodies. This divide, of course, is in reality a fuzzy one, and the strict delineation of audience from public speaks as much to ideological concerns as to any social facts. The distinction is deeply mixed up with gender norms and the related public/private divide: the "mere watching" of audiences has classically been constructed as passive through its association with domesticity and women's worlds whereas media publics have been traditionally associated with activity and political engagement, as defined through a discourse of political speech as manly expression.[49] The publics that formed around the murder of Matthew Shepard illustrate the slipperiness of these categories. The way in which people came together, as evidenced both in the visibility of bodies in the streets and in the texts of letters to the editor invoking a collectivity (a "we") and the need for action, fit within the idealized definition of publics within public sphere scholarship. Yet these responses were couched and enacted within the language of sentiment, from mourning to expressions of shame—an idiom that, as emotional and feminized speech, is often conceptually divorced from the political. In Laramie, such a discourse of shame emerged on the local level. It would be easy to read this as a privatization of the public sphere, convening a collective merely to discuss matters of public concern as issues of private morality.[50] The basic premise that expressions of feelings are not automatically and always private and personal provides a different view. It asks us to look at the political origins and deployments of expressions of feeling in public venues and in relation to public issues. In the case of Laramie, the development of a discourse of shame worked primarily not to privatize or put the lid back on the matter but to make a demand of collective responsibility and action.

To be a member of the liberal—or, as one *Houston Chronicle* editorial put it, "right thinking"—public, people were asked to have the right feelings. These proper feelings were mourning and kinship with Shepard and distance from his killers and, by extension, Laramie. National media articulated homophobia as outside national values and as something that should be expelled from the national body. This expulsion was articulated through the localization of homophobia and danger in Western geography, masculinities, and sexualities. The repeated media localizations became a cumulative "shame on you" (rather than, say, shame on a larger "us") that was echoed by many letter writers, who collectively identified against Laramie and Wyoming—or at least the illiberalism it had come to stand for. While these are examples of a type of scapegoating or national exoneration on the national level, the rhetoric of shame hit home and was taken up in Laramie in productive and unexpected ways (explored here and in the next chapter).

Shame is, by most accounts, a particularly social and norm-invested emotion. Shame is a felt failing or interruption. It is deeper and more pervasive than guilt or embarrassment, which are more localized feelings. Shame implies imperfection. It also implies relationships of desire. One is always shamed before an other, whether that other is a specific person, a generalized other, or a social norm. It is a failing, though one that only makes sense in relation to an object of desire or admiration. People feel shame about failing to meet a desired standard, but not about failure to meet a despised one.[51] Hence its connection to social norms, in both their oppressive and more beneficial moments—shame is about meeting expectations, within a micro or macro context. In the media discourse on homophobia and Laramie, shame was the consequence of a failure to live up to liberal ideals of equality and openness and hence to be part of the national body. The normativity in these texts is interesting in part because of the way that national ideals and membership are deployed to explicitly exclude homophobia, at least in its most physical and violent manifestations.

This shows up in the letters written to local papers. The construction of a mainstream, liberal public against a smaller, geographically defined illiberal public is clear in the contrast between letters to the editor in the national press and those sent to Wyoming papers. While the letters published in editorial pages are not transparent representations of opinion but a melding of public expression and the institutional logic of the newspapers, they trace and propose broad outlines of relationships. The mode of address in editorials and letters to the editor in national publications (*New York Times, USA Today, Time, Newsweek,* and *U.S. News & World Report*) was one of commonality. In contrast, many letters sent to the Wyoming press addressed Wyoming residents through distance, frequently through hostility and disdain.

The majority of writers in the editorial pages of national publications used the inclusive "we" to address implicitly like-minded publics defined by sexuality (for example, addresses to gay/queer readers) and by political values (addresses to "Americans" who ought to fight homophobia). The letters to the Laramie and Cheyenne papers from out of town included offers of sympathy and condolences but also condemnations that explicitly addressed the Wyoming public as other and opposite to the writers' political and national identities. The Cheyenne paper devoted two days of its editorial pages (October 14 and 15) to letters from out of state. Most were composed as pleas for a heavy penalty for the killers and for acceptance of gay neighbors. Several addressed Wyoming in accusatory tones. A letter writer from Austin, Texas, challenged "Wyoming" to show what it was "made of," asking, "Are you a bunch of back-water hicks with a tribal form of government?" Another, from Salt Lake City, argued that "the good people of Wyoming" were accessories to murder for failing to pass a hate crimes law, concluding, "Shame on you, Wyoming."[52] Both letters were striking in the distance implied in their grammar and content.

Letters from out of state to the local daily, the *Laramie Boomerang*, urged residents not to view the murder as an isolated incident but to punish the killers, to pass a hate crimes law, and to express, as an October 25 letter writer put it, "shock and disgust with the politicians and people of the state of Wyoming."[53] The different ways people addressed the national public and Wyoming residents illustrate the way that the national public was constructed to the exclusion of Wyoming (as an intolerant locale). News texts and these citizen epistles argued that Wyoming and Laramie failed to live up to national ideals, values, and/or membership. Their rhetorical exclusions invited and, not surprisingly, produced expressions of shame on the part of some residents of Laramie and Wyoming.

Shame was not the only public affect displayed in Laramie after the murder. There were other modes of expression, protest, and conversation. These are deftly described by Beth Loffreda in her ethnographically based account of local reactions to the murder, *Losing Matt Shepard*. Loffreda's account contrasts the complexity of local responses to the often reductive media representations. In charting these responses, she focuses on the impact of the murder on gay and ethnic/racial minority residents. For some, the attack was the eruption (and incontrovertible proof) of long-felt prejudice, linked not only to gay men and lesbians but also to people of color and of other nationalities living in Laramie.[54] For others, it was a chance to speak out and transform aspects of local culture they found wrong or just suffocating. In these conversations, there is a sense that the national media attention forced mainstream Laramie to look and listen to, if not the voices of minority residents, at least the general concerns of sexual and racial minorities. There are many moments of politicization in these pages: young people who felt compelled to organize or otherwise devote their time and energy to fighting different sites of violence and homophobia. There are also more ambiguous responses, such as participation in vigils and other memorial events. In these events, the normativity of expressions of feelings comes across; there is an expectation that liberal-minded or cosmopolitan residents should participate and publicly mourn.

The normativity of this expression is what interests me here; there were many expected responses to the murder. Shame was among the most frequent and the most productive. Expressions of shame are particularly interesting in their invocation of normativity and the power of media publicity and in the way these expressions were linked to the mobilization of public, collective political responses to the murder. Writing about the way shame functioned within Laramie is tricky and fraught with various analytic and ethical issues. In writing about the circulation of shame in public and the way that expressions of shame functioned as claims on the whiteness and class of the public sphere, I do not mean to negate the highly personal experiences of all of these feelings. I am not suggesting that people in Laramie behaved in any more shameful a manner than anywhere else. Nor do I wish to obscure the many other feelings, such as recognition and anger, that were local responses to the murder. Rather, I am interested in looking at how the national discourse produced local expressions of shame as a response. I offer a critical look at how deployments of caring and the expression of shame function as technologies of belonging (and to what). Looking at how expressions of feeling are invested in relations of power and in defining the parameters and rules of political discussion, ideals, and critique does not mean that these feelings are "tainted" or useless. This analysis, after all, is based on the premise that emotions are at least in part discursive and hence always products of social structures and relations of power.

Shame is a highly political feeling. Shame is well known to be involved in the policing of what are deemed to be socially inappropriate behaviors and desires; this aspect of shame has a history of policing queer sexualities and has been an important tool of closeting. This track record makes shame a tricky political subject and makes ideas about who should feel shame, and for what, particularly hazardous.[55] However, the politics of expressions of shame are not easily reducible to conservative forces. As scholars such as Sara Ahmed and Elspeth Probyn point out, the very sociality of shame gives it a mobilizing potential. When people (or even institutions) that exist within hegemonic social positions experience shame for failing to live up to ideals of justice, the intensity and reflexiveness of shame may goad action toward self-transformation. For example, expressions of shame about historical wrongs such as slavery or Ahmed's example, Australia's notorious policies aimed at "integrating" aboriginal peoples,

mark a recognition that the nation and the people who populate it have failed
to live up to their own principles and mark these historical abuses as something
one ought to feel shameful about. The potential of such discursive moments to
be reflexive and critical is not a guarantee; expressions of shame can stop short
of actual critical self-evaluation or efforts to right political or cultural wrongs.
In Ahmed's example, the apology to aboriginal peoples was worded to carefully
avoid expressions of responsibility that would require the state to take concrete
steps toward making amends.[56]

As with any emotional discourse, the politics of shame must be judged by
its products. In the case of shame, this question has two components: shame's
products are both the articulation of a desired or valued object, person, or idea
(which is failed) and the actions or other outcomes enabled by expressions
of shame. In order to understand the first of these, how expressions of shame
worked as arguments or instantiations of social value, it is necessary to explore
the way that the discourse of shame circulated in Laramie as a response to the
national media coverage. The political actions enabled by this expression are
further explored in the next chapter.

## The Expression of Shame and Civic Identity

In order to examine how shame functioned in Laramie, it is necessary to look at
the clash between locals and national media over the characterizations of civic
identity. I have already discussed some of the ways that national media characterized Laramie as a dangerous relic of the Old West, as home to violent and
homophobic masculinity, and as economically desperate. This was not how residents depicted themselves in the local press and in their statements to/discus-
sions with outside reporters documenting the situation (reporters for national
and regional publications as well as playwright-ethnographers).

The police chief told a reporter for *Vanity Fair* that Laramie was a trusting
and traditional community: "We are what America used to be. And we want to
stay that way."[57] As the *Denver Post* noted, the chamber of commerce boasted a
local murder rate of 0 before the attack on Matthew Shepard. Responding to the
attack, county judge Robert Castor told *Denver Post* reporters, "Obviously, I'm
shocked. Laramie usually is a very quiet town. We don't have any violent crime.
No gang activity, very little drug activity. . . . It's a nice little community to raise
your children in."[58] The article contrasted his view of Laramie with statements
from members of the campus LGBT group, who noted gay and lesbian couples
did not feel safe holding hands in Laramie. City Councilman Jim Rose also defined Laramie in terms of safety, telling the *Rocky Mountain News* that "he and
others have felt insulated from the violence of crime in America's urban area.

'What makes this sobering is that it does not recognize geographic boundaries,' he said. 'If it can happen here, it can happen anywhere.'"[59]

The claims of safety were inflated perhaps, as part of civic image construction. Drugs, murder, and violence do happen in Laramie. Wyoming, even at the time, had a higher rate of youth crystal methamphetamine use than the nation as a whole.[60] While the advertised murder rate was 0, another notorious murder had taken place only a year earlier, when 15-year-old Daphne Sulk was stabbed 17 times by her 38-year-old boyfriend and left in the snow to die. He was only charged with manslaughter, an issue that would surface many times in discussions of Shepard's death. Further, the rate of domestic violence is quite high: in 1997, Wyoming was ranked eighth in the nation in the number of domestic violence murders.[61] Of the 163 incidents of domestic violence reported in Wyoming in 1997, over 100 included serious physical harm. Not all incidents are included in these statistics: Stop Abuse for Everyone (SAFE) reported fielding 4,000 calls involving domestic violence from Laramie alone in the same year.[62]

Given these facts, statements such as Castor's and Rose's require a very particular definition of safety. They in fact posit Laramie as safe through its difference from big cities (no gangs, few drug problems, no street crime), implicitly framing the assault as a type of crime associated with the so-called random violence of urban crime (also probably racialized as black, not white, crime) rather than a crime associated with the relative intimacy and knowledge about the neighbors, associated with small towns. By focusing their definition of danger on urban drug use and crime, they are able to ignore issues of domestic violence and crystal methamphetamine use (a drug that is constructed as rural and white rather than as urban and black) as safety issues.

Incongruously, as prominent Laramie residents were defining danger in terms of the urban, outside world, that outside world was defining Laramie as a dangerous, hate-filled place, defining danger in terms of masculinity and class. In the national press, Laramie was becoming the other against which the national public of tolerant citizens was defined. Articles with titles such as "The Road to Laramie" in the *New York Times*, "To Be Young and Gay in Wyoming" in *Time*, or "The Lessons of Laramie" in the *Boston Globe* focused on the question of whether such a crime could have happened anywhere or whether there was something particularly wrong with the city or state.

This news coverage provided a stark contrast to local identity. National media coverage challenged community identity as safe, harmonious, happy (even an ideal of what the nation should be). Formerly invisible or ignored gay and lesbian residents had platforms to speak in local and national media, at times providing a different (and less friendly and secure) vision of life in Laramie.

And out-of-town journalists came in with preconceived ideas about Wyoming culture, expectations of class and culture based on urban and often East Coast standards, or just the imperative to put together an attention-grabbing story. The clash of civic visions started to surface in the local media discourse when the *Boomerang* editors ran the October 18 AP story on class divisions within Laramie as an indicator of what the rest of the nation was reading about the town. The minor errors of fact and exaggerations in the story served as a flash point for complaints about journalists' sloppiness and use of stereotypes.[63] After the AP story ran, the *Boomerang* published five letters rebutting the article, one upset that it "bash[ed] many of the good people of Laramie in an attempt to place them in a lower social class." Almost all of the letter writers' complaints focused on the portrayal of Laramie as poor or "low" class. Concern continued in the following weeks, as the national news began to turn elsewhere. On October 29, an article ran in the *Boomerang* ("A Media Tale: Businessman, Reporter Tell Versions of National Broadcast") in which the owner of a local bar complained of harassment (phone calls, being yelled at by strangers, having a beer bottle thrown at him) after an NBC broadcast featuring an interview in his bar. The October 9 *NBC Nightly News* segment had contained a brief interview with a young bar patron, who was quoted as saying that being gay in Wyoming was asking for trouble; this was taken as a disturbing display of anti-gay sentiment by locals and journalists alike. In the local discussion, the quote was attributed to the bar owner rather than a patron. The bar owner accused NBC of knowingly painting a one-sided and negative portrait of the town, picking the most inflammatory quote to air. He was not alone in this. The feeling that Wyoming (and Laramie in particular) had come under unfair attack was also circulated in an October 22 community forum, "Hostility Bites." Participants debated about the media coverage of the murder, some finding the effect favorable in that it turned attention to the experiences of gay and lesbian residents while others focused on stereotypes and insults circulated by national media.[64]

The discursive construction of Wyoming as outside of the national (right-thinking) public helped to construct a local public, defined in relation to the national one. Surprised and unhappy about the image of themselves, residents publicly addressed each other in the local media as the subjects of national media mistreatment. In the news, public memorials, town meetings, and letters to the editor, people addressed a public of strangers commonly defined by some level of assigned responsibility for Shepard's murder. There were community forums, campus rallies, city council meetings, and articles in the newspaper about local discrimination against gay men and lesbians. Directed and primed by the images and language of national media coverage, shame and indignation ran through these forums. Banners from windows and business marquees held slogans such as "Hate is not a Laramie value" and "No hate in our state" for camera crews and community alike. Protesters and vigil keepers also carried signs such as "Wake up, Wyo., hate happens here" as interventions within the local struggle to understand the crime and what it said about the community.

Some of this discussion was an effort to disown the crime, to distance Laramie residents from the killers. In essence, it was a repetition of the way the press distanced Laramie from the image of the nation. At the same time, something else interesting happened with the shaming discourse. Some people used it as a call to self-reflection and political critique, attempting to open up a space for conversation, self-examination, and even change. This conversation went on, among other places, in the letters to the editor of the *Laramie Boomerang*.

> Many people feel the tragic event of Shepard's death gives Wyoming a bad name. However, there is one grand way to cure that impression. If our legislature will pass a hate crime bill, we'll be able to show the nation that we in Wyoming are just and good people. Evidence of that is the statewide expression of shock and grief in recent days.[65]

And:

> We who allowed this dreadful deed to happen must share the guilt, in the shame of it. For we did not recognize in the aggressors the potential for violent, unprovoked, and repeated aggression. . . . Out of neglect and indifference, we of Laramie and Wyoming have allowed young twisted, damaged children to take the life of another.[66]

These snippets of public communication, from individuals to the other community members similarly engaged in concern about the murder, parse out responsibility to the community. Some take the opportunity to distance themselves from the community while others engage in a critical self-reflection. Some express these failures in terms of private, domestic lapses while others more expressly focus on public mores and legal structures. They all address neighbors and strangers as a public defined by common attention to and concern about Shepard's murder and the national media discourse surrounding it.

Such local expressions of shame perhaps explain the eagerness to address a broader public and to clear the community's name. The national media coverage had asked residents to see the crime as a barometer of local political values and civic identity. The attack and its mediation came to speak to and about the community in a way that other recent murders had not. The nature and extent of the public displays of mourning for Shepard had to do with shock and horror at the crime but also with the national spotlight. The shame residents expressed in public was not simply before other community members but also before a public defined as national. As many disgruntled residents noted, similar articulations and displays had not been made for other recent, brutal killings that received much less media attention. Most notably, they compared the coverage of Shepard's murder to that of Daphne Sulk, the pregnant teenager who was stabbed by her boyfriend. In addition, 8-year-old Laramie resident Christin Lamb was sexually assaulted and killed while visiting family in Powell, Wyoming, in the summer of 1998. As some commentators pointed out, these murders were also brutal and sensational. People cared about these killings and the victims. For many, these murders (especially Sulk's), their investigations, and outcomes spoke disappointingly about gender and the politics of class and influence in Wyoming. These murders did not instigate the same public expressions of shame and soul-searching about the rates of and attitudes toward violence against women or about the local justice system's ability to serve citizens with less means. Sulk's case was hardly covered even in the local paper.[67] Neither Sulk nor Lamb was affluent. Sulk was described as a runaway from her rundown (and reportedly unheated) trailer home and as sleeping with several older men before her murder. There were no organized expressions of public outrage at the time of her killing or when the court sentenced her boyfriend/killer with voluntary manslaughter. The crimes were, in general, discussed within local media as private tragedies (in Sulk's case, at times as her fault) rather than as parts of a larger pattern of violence against women, as a public social problem.[68]

The major difference between these murders and Shepard's was the media coverage. Shepard's death was framed as a social problem rather than a private one. Further, this social problem was framed as a symptom of local culture and masculinity. The local culture had been stereotyped and used as a foil for defining the tolerant (right-thinking) public, positioned as outside the ideal or even norm of citizenship. This ideal, however, was shared by many Laramie residents. Hence their expressions of shame focused on how Laramie failed to live up to these ideals: to raise good citizens, to embody the ideals of liberal tolerance. The latter was particularly fraught, as the "live and let live" form of liberal tolerance is key to regional identity as well as national identity.

I noted earlier that shame is particularly social and manifests itself in relation to others. Laramie had been shamed before the nation. The national media, and individuals speaking to that media (in quotes and in letters to the editor), had spoken about Laramie and Wyoming as a separate (illiberal, not quite modern) public. People in Laramie spoke to one another about this national media coverage in interpersonal spaces as well as in local media. In this, two sets of publics were discursively addressed and constituted. The national media texts and letters defined a public through kinship with Shepard and distance from Laramie and Shepard's killers. These same calls formed a second public, one that was the target of the shaming, roughly limited to residents of Laramie and Wyoming. In letters to the editor and community forums, Laramie residents addressed one another as a public in response to the national media.

Both sets of texts structured emotion in hierarchical ways, through shaming, because they were mostly constructed as monologues. The nation barely spoke to Laramie. The hierarchy of shame relied on the effective othering of the shamed party, on their stereotyping. But not all interactions between the nation and Laramie were monologues. The ethnographically based play *The Laramie Project,* based in post-Brechtian theater, offered a dialogical construction of Laramie and its response to the murder of Matthew Shepard, brokered by the New York theater troupe and the Laramie residents they interviewed as the basis for the play. The production of *The Laramie Project,* as a play, and then in 2001 as a "quality" TV movie on HBO, became a venue for Laramie residents to address the broader national public, in conversation with members of that public.

## A Normal Town:
### Articulating Membership through The Laramie Project

The *Project* merits extended consideration for the way it was discussed and received within Laramie as a chance to redeem the community and erase the mark of shame that had defined it. In talking to representatives of local media outlets, locals discussed the *Project* as a chance to set the record straight, for the town to represent itself in a better light. One of the critical appraisals of *The Laramie Project* was that the respondents were not authentic, that their voices were too pat and polished.[69] The criticism that the subjects' statements were too rehearsed means that the subjects were thinking of an audience beyond the interpersonal space of the interview. In a sense, the complaint is that the interviewees were self-consciously addressing a larger public. That is what makes the dramatization so interesting. Through the production, residents attempted to address the audience of national media, to speak back to the media coverage and point out that Laramie was part of the normatively defined nation.

The media coverage of the murder attracted the attention of Moisés Kaufman and the Tectonic Theater Project, who saw in the events unfolding in Laramie a flash point that might illuminate contemporary attitudes about sexuality, class, violence, and privilege.[70] Such was the project he and members of his theater troupe undertook when they traveled to Laramie a month after

Shepard's murder. They returned several times in 1998 and 1999, collecting over 200 hours of interviews, which they then worked into a dramatization. The story focused not on what happened to Shepard on the night of October 6 but what happened to Laramie afterwards. The result was a fragmented and fairly complex layering of different understandings of the murder and different personal and political aftershocks. When it aired on HBO in 2002, Laramie residents got to speak indirectly to a national public. Many of the aesthetic and ethnographic complexities of the play were ironed out in the cable TV production, the short, abstract fragmented voices of residents being woven into longer scenes and a narrative that focused on the personal transformation of several individuals. Even so, the ethnographic production, and multiple perspectives offered by it, maintained a dialogic form.

The hope that the *Project* might articulate Laramie's normalcy and membership in the nation from which it had been excluded is exemplified in the local reactions to the stage production and the debut of the *Project* on HBO. The news coverage had left many people feeling that they had been portrayed as "rednecks" or "hicks," and the MTV movie about the murder was met with local dismay for its unfavorable depiction of Laramie and misrepresentations of the investigation.[71] But local reaction to the *Project* was more often one of pride—specifically, restored pride before a national audience. The local paper printed excerpts of reviews of the Denver premiere of the play written by Laramie high school journalism students; the students remarked that the play restored dignity to Laramie and made them feel proud to live there. One noted favorably that the *Project* portrayed Laramie as a "normal" small town just like any other; another was happy to see Laramie portrayed as a community in which people felt safe.[72] Expressions of pride had to do with the way that Laramie was being represented to others: socially speaking, pride is available though a public alignment of the self with a collective ideal.[73] What this collective ideal was is suggested by the role of normalcy in the reception. The interest in being normal is an interest in being like the America Laramie had symbolically been separated from in the mainstream media discourse. At least some of the positive local reception of the *Project* had to do with the desire to be like (or be a member of) the public addressed by the national media and to be able to fully inhabit discourses of whiteness, class, and culture/education.

Perhaps part of the reason that *The Laramie Project* was as well received as it was lies in distribution. The *Project* addressed a specific public or set of publics. As a play, it was performed before audiences across the United States (and beyond, in Japan, the UK, and Australia). As an HBO movie, it was exhibited as part of the network's upscale "quality TV" programming. Expressions of pride at the representation have to do with the content of the *Project* (how Laramie residents were positioned as "normal") but also its address and circulation. It was directed at the same public that the earlier discourse locating shame and responsibility in Laramie had been (one imagined as upscale, white, cosmopolitan, and largely straight), but rather than engaging in shaming and othering, the invitation was to understand (if not to identify with) Laramie residents.[74]

Toward this end, the producers of both the play and the movie positioned Laramie as a "microcosm" of the United States (the term used by multiple reviews of the play and by the HBO marketing department). But even within the population of Laramie, the interviewees featured in the narrative represented some parts of the community more than others. Speakers from the poorer, rural, and conservative members of the community received less prominent places than did professionals, university students, and professors. Zubaida, a young Muslim woman, stood in for the ethnic diversity of Laramie; her words on the difficulty of facing some of the implications of Shepard's murder provide an epigraph to this chapter. Poor whites were poorly represented; there were no voices of poor or middle-class Latino residents (not even the young Latino men Henderson and McKinney attacked after they left Shepard). Likewise, Laramie's Asian/Pacific Islander communities do not appear in this microcosm, although testimony from Asian Americans played a prominent role in the city bias crimes ordinance.[75]

Given the exclusion of segments of the Laramie population, the "microcosm" presented is somewhat limited, in terms of both Laramie and the larger nation it is supposed to stand in for. The *Project* was addressed to a similar subset of the nation as the mainstream news coverage had been: what might be termed an elite audience. This is underscored by the political economy of audiences. HBO banked on the assumption that those who felt interested in and addressed by the *Project* overlapped with the audience of their own "quality" programming when it contracted Tectonic director Moisés Kaufman to direct the movie version and to employ a full house of Hollywood stars in the leading roles, including Peter Fonda, Janeane Garofalo, Steve Buscemi, Christina Ricci, Dylan Baker, Laura Linney, Camryn Manheim, and Clea DuVall. These stars were for the most part from independent film and high-end television, likely to appeal to a "highbrow" audience. Promotional materials carefully positioned the *Project* as, in the words of Clea DuVall, "important work."[76] The importance of the work was measured not only by public involvement in the immediate political issues of gay rights and anti-gay discrimination in America but also by the economic logic of the movie's appeal to liberal upper-class audiences.

For many, the play allowed Laramie back into this particular political and cultural demographic. For others, it was another example of the liberal outsiders getting it wrong.[77] The two responses mark distinct reactions to and feelings toward the national public addressed in mainstream media coverage. For those who expressed a sense of restored pride in the scenes of Laramie circulating the nation through theaters and screens, the "national" public addressed in this circulation was an object of desire. Pride, like shame, is only felt before a desired or respected other.[78] This national public was a collectivity they desired greater proximity to, and the *Project* seemed to offer that proximity. For those who rejected the vision of the nation in the national media coverage, the *Project* offered nothing but another image of Laramie by outsiders, who were bound to get it wrong. They had less desire to speak back to this nation through participation in the *Project* or otherwise. Similar differenices in desire for proximity to (and dialog with) the national public animated the local debates over the need for a local hate crime ordinance, as demonstrated in the next chapter.

## Conclusion: The Politics of Mourning

The murder of Matthew Shepard spurred a spate of media texts and public discourse. This discourse was about establishing a relationship with Shepard and defining, inciting, and exhibiting proper feelings in response to the murder. As the first nationally iconic representation of anti-gay violence as an example of illiberalism, the work of establishing the proper response was pronounced. The accumulation of media texts defining the murdered man and the circumstances and meanings of his death worked as much as any state ceremony or media event to help define the political community. In articulating relationships between dominant publics and the murdered man, media texts were giving shape to the political values and culture of those publics—projecting a certain picture of "liberal tolerance" and inviting readers and viewers to identify with that picture, to see and make themselves in that image. This affective work of mediation was not external to politics but constitutive of politics.

The national media texts encouraged a feeling of kinship, similarity, and proximity to Shepard, as a sympathetic (like "us") victim of illegitimate violence. This rhetoric of kinship and the specific images and words used to define and describe Shepard and his death demonstrated that it was normal to care. At the level of national politics, this invitation was tied to an expansion of the definition of the national community. The mediation invited the nation to feel for a man who represented a minority group in many ways legally and symbolically excluded from the mainstream, the national, asking a public imagined in terms of heterosexuality to identify with a man whose sexuality would otherwise mark him as other. This element of the mediation encouraged an expansion of the normative imagination of the political community. These very rhetorics and images, however, were built upon exclusionary logics of membership and value, inviting this expansion through the lens of a similarity and value rooted in whiteness and markers of class privilege. The expressions of feeling traced here were not ahistorical or apolitical but rather embedded in the sociohistorical political climate and in other structures of belonging. They were tied to the distribution of material and symbolic goods.

This image of the political community provided the ground for the political responses, from the national discussion of anti-gay violence (particularly in schools) to the passage of a local bias crimes ordinance in Laramie. The vision of this political community became an object of desire, and the desire to be within that community became the motivation for the political actions (and inactions) that followed. These images of political community and the sets of feelings circulated in media texts provided the impetus and engine of public formation. Publics appeared on pages and screens mourning, and publics gathered outside of media spaces to join in this mourning across the nation. People testified to their feelings, wrote letters, sent flowers. These unusual displays of feeling for a stranger underscore a broader point: that the formation of publics relies on an affective impulse, a recognition and identification.

The formation of public opinion, active publics, and a social movement type of mobilization are very much the forms of action prized in political theory and idealized popular representations of democracy: actively engaged bodies of citizens arguing about the shape and tenor of the institutions of government. Yet the very self-reflexiveness that is the hallmark of publics is not a product purely of reasoned discussion; it is also the engagement of emotion. The very logic of public formation, the double articulation of first and third person exemplified in the phrase "we the people," presumes an affective moment of identification with "we." This recognition of oneself as part of a larger group, whether it is united by mourning or by debate, is a felt proximity or community. This imagined community is based upon the representations of media texts. The representations are both depictions and projections. That is, the depiction of a feeling public in these texts both represented and produced a public defined and united in terms of feeling.

The formation of publics is one of the basic building blocks of democracy, the vehicle by which citizens participate in governance, and hence it is key to the legitimacy of democratic order—or at least Western liberal versions of democratic order. Yet these "fuzzier" aspects of public formation—the social relations imagined within them, the impulses that move individuals toward an identification as part of the peculiar collectivity of publics—are underexamined as parts of political communication and the role of media in politics. The discussion of the political function of media, or what democratic media communication should look like, is dominated by concerns with information, access, and deliberation. The question of access to the media is, of course, very important: it is key to what extent media and everything conveyed therein (including emotional discourse) functions as a top-down or a bottom-up process. Openness and quality of discourse are benchmarks of how well the media serve the public sphere. It is true that information is necessary for better decisions. But decisions are not based on information alone. Failures of information are not the most serious threat to civic and political life. The biggest failures that haunt the unaccomplished democratic ideals and institutions of at least the United States' political history are not failures of information.[79] Poor information does not explain the selective interpretation and application of enfranchisements and other rights. These failures are better explained by perceptions of membership, proximity, and the necessary commitment to others.

The importance of proximity of others is implicitly recognized within deliberative models of democracy, which argue that there is a political good in the process of deliberation that goes beyond the information exchanged. The benefit of deliberation is that it can lead to a legitimate consensus. This ability is, at heart, based on an idea of the ethical pull of dialogue.[80] Whether explicitly acknowledged or not, the ability of deliberation to pull us outside of our own interests toward a consideration of the collective good and consensus prized in deliberative democratic theory is based in the ethics of reciprocity that form the norms of face-to-face conversation in which two or more others speak and listen to one another. The actual presence of others constitutes the demand to listen, to provide reasons, to enter into exchange. To put this point in Habermasian terms, the rationality of communication is a function of proximity.[81] This model of deliberation (and its inherent ethics) works well for the town hall meeting and other small-scale political conversations. But the communicative workings of large-scale democratic "conversation" rely on projections of proximity in addition to the proximities of the face-to-face sort. The role of media in constituting the sense of proximity to those whom we do not meet in daily life, of defining normative feelings, is key to the creation of commitments that form the conditions of possibility for public action, political participation, and the enactment of citizenship.

Commitments to Matthew Shepard formed the basis for a number of political actions. These commitments are not explained by access, information, or deliberation. Different commitments and actions were authorized by the way media texts positioned different audiences as publics in relation to Shepard, as an icon of the nation and object of identification. The rhetorics of kinship and discourse of shame produced through the circulation of media texts exceed these ways of talking about the political role of media. This emotional discourse provided the impetus for politicization, for individuals to form publics, to see themselves addressed and involved in a public event. It also provided the grounds for political action. At the national level, these political actions are varied and dispersed. At the local level, they were specific. The next chapter examines the type of public and political action enabled by this emotional address. In doing so, it suggests a politics of media communication that goes beyond access, information, and deliberation.

# [ 2 ]

## "Hate Is Not a Laramie Value"
### *Translating Feelings into Law*

The Laramie Bias Crimes Ordinance was a process of legal epistemology, you know. How do we know there has been a violation of an equality principle, and how do we know what our equality principles are? That process doesn't have to be in the criminal courtroom. It can be, but it can also be in this training and statistics process, and in the process by which there is a public reporting. . . . It's like, okay, this event is over, now let's mourn but organize because it's gonna happen again, and when it happens again, we're going to want to have a site of discourse or something around which to organize, establish what our equal rights values are.
—Bern Haggerty, interview with author, November 2005

We had this intense national lens on Laramie, this hate crime. And here's this very innocuous ordinance for which we had already made a compromise. If you can't pass it, all of this language about being a caring community, all of this "this isn't us" stuff simply becomes sort of hypocritical. You know, wait a minute; I mean if this really isn't us, how come you couldn't pull off something as simple and as innocuous as this small element of penalty enhancement?
—Jeff Lockwood, interview with author, October 2005

IN THE LAST CHAPTER, I traced the circulation and workings of attachment, identification, and shame in a slice of the national and local discourse about the murder of Matthew Shepard. In this chapter, I take this one step further: to look at the structural products of this discourse. There were many local reactions to Shepard's death and the national press—and shaming—that followed, from the football team's participation in rituals of mourning to the founding of a community diversity task force. The one most frequently referenced as evidence of "real" change, though, was the passage of a "bias crimes" ordinance by the Laramie City Council in May 2000. This ordinance, which came almost two years after the murder, was certainly the most publicly debated, documented, and fractious of the responses to the murder. It was the one that residents repeatedly turned to in order to say that the city had "done something" in response to the murder and, I would add, its mediation. It is also the central concern of this chapter.

The ordinance was a highly controversial and hotly debated addition to the city legal code. It was the subject of months of impassioned debate in local spaces and in city council meetings and took on great import locally as a concrete community response to the murder. Debates over the ordinance endowed it with great affective and symbolic power, alternately claiming that it would redefine the norms of community membership; demonstrate that Laramie was a caring, tolerant, or modern community; or "set the record straight." Yet power to do any of these things is not to be found in the simple language or enforceable provisions of the ordinance. In fact, the ordinance in itself did very little. The text of the ordinance that was eventually debated and passed reads:

> The City Manager or his designee shall:
>
> Establish guidelines for the collection of bias crime data, including the criteria which must be present to find evidence of prejudice;
>
> Provide training for police officers and other personnel for identifying bias crimes;
>
> Require the Chief of Police or his designees to acquire data on the incidence of bias crimes in the City; and
>
> Provide a statistical summary of data annually, for inclusion in the City council's minutes, concerning the incidence of bias crimes in the City; and make available a summary of actions taken under these sections.[1]

In other words, the ordinance required that the police department define bias crimes, train police officers based on this definition, create procedures for collecting data on these crimes, and report them annually to the city council. It was a very modest law. This limited scope is what led some people I spoke to in Laramie to dismiss the ordinance as a "feel-good law": one that let people feel good but did little else. Even in this dismissal, the ordinance is imagined to do affective work. The way that this affective and symbolic power was inscribed in the law through the processes of deliberation and discussion is an important part of this chapter. However, it is also important to understand how this was a product of the media discourse. Neither the ordinance nor the broad powers ascribed to it would make sense or have taken place without the media coverage. Neither would have taken the shape they did without the particular affective tenor of the media coverage.

The pressure to pass the ordinance as well as the idea that this should be some version of a hate crimes law came in direct response to the media coverage. Arguments for the necessity of the ordinance drew on the media coverage, notions of publicity, and the idea that the ordinance could and would place Laramie within the norm, through enactment of proper feeling.

The way that feelings became the basis for demanding, then passing, the ordinance and the way that the ordinance was positioned as able to define relations of membership and show feeling are provocative. These aspects of the local discussion and meaning of the ordinance show that the work of emotional mediation had an impact not only on the more ephemeral site of cultural politics but also on the more concrete and sober institutions that provide symbolic and procedural legitimacy for our political system. In fact, in the case of Laramie, the idealized procedures of democratic governance were arguably how the ordinance came to be inscribed with an affective register. Here, in the specific history of the hate crimes ordinance in Laramie, it is possible to see the deep connection between the constructive, projective aspects of communication, often addressed as the poetic or ritual aspects of communication, and the supposedly dry, functional processes and deliberation that constitute the norms of political communication and the public sphere.

By focusing on the local responses to the emotional mediation of the murder of Matthew Shepard, I want to show specific ways in which local residents took up and responded to the media texts discussed in the last chapter. Looking only at the national media texts and surmising political impact based on these texts alone risks overlooking how these texts have variable impacts in different cultural and geographical locales. Remaining at the level of the national, it is easy to conclude that emotional mediation privatizes or enables a politics of sentimentality. What emerges in the case of Laramie, however, is much more complex. In the last chapter, I suggested that a local public organized around expressions of shame emerged in response to the national media coverage: specifically, the affective politics of media coverage that represented Laramie in terms of a masculinity and geography distant from national ideals and self-image. The local discussion of the bias crimes ordinance helps flesh out questions about the politics of emotional mediation, such as: What kind of publics are enabled by affective discourse? What types of political actions are enabled through affective discourse? How does this mobilization impact democratic processes? In order to answer these questions, this chapter examines the debates surrounding the passage of the ordinance, the reasons (convincing arguments) for its passage, and contemporary understandings of the ordinance's impact.

The chapter examines the formation of this affectively constituted public and the politics of its actions, describing how some members of this public organized to lobby the city council for an official response to the murder and analyzing the different arguments and statements deployed in the debates. I piece together this story through public documents and interviews with those involved in passage of the ordinance. The chapter draws on letters to the editor in the local newspaper, city council minutes of the debates attending each reading of the ordinance, and archives of the correspondence between advocates and the council in addition to the interviews with key actors.[2]

## Mediation and Activist Publics: A Brief History of the Ordinance

That Laramie passed a bias crimes ordinance, no matter how modest, was the outcome of the activism and political involvement of local residents. The Laramie City Council was not eager to take up the issue, preferring instead to leave policy changes to state legislators. It was local residents who felt something had to be done and pressured the council into drafting an ordinance. These local residents formed a public around both the media coverage and the local reality of the murder. This was not just any public but the active, policy-oriented type of public that forms the political ideal of the public sphere and many normative visions of democracy. A bit of history of the activism and politics of the ordinance shows how this public formed around and in reaction to mediation and provides background for the debates that followed.

In the immediate wake of the murder, letters to the editor of the *Laramie Boomerang* expressed outrage and shame that the murder had happened locally and requested some form of community action. These letters yield some of the first clues as to how people began to see themselves as a public and how the newspaper became a shared textual location from which people spoke up, addressing others within the community and the nation. It was within this local discursive context that the issue of the hate crimes ordinance arose, in response to the city council's apparent inaction. The day after Shepard's death in a Colorado hospital, in what was at least perceived locally to have been a closed session, the Laramie City Council endorsed a nonbinding "Resolution of Sympathy for the Death of Matthew Shepard and Declaring Support for the Laramie Community."[3] (It is notable that in the grammar of this statement, the community is positioned as an injured party, along with Shepard.) At the meeting, council members discussed and decided against issuing a statement supporting passage of a state hate crimes law.[4] Several residents protested the closed session and what they saw as an attempt to sweep the issue under the rug, writing letters to the editor and attending the next scheduled council meeting to demand a more public discussion of the hate crimes law issue. These residents began meeting to discuss what the city could and should do, forming what they came to call the Laramie Coalition.[5] Giving themselves a name and a cause, a subset of the local opinion-forming public coalesced to demand formal action on the part of the governing body (here, the city). The Laramie Coalition was a loose and shifting grouping of people, driven by the actions of a few local residents, Bern Haggerty, Jeanne Hurd, and Jeff Lockwood key among them. This group worked closely with religious leaders Sally Palmer and Roger Schmidt and loosely with local LGBT organizations and many other residents to advocate for the ordinance.

When I spoke with the leaders of the Laramie Coalition about how and why they decided to come together to demand a hate crimes ordinance, each responded that they simply felt something had to be done. A response was demanded. This was an effect of both the proximity and horror of the crime and the tenor of media coverage—the two were inextricable. The basic sense of obligation was tied to the understanding that the murder was a hate crime, an awareness all those I interviewed attributed to the fact that it was labeled as such: most people in Laramie learned about the murder through the news media, as did the rest of the nation. While it is arguable that coverage at the national level invited a spectatorial public through distance from the crime and imagined proximity to Shepard, the publics that formed in Laramie were of necessity very different. If the news texts invited a public distant from Laramie, residents were not the recipients of this invitation. While the primary objects of othering were the killers, Laramie and the West were also constructed as distant from the national public, as imagined by mainstream media outlets. One of the key ways the media functioned was to make Matthew Shepard seem like the boy next door. Within Laramie, this was unnecessary. He *was* the boy next door. Yet the local implications of the alignment of Shepard with the nation and (violated) liberal principles were to distance Laramie residents from Shepard as well as from the nation and those principles.

For progressives who held left-liberal ideals of equality and justice dear, this distance formed a demand. The leaders of the coalition were already activists, involved in different social justice campaigns. This perhaps predisposed their sense of obligation. However, this sense of a sort of communal obligation can also be seen in letters to the editor from unaffiliated individuals that urged action. This obligation is premised on a felt failing: shock that the murder had happened within the community and a sense that there was an element of shared responsibility, as members of a small community, and that something could be done. Those who responded to make organized demands of legal change, forming the Laramie Coalition, came from other venues of activism: environmental justice, civil rights, and socioeconomic justice. The murder put gay and lesbian issues and residents on the radar of these local (straight) social justice activists, bringing them into conversation with the university LGBT group and in essence making sexuality more central to local definitions of and agendas for social justice. It also compelled action: these activists felt the need to come together to do something, spending hours of their time lobbying for the ordinance in official and unofficial venues. Beyond this small band of advocates, many other residents mobilized in different ways. Private spaces were full of talk about the appropriate public response to the murder,[6] and the city council meetings were packed with residents waiting, watching, and offering testimony on and about the ordinance. What drew people out into discussion, into active publics, was not simply the murder, as horrible and shocking as it was, but also the presentation of the murder through media texts.

The compulsion to testify, the expressed sense of obligation, makes sense within the discourse of shame, in which shame is a felt failure to live up to an ideal before another. To tie the mobilization of the activists to the discourse of shame is not to suggest that anyone individually felt guilt or shame but rather that the fact of the murder violated the liberal political ideals held by progressive activists in a very public way, demanding some action. Those involved did not necessarily believe that the murder could not have happened anywhere else, but they did say they felt an ethical responsibility for the fact that it had happened there. The fact that the murder and its coverage pulled people into discussion and action was frequently described by these activists as one of the most important outcomes of the murder. Lockwood discussed how the process of coming together around the murder and the ordinance as a response defined an activist subcommunity that crossed many organizations and issues. He described his impression of the response to the murder and its mediation as a 20-60-20 split: 20 percent of the community rejected the coverage of the murder as an overblown response and turned away, 60 percent were affected but bemused, and 20 percent felt a political and ethical compulsion to act. Bern Haggerty similarly noted:

> There probably were individuals who experienced a transformative, empowering episode when they got to go become an advocate or activist in their young life or for the first time or their old life. And, you know, that's not to be taken for granted in America today. There's so much mind-numbing shit, and we're not given much of a chance to actually be human beings—really practice democracy. And that's important. And that process by which people did that, came out either as human beings and activists, citizens, whatever you want to call it, or came out in other senses. That process is documented and it's an example and sort of a statement by a collection of people about what's right and what's wrong and the way things should happen and shouldn't happen.[7]

That it was the Shepard murder that pulled people into publics, pushed them into really practicing democracy, is deeply linked to the emotional mediation of the crime. There had been other brutal murders in Laramie, many of them linked to gender violence. None had been publicly presented as a social issue, linked to discrimination or local culture, with the same force. The discussion of Shepard's murder as a homophobic hate crime articulated it as an instance of discrimination and inequality. The projection of Laramie as the home of this discrimination, and as distant from national ideals, rhetorically placed responsibility in the community. This sense of responsibility was echoed in political action and in local invocations of a discourse of shame, with its attendant call for self-examination and public redress.

That the ordinance was the form of this action and public redress was an effect of the media coverage and the larger state and national political contexts. The murder was immediately and repeatedly framed in the news as a hate crime.[8] Particularly the TV news discourse, in its juxtaposition of the coverage of the murder with the fact that Wyoming had no hate crimes law, placed the attack within a context of legal causality and remedy. This framing linked the crime directly to issues of policy and a series of national political discussions.

Not only was Shepard attacked almost four months to the day after James Byrd Jr.'s murder ignited a national discussion on hate crimes, but it also occurred at a moment of increasing national political discussions on sexuality and hate crimes. Conservative leaders had been vocally promoting anti-gay politics and policy before Shepard was killed. The preceding June, Senate majority leader Trent Lott had called homosexuality a "sickness" akin to alcoholism, sex addiction, and kleptomania in pathology and curability; this comment was defended by Texas representative and House leader Dick Armey. The month Shepard was attacked, a national anti-gay ad campaign debuted on TV featuring "ex-gay" spokespeople and advocating a "cure" to reverse same-sex sexual orientation.[9] On the other side of the aisle, President Bill Clinton had, in 1997, backed a call to expand federal hate crime laws to cover attacks based on sexual orientation, in the form of the proposed "Hate Crimes Prevention Act." Immediately after Matthew Shepard's death, Clinton linked the attack to the need to pass the legislation.[10]

A more localized version of the federal push for hate crime laws had been going on in Wyoming during the 1990s. Democrats and a coalition of progressive religious and civil rights groups had been trying to pass state laws that protected gay men and lesbians from harassment and violence throughout the decade. The first attempt to pass an official hate crimes law at the state level came in 1994, without much success. In the wake of Shepard's murder, supporters hoped the national attention might push the legislature to pass a similar bill in the 1999 session. In this session, seven versions of such laws were forwarded; none passed, although one bill came closer to passage than any previous measure, finally losing in a tie vote of 30–30. As with the history of the James Byrd Jr. Hate Crimes Act, those close to the bill suggested it was the inclusion of sexuality, and not the idea of hate crime laws in general, that made the bill so controversial.[11]

These contexts set the backdrop for the local turn to law as the site of proper political response. At the city level, the idea that proper response was a hate crimes ordinance emerged soon after the attack. This was no doubt linked to pessimism about a bill passing at the state level. It was also no doubt linked to the politics of those advocating the ordinance. From the beginning, Bern Haggerty and Jeanne Hurd took on prominent roles. Jeff Lockwood, a University of Wyoming professor and president of the Unitarian Fellowship, soon joined them. Haggerty, an attorney for the state attorney general's office, was running for city council in the fall of 1998, on a platform that included passage of a hate crimes law. Hurd was an activist involved in economic and racial justice projects in Wyoming and Montana.[12] Aware of the systemic local socioeconomic and racial/ethnic disparities that they felt were often glossed over in local media and politics, all were attuned to structural causes of community inequality and individual suffering, expressing a sense that the murder had exposed some real community problems that needed to be addressed.[13] When the council effectively refused to address the issue, first waiting until the newly elected council members could take their seats in January 1999, and then not putting the issue on the agenda when the new council convened, the Laramie Coalition decided to take charge and submit their own hate crimes proposal.

Bern Haggerty drew upon other city hate crimes ordinances and consulted with Equality Colorado and the United Gays and Lesbians of Wyoming (UGLW). The Laramie Coalition submitted what they titled a bias crimes ordinance to the council in January 1999.[14] This original draft would have (1) defined bias crimes as a manifestation of prejudice based on perceptions of race, religion, national origin, age, ancestry, gender, sexual orientation, or disability; (2) created stiffer penalties for crimes defined as bias crimes; (3) established provisions for increasing penalties for crimes motivated by bias; (4) created opportunities to file civil cases in bias crimes; (5) allowed the city or an individual to file an injunction to stop an ongoing bias crime; and (6) required the police to train officers on how to handle bias crimes as well as track and publicly report the number of bias crimes each year.[15] The aim of this original draft, which would be significantly watered down over the next year before it passed, was to construct a comprehensive measure that went beyond criminal law and procedures, to put more power into the hands of targeted individuals.[16]

The council still refused to publicly consider the measure; in response, members of the Coalition issued press releases, wrote letters to the Laramie,

Casper, and Cheyenne newspapers, and began a sort of filibuster strategy, gathering people who wanted to testify before the council meetings and taking up the public comments part of the session with comments and requests for a hearing on the bias crimes ordinance.[17] Eventually, City Councilman Tom Gaddis proposed a compromise: he would place the measure on the agenda if the Coalition would postpone lobbying until after the trials of McKinney and Henderson and the attendant media attention.[18]

In the yearlong wait until the end of the trials and the reintroduction of the ordinance, the measure went through a series of compromises and a fair amount of discussion. Gaddis backed off on his support, then worked out a compromise that many in the Coalition did not approve: he would sponsor a revised version of the ordinance in which all but the reporting and training requirements were removed. This, he argued, would increase the chances of the bill passing. The bias crimes ordinance (city ordinance #1506) that resurfaced at the March 21, 2001, city council meeting was the one that would eventually be passed. The alterations took out the definition of bias crimes (leaving this definition up to local police) and with it any mention of sexuality, leaving a compromise version of the bill focused on police training and procedure. This version, included at the beginning of this chapter, was derided as "mere bookkeeping."[19] The text of this final version of the ordinance was carefully separated from Matthew Shepard, yet the discussion and debate would continue to define the measure as being about his murder.

Following typical legislative procedures, this watered-down ordinance was read three times over the course of the next three months to packed and passionate council meetings on March 21, April 4, and May 2, 2000, eventually passing each reading by a narrow margin. It became part of the city legal code when it passed the third reading by a 5–4 vote on May 2.[20] During this time, a debate raged in the city. While many of the important conversations took place one-on-one, in private interpersonal spaces, much of it was carried on in public. The council meeting minutes archive these debates. The opinion section of the *Boomerang* was dominated by exchanges over the ordinance and sexual orientation during this period. These documents as well as the interviews described above provide my record of this debate. The issues of contention in this debate, and the perceived outcomes of the measure, show that much of the concern over the law and its perceived work had to do with establishing normative feelings and defining civic identity.

While the debate over the ordinance was clearly part of a discussion of how Laramie would continue to respond to the national media discourse, it was also in some ways simply politics as usual. I don't want to suggest that the only things going on in the debate were reactions to media coverage and attitudes about sexuality (as well as race, ethnicity, and religion). These were present at every moment and are evident in the debates discussed here, but so was the background of Laramie—and, more broadly, Wyoming—politics. Much of the debate followed well-worn patterns of libertarian arguments against state intervention versus progressive arguments for support of the public good. Some of the major arguments against the bias crimes ordinance were the same as those used against other contentious local issues, such as the proposed leash law and the recently passed smoking ordinance in Laramie: namely, concerns that the ordinance went beyond the jurisdiction of the city or took the first step down a "slippery slope" into an Orwellian nightmare of thought policing. One council member gave a typical example of this form of reasoning:

> And one of the things in terms of citizen participation, one of the things that was advocated by a certain group, was, well, you pass this, you city council people, and the next thing you do, you'll take away some more of our rights, and then it'll snowball and pretty soon everything's a hate crime, etc. . . . Incidentally, that particular response to proposed ordinances is not infrequent. You know, "you guys up there in this council pass this, then the next thing you know you want to put a leash on my horse," you know, and so on. They argue against anything on the basis that it'll snowball.[21]

This general libertarian sentiment was a factor in the legislature's decision not to pass a state hate crime law. In my interviews, several progressive activists reminded me that Wyoming politics tended to be evenhandedly libertarian: that even though there was a fair amount of overt homophobia in the legislature, lawmakers' libertarianism kept them from passing overtly anti-gay measures, such as laws that outlaw same-sex sex and marriage.[22]

## The Politics of Affective Discourse

The way that advocates proposed and argued for the ordinance hinged upon both the coverage of the murder and a sense that the ordinance would do a great deal of symbolic and cultural good. This latter idea also provided the basis for the opposition. How each side became convinced that an ordinance some dismissed as "merely" recordkeeping would do so much is only understandable within the context of the media coverage. The specific cultural, symbolic, and material outcomes attributed to the law show that, in keeping with its roots in emotional mediation, the ordinance was understood locally to do much more than simply require police to keep track of hate crime statistics. Rather, the ordinance was seen as articulating relationships and defining emotional norms of membership and political performance. These affective powers were inscribed in the ordinance through the political process of public debate, deliberation, and voting.

The argumentation on each side was wrapped up in differing reactions to the media coverage, particularly to the way the social and physical landscape of the rural West was othered and the killers' violence was tied to the community. The discussion of the hate crimes ordinance was deeply enmeshed in this discourse, either in professing shame and the requirement to own the crime and attempt to make some kind of change, or in rejection of community responsibility and shame. Analyzing the terms of the debate illustrates that what was at stake in the ordinance were the official interpretation of the crime and definitions of community norms.

## SHOWING THE WORLD

The issue of how the ordinance and its discussion represented Laramie was central from the start. When the Laramie Coalition sent a letter to the editor and city council in January 1999 outlining why the city should consider a bias crimes ordinance, they laid out what they considered the most compelling arguments for doing so. The letter, which advocated the original, more ambitious bias ordinance proposal, argued first the need to have city measures to deal with misdemeanor bias crimes not covered by state law. To support this argument, the letter offered an example of what had become a notorious piece of anti-gay graffiti. In 1993, a sign by the highway inviting tourists to "Shoot a Day or Two" in Laramie had been altered with spray paint to read "Shoot a Gay or Two."[23] A former resident complained about the vandalism; when officials did not respond to his complaint, he took up a can of spray paint to blot out the word *Gay*. Shortly after Matthew Shepard's death, this story was circulated nationally by the *New York Times*, a part of the media coverage that residents thought painted a picture of Laramie as an illiberal outpost. The letter stated that the proposed ordinance would provide tools to treat misdemeanors like this seriously in the future. Second, the letter argued that bias crimes tended to manifest in attacks by groups on individuals and beget violence in return, using the beating of Rodney King and the retaliatory beating of white truck driver Reginald Denny as an illustration. Finally, it argued that the ordinance gave Laramie a chance to refute its reputation as a "hateful, inhospitable" place and a chance to make life in Laramie more livable for all.[24]

The letter is interesting in the rhetorical strategies it uses to present the ordinance, relying quite heavily on appeals to concern over public image and to comparisons with racial violence. While the first reason given has to do with the need for a mechanism to treat hate- or bias-related misdemeanors more seriously than other misdemeanors, the example given pointed more toward the issue of national image. This example, the "Shoot a Gay or Two" graffito, had been cited in three *New York Times* articles as a smoking gun pointing to the violently homophobic character of Laramie. While the public image of Laramie was listed as the last reason, it was in fact invoked in the first. And the use of recent examples of black and white racial tensions and violence in the King and Denny beatings both suggested the possibility of retaliatory violence if no action was taken and invoked the legitimacy of civil rights social action and laws in forwarding the local bias crimes measure. Here, the rhetorical effect is to argue that Matthew Shepard's beating was in fact a civil rights issue and, in turn, that to refuse to discuss and pass the bias crimes ordinance was a refutation of civil rights goals and politics.

The emphasis on public image is very much in reference to the media coverage; there could have been no discussion or concern over Laramie's image before a larger public without this coverage. The effort to frame the issue as a civil rights issue does more than place the ordinance on firmer ground. Civil rights have an established discursive history as a desirable social good, even if this desire does not always go beyond the symbolism of civil rights to the substance of those rights. The invocation of civil rights also carries with it reference to publicity. Within popular memory, after all, civil rights are tied to media publicity: the idea that the media images of police and other white officials' brutality against black Americans in the South evoked outrage across the nation and moved many white Americans to support civil rights may have had some resonance with the experience of media coverage in Laramie. What was at stake in this discussion was the place of Laramie on the national cultural and political map.

The references to image were not limited to the Laramie Coalition. Letters to the editor and the minutes of the city council meetings were full of talk about what sort of message Laramie was sending to "the world" and whether or not this was important. Continuing expressions of shame were linked up with proposals for atonement, self-reflection, and improvement in these exchanges. One letter to the editor, bemoaning the inadequacy of the bias crimes ordinance, expressed this in a particularly colorful way:

> If we had passed a timely misdemeanor law, we would have become a "city on a hill." Now, thanks to the usual guile and inertia, we look like one of those devil towns featured on *Twilight Zone*. We missed the brass ring because we were blinded by right-wing notions and religious bigotry.[25]

More is at issue here than the content of the bias crimes reporting ordinance. The connection between Laramie and a *Twilight Zone* "devil town" is a statement about Laramie's civic identity. It suggests marginalization, a sort of freak-show status, which the author accuses local politicians of bringing upon the community. A similar statement in another letter to the editor references both hope for a concrete outcome and the notion that the measure could and should represent Laramie, as a sort of response to the media coverage:

> I hope this could be the beginning of a safer environment for all Laramie citizens. I hope it could be a reversal in public opinion—global public opinion—about the connection between Laramie and hate (think Jasper, TX and Coeur d'Alene, ID). I hope it could be our opportunity to set the record straight. Let's say to the world "yes, this hideous crime happened here and we are not willing to let our differences and doctrine alter the fact that a human being was brutally murdered on our soil."[26]

In each of these examples, the core argument for passage of the ordinance centers on the relation of Laramie to the rest of the nation; each also is clearly a response to the national discourse. In endorsing the need to change, the authors express shame before the nation at the community's failure to live up to liberal ideals. Each positions the ordinance as a way of repairing that failure: in the first, the council's failure to act would add further shame, and in the second the ordinance could provide a way to endorse and reclaim the very ideals the murder seemed to flout.

Considering all the talk about making a statement or showing "the world," it is striking to note that there were no national media cameras present during these debates and that the ordinance received little to no national media coverage. Despite the notable lack of cameras and reporters, the notion remained that the ordinance was somehow making a statement or taking place before a media audience. In reality, the community was speaking to itself, about itself, through the spaces of the local newspaper and council meetings as well as those face-to-face venues such as coffee shops and domestic spaces that leave no archives behind to study. Yet the rhetorical figure of the media in general remained. While the media were often referenced in my interviews and in the archives through the synecdochal figure of the camera, what this figure referred to was always a more general sense of publicity and symbolic power associated with the various institutions and channels of mass media, plural. Within the context of Laramie, TV cameras also connote national media, as there is no local television channel (the closest is in Cheyenne).[27] The many references to phantom cameras and reporters place the discussions of the ordinance within a symbolic media frame:

that the discussions were the legitimate purview of media coverage, part of the public social world. Yet what placed the ordinance within this frame was not actual media coverage (there was little) but rather the words of locals, in statements that the ordinance would "show the world" and references to the prior media coverage. The persuasiveness of these statements no doubt rested on the context of the prior media coverage of Laramie. The references to global opinion reveal the felt normativity of that media coverage. The coverage articulated norms of feeling and commitment, which were taken up by proponents of the bill. This normativity did not radiate from the texts alone but was a side effect of their circulation within media channels and association with highly symbolic media institutions.[28] Conscious or not, these invocations of a missing media presence rhetorically harnessed symbolic power associated with large-scale media, even without actual cameras or reporters.

The notion of a national audience was persuasive, cameras or no. If Laramie had been discursively excluded from the (virtuous, liberal) national public invoked in the press coverage of Shepard's murder, the ordinance appeared to some to be a way of reconnecting with that national culture. It became a way of reintegrating Laramie with the image of the nation from which the news coverage had othered the community, by establishing proximity between Laramie and the national ideal invoked in the news coverage. This ideal was, of course, more mythology than reality. In defining Laramie as an aberration, the news media produced an image of the nation as inhabiting liberal ideals that in fact are violated daily in life and law.[29] The ordinance was also in some ways a form of agency. Laramie had appeared in the national news as a sort of symbolic backdrop to a story that many felt was written elsewhere, with the moral of the story decided in advance.[30] The ordinance was a reply authored and debated by residents.

The sense that the ordinance was in some way a media event or that the light of national publicity continued to shine was clearly a part of the strategy of the activists. Hurd, Lockwood, and Haggerty all noted the tactical importance of the potential for embarrassment to move the council. From the first opposition to the council's closed meeting to the first Laramie Coalition petition's emphasis on public image to the council's agreement to consider the ordinance in exchange for silence during the media-saturated trials of Henderson and McKinney, the issue of appearance before the media, and by extension "the world," was a central concern in the efforts to press the council to action. The activists hoped to use this sense of publicity to keep the council on its best behavior. Lockwood noted the council wanted the deliberations to be as private as possible whereas the activists wanted them to be as public as possible:

> We had this intense national lens on Laramie, this hate crime. And here's this very innocuous ordinance for which we had already made a compromise. If you can't pass it, all this language about being a caring community, all of this "this isn't us" stuff, simply becomes sort of hypocritical. You know, wait a minute; I mean if this really isn't us, how come you couldn't pull off something as simple and as innocuous as this small element of penalty enhancement?[31]

The idea of using publicity to force the council to act in line with their expressions of feeling was echoed by others. Haggerty called the original ordinance a sort of dare: to dare the council to vote against it in front of the media attention to force a conversation.[32] This threat, that the community and its representatives on the council would look hypocritical at best, seems implicit in the letters to the editor that reference global public opinion as well. That these arguments were persuasive even in the absence of actual cameras or reporters suggests the extent to which everything around the murder had been placed within a frame of mediation: that is, understood within the continuing impact of the media coverage and always subject to a return of publicity.

To say that these invocations of civic representation and global opinion were strategic is not to say they are not real. Whether the role of feelings is heartfelt and authentic or not is not my point here. The effectiveness, politics, and ethics of these deployments of feeling are. The very fact that these arguments are repeated so frequently suggests the currency of a sense that Laramie's image needed to be cleansed and that the city was subject to shame. That these arguments may have been attempts to win over those invested in civic reputation rather than civic reflection and reform does not mean they are not affective. Rather, to the extent that they were strategic, the very strategies of argumentation were based upon and supported by affective responses to the murder. That people troubled to make the arguments at all is also significant; it was an example of citizen demands that are supposed to be at the heart of democratic politics. This action is again evidence of the motivating impulse provided by the media coverage, specifically its emotional mediation. These invocations of public image and representation were effective, as evidenced by the fact that these arguments were taken up by the council members and cited among the reasons why the council passed the ordinance.

For local politicians, the media coverage cast a long shadow over the town and over the deliberations about the bias crimes ordinance. They were highly sensitive to the fact that the murder, and the media coverage of it, had given the community a "black eye."[33] Dave Williams, a council member who opposed the bill, remembered one of the major arguments for the bill as "We need to track this. We need to show people that we're not biased here."[34] Williams had been

vice mayor at the time of the murder, and he became mayor during the trials of
Henderson and McKinney, so he was particularly attuned to the negative publicity, noting that Laramie had gotten a lot of bad press and that ways of improving the city's image had been a major topic of concern for the mayor's office and
the council. Other former council members similarly remembered this concern
with public image. The council and other public officials were under intense
national scrutiny: the mayor received a phone call from President Clinton's office, University of Wyoming (UW) president Phil Dubois received a 45-minute
phone tirade from pop star Madonna, and the council members were getting
letters and phone calls from across the country asking what they were going to
do in response to the murder.[35] In response, the council tried to present a positive image of the community through statements of sympathy for the Shepard
family—literal statements that did not promise any action or change by the city,
as the Laramie Coalition pointed out—and, eventually, through the passage of
the ordinance. That the decision was part of a desire to respond to this national
pressure, to "make a statement," was clearly articulated by the former council
members. Shumway, for example, explained:

> And when it came down to the vote, I don't think we were voting on
> whether we were going to put teeth in the laws of the city of Laramie. It was
> just whether there was a message going out that we're going to be vigilant and
> diligent in trying to do the very best job we can in keeping this from happening
> again, discouraging this because you really can't prevent it. If it's gonna happen,
> it's gonna happen. But you just have to say we won't tolerate it.[36]

Of course, it is ironic that the law that came to say "we have done something
real" did so little. The original measure, which council members dismissed because it wouldn't have done much (the enhanced penalties would have applied
only to misdemeanors, as that is the extent of the city's jurisdiction), would in
fact have done something toward asking law enforcement officials and politicians to take more seriously the most frequent instances of homophobic and
racist harassment. None of the council members I spoke to seemed to grasp
this irony; instead, the supporters of the measure said that they had done all
they could and that their hands were tied by the limits of city governance. For
example, a supporter of the measure on the council noted that they could not
"completely ignore the issue and say that just because we can't implement effective penalties, we did not want to ignore the issue, so that's why we came up with
the compromise."[37] While there is certainly some duplicity, conscious or not, in
the council members' invocation of the ordinance they had watered down as
proof of their commitment to action, their statements are not necessarily purely

disingenuous. There is a logic to the idea that the importance of the ordinance lay in the statement it made.

The idea that the ordinance made a statement positions it as a communicative act meant to convey something. To judge from the way people talked about the law as really doing something, this statement was important. For some, it was the establishment of an interpretation and record of the crime, documenting the murder as a hate crime within the official record. However, if communication does more than convey information, also constructing relationships and orienting us toward some others and away from others, then the statement the ordinance made needs to be viewed as more than just establishing meaning. Despite the many references to making statements by those involved, perhaps the most important thing that the ordinance did was to construct relationships, both externally and internally. The ordinance, it was hoped, would redefine the relationship of Laramie to the rest of the nation by showing that Laramie cared. However, the way that the ordinance constructed relationships played out in yet another register, in how it was understood to define and delineate relationships between the city and its citizens and among those citizens—in particular, through the discussion of community membership.

### Defining Community

While supporters of the ordinance argued that it would bring Laramie closer to the liberal ideals associated with the nation, many of those who objected to it saw these goals as constructions of what they termed the "liberal media" or "homosexual activists." As such, these goals were not desirable, and any attempts to move Laramie closer to this vision of the nation were wrongheaded. To pass the ordinance would endorse the framework of hate crime and adopt an undesirable vision of the nation expressed in media coverage. It would also remap the contours of community and redefine membership in the terms espoused by outsiders. Opponents read into the ordinance undesirable norms of feeling: the need to express shame or repentance but also to feel for gay and lesbian residents. Within this context, passage of the ordinance meant that something was askew in the established organization and norms of the community, that something *should be* changed. What it was that they felt the ordinance sought to change can be read in their concerns that the ordinance would recognize the "legitimacy of homosexuality" and create "special classes" of citizens who would be more protected under the law than others. For opponents, these were changes that should not take place. The objections raised by these opponents are remarkable in many ways, not least of which is that they read so much legal (creating a separate class of citizen) and cultural (legitimizing same-sex desire and relationships, drawing boundaries of community) power into a law that essentially asked the police to train officers in responding to and reporting bias crimes. These protestations also show that the challenges to the ordinance hinged not on its concrete provisions but on its felt power to redefine norms of feeling and community. The anxiety here is not reducible to the meaning of the ordinance. It concerns how the ordinance would draw new axes of proximity and distance, defining some citizens as more desirable, more central to the law.

Many of the objections to the proposed ordinance circled around issues of who the "real" or central members of the community were and often an apparent fear that what was considered "normal" for white, heterosexual Christians (the concern surfaced most intensely, though not exclusively, in regard to men) might be criminalized or at least marginalized. Objections articulated in terms of insiders and outsiders expressed a fear that outsider norms (those of the "liberal media," "homosexual activists," or some other cultural "elite") were being forced upon the community. Council member Bell frequently and rhetorically claimed that the measure had been proposed by "duplistic interlopers." The rhetorical suggestion that the ordinance had been proposed from outside the bounds of the real community marked a point of contention in the discussions over whose interests the city had a duty to protect as its citizens. It also evoked a sort of cultural divide between the university community (professors and students, figured as leftist cultural elite) and the "real" town.[38] More subtle invocations of insider and outsider rhetoric showed up in the belief expressed by some council members and locals that the media had "gotten it wrong." This outsider rhetoric drew strength from local knowledge, rumor, and the general sense that the ordinance was a response to the media coverage, which had been an imposition from outside, welcomed by some and not by others.

The majority of the objections based on the idea that the ordinance recognized homosexuality came cloaked in constitutional language: in the idea that the measure created unconstitutional "special classes," who would be granted greater protection under the law than others. In the debate surrounding the ordinance, the special class of concern was gay and lesbian residents. In its rhetoric of formally neutral legal principles, the language of special classes is an example of how private interests get cloaked in the language of rationality, disinterest, and neutral principles. The objection that special classes are unconstitutional or otherwise illegal was a reaction to the sense that the ordinance would recognize and sanction gay and lesbian individuals and relationships or even undermine the rights of straight or Christian residents. As is frequently the case, the language of disinterest and legal principle was a vehicle for forwarding a particular set of sentiments and interests. These opponents wished to see their own feelings of aversion reflected and legitimized in the law. Further, within the language of special classes and equal protection, it is possible to see a politics of fear and attachment: fear of being left out of visions of the community seen as imposed from outside and the politics of what larger public Laramie would be attached to.

These objections were based on the idea that to be gay was a sin and that the ordinance was somehow "pro-gay," that it would recognize or normalize the inclusion of gay and lesbian individuals. Many were angry to have to recognize homosexuality in their midst, wishing, as council member Williams put it, to keep sexual orientation "within the walls of your own home" and out of the public concerns of the community. The most explicit objections of this type can be seen in the words of the most outspoken local opponent, who argued that the ordinance was solely "for the purpose of legitimating sodomy" and that "the activists have a five-point plan to force approval of the homosexual lifestyle."[39] Others argued more generally that the ordinance was caving to the "liberal media," which had used the murder of Shepard to forward its own agenda, which had little to do with Laramie.[40]

The idea that the ordinance would create special classes of citizens with special rights no doubt was lifted from the anti–hate crimes discourse circulating in national politics. The way this idea was deployed in the local debate betrays a set of concerns about shifting norms and definitions of community. Concerns about the creation of "special classes" were twinned with concerns about discrimination against heterosexual, white Christians (more often than not, men), who expressed concerns that the law would target them. In one such claim, vocal opponent Steve Westfahl objected that "when homosexuals' rights are over-protected, those who hold moral or religious objections to homosexuality are discriminated against."[41] Council member Bob Bell warned that good citizens would be oppressed by "thought police" if the ordinance was passed. Another resident speaking in the public comments section, Tim Hale, expressed concerns that Laramie might become more like Laguna Beach, California, where he asserted "local police were instructed to keep records on the political views of city residents who voice disapproval of government-designated protected groups such as homosexuals."[42] The paranoia of these comments may be hyperbolic or uninformed, but the comments express a fear that is astounding considering the circumstances. These opponents understood this to be an ordinance about the murder of a gay man, yet they felt vulnerability based on their beliefs. Opponents such as Bell could consider or present themselves as the real minorities, not represented in the national culture depicted by mainstream media.[43]

The idea that the ordinance would marginalize them was dependent upon both a disavowal of structural privileges of race and gender (all of these speakers were white, and the majority were men) and the way that the ordinance was framed and discussed as an endorsement of the national media narrative and affective norms. It was also based on a notion that the ordinance could and would do far more than it did. The stripped-down ordinance did not in fact create special classes or otherwise name axes of discrimination to which the ordinance would apply, though it required police to define these. Even if it had defined these axes of discrimination and included crimes against gay men and lesbians, it would not have done what the opposition feared it would: criminalize their beliefs or the behaviors they considered normal.

The fear of criminalization can be seen in Hale's worry that the ordinance would make Laramie like his image of Laguna Beach, a community where to be gay was the norm within the law and where police carefully monitored the straight population. Similar fears of criminalization were expressed by Carol Jensen, who told the council: "Bias crime legislation could result in people being persecuted for sharing their beliefs. . . . Homosexuals are already protected under present laws and there is no need to waste time with labeling."[44] In these statements there is a fear that what the speakers considered to be normal and permissible might be moving into the territory of the illegal. Each of these comments suggests that the current legal framework is sufficient as well as a fear that (white) conservative/Christian heterosexual men and women were under attack in the measure. Of course, not all objections to the ordinance, or special classes, were linked to conservative religious politics. And not all the religious groups and actors involved opposed the ordinance. The churches in Laramie were split over the bias crimes ordinance. The Unitarian Fellowship, United Church of Christ, and local Catholic priests were strong advocates for the measure, whereas at least one of the local Baptist churches was a strong source of opposition, as was the Mormon church. Even though the debate did not hinge on a religious-secular divide, many opponents were concerned about anti-religious discrimination.

Council member Williams, who was mayor at the time of the vote, located his opposition to the ordinance in fears that it would criminalize otherwise normal behavior, in particular what he considered normal masculinity. When discussing how he understood the impact of the ordinance and his misgivings about it, Williams referred to a scenario in which a gay and a straight man get into a drunken brawl and the straight man is arrested for unwittingly committing a bias crime. While this scenario could not happen within the provisions of the bias ordinance, this statement illustrates the concern over "special protections" in many statements of opponents: that simply being white and heterosexual (and/or embodying a "tough" masculinity) might make them perpetrators under the law.

The expression of fears that the ordinance would criminalize "normal" masculine behavior or conservative Christianity is difficult to connect up to the content and stated intent of the measure. These fears make more sense as fears about change in the norms and definition of community. The city council's support of the bill would signal both community responsibility and an acceptance of the story that the murder was fueled at least in part by homophobia (many still rejected this story, using a zero-sum logic to argue that the real reason for the attack had been a drug deal gone wrong or just an instance of "boys being boys" getting out of hand) and a consensus that homophobia was wrong, outside the bounds of normal or acceptable behavior. The worries about fighting and criminalization of anti-gay religious views were perhaps more a fear that these "normal" behaviors and masculinities would be found to be deviant or undesirable within the community itself. This fear appears in discussions of who was not protected under the ordinance; Jensen complained that she would not be protected if the measure passed, noting that, as a European-American pro-life Christian, she experienced prejudice but would not be protected, as the ordinance did not recognize "Christians and pro-lifers."[45] As with many of the objections, hers is to not being included in the imagined protected classes (others argued that the ordinance would create tensions between those considered special classes and those not included); the concern is about being left aside and not protected by the law. Of course, the ordinance actually did not define any special classes or otherwise contain any language about who the targets of hate crimes were. In the way the debate unfolded, with the intense focus on the makeup of these special classes (namely, gay men and lesbians and, to a lesser extent, racial minorities), it is tempting to read an implicit recognition of structural discrimination. Whether consciously or not, objections to being supplanted in the law by "special classes" were organized around a fear of loss—that the recognition of gay and lesbian citizens in the city legal code would signal a loss of the privileged assumption that white and heterosexual status equaled that of universal citizen under the law. These fears are that new cultural and legal norms would make white heterosexuals (often implicitly male, and often explicitly Christian) more vulnerable—a fear expressed in terms of becoming more like places such as California, of being mainstreamed into what was perceived as a left-leaning national culture not desired by many residents.

The comments excerpted above all have in common a fear that terms in which protection under the law were written would change: that gay and lesbian subjects would become too central to the law, their rights too protected, and that the very definition of the safety of the community would be recast away from protecting those who had previously assumed centrality to the law (as "universal" citizens) toward protecting those members who had previously been assumed to be on the fringe.[46] The idea that the ordinance might make Laramie more like Laguna Beach encapsulates the way in which the discussion of the ordinance became a debate on how it might threaten or even redraw community norms and boundaries. The ordinance itself, in its modest requirements, had no such formal legal or jurisdictional power. These concerns had to do with the way that the ordinance archived a particular interpretation of the crime as well as with how the ordinance represented a normative vision of the community. These concerns, however, go beyond the bounds of representation as it is normally understood; the concerns were about what types of hierarchies and relationships were implied by the ordinance. In the balance was the question of how the ordinance would define the normal citizen around whom the law revolves, who would be defined as vulnerable, and who would be defined as a potential threat. In sum, it defined who is within the law and who is outside it.

### Performing Care, Being Modern

In the end, the desire to realign the community with national norms, as expressed through the media coverage, prevailed. The ordinance passed. The reasons that the former council members gave for this passage and for how the ordinance changed Laramie, generally for the better in their estimations, suggest that the ordinance was indeed a way to make a statement directed at "the world." The statement was that Laramie was a caring community. The need to express caring and its relationship to being modern are indicative of the ordinance's intricate affective politics. The fact that the council felt a need to display sentiments of caring, even archive them into law, is tied to the way that the media coverage constructed norms of feeling for Matthew Shepard and the desire of locals to show that they too joined in this feeling and so were normal and reasonable people. It was also linked to attempts to articulate a modern and civilized civic identity, a response to the rhetoric and iconography of the media coverage.

Laramie had been represented as out of synch, out of time, out of feeling with the nation, particularly with the liberal public that formed around Matthew Shepard's death. The backdrop against which a predominance of media texts addressed their reading/viewing publics was an iconic geography: namely, the West. This geography conveyed romantic visions of the past but also of ambivalent masculinity, gender and racial violence incompatible with liberal ideals of tolerance and notions of being civilized. The idea that the ordinance was a statement of caring seemed to offer the opportunity to speak back to this representation, to connect Laramie to what were locally seen as nationally normative responses to Shepard's death. Caring was a central term for connection, from the exhortations of Father Roger Schmidt and Rev. Sally Palmer for the council to take the "opportunity to show that Laramie notices and cares about everyone," to the urging from UW president Phil Dubois for the council to pass the ordinance in order to "affirm, in the wake of the murder of Matthew Shepard, that this community cares about what happened here and that we are committed in the most profound way to preventing similar crimes from happening again."[47] Each invocation of caring was articulated as a display, in Palmer's case to "show" an undefined public or audience the good character of the community and in Dubois's case to show potential students and faculty recruits that Laramie was not a bad place. The ordinance was treated as a way of institutionalizing the proper display of feeling about the crime; that is, it would create an institutional structure that reflected normative feelings on the crime, demonstrating that Laramie was not a "bad" place but a place like others, within the norms of sentiment.

The national discourse had cast some doubt that the city (and its officials) cared enough about Matthew Shepard's death and about potential issues of inequality and prejudice within the local culture. Several council members discussed the ordinance as a way of offering proof that they did indeed care. By doing so, they hoped to move Laramie closer to the national image of liberalism. Articulation and institutionalization of a particular affective response was the method for closing this gap. Council members felt this need acutely, referencing the need to manage the community's image through demonstrating feeling. Perhaps most attuned to this, as the mayor at the time that Matthew Shepard was killed, Trudy McKracken said that her own swing vote to support the bill was the outcome of empathy and the need to show others that she, and the city, cared. McKracken was, in many ways, a member of the opposition, holding that the label of hate crime had been imposed by a liberal media, when the murder was really a robbery gone wrong, and expressing concern about "legitimating homosexuality." Yet in the end she voted for the ordinance, over the objections of her church and many members of her community, providing the swing vote that allowed the ordinance to pass. She explained why she felt compelled to vote for the ordinance in terms of the need to be fair and in terms of feeling:

> Because of the way the news had positioned it, if you're sitting there saying it's a robbery gone wrong but 99 percent of people think it's a bias crime, it doesn't matter what you do or don't do. The less we did, the more we were seen

as accepting it just being okay. . . . That's where it hurts. It never was okay. How could you say it was okay? You'd have to be like that Reverend from [Kansas].[48]

What is particularly striking in McKracken's vote is that the question of what the ordinance said about Laramie, in particular the norms of feeling within Laramie, came to be the central issue. McKracken's decision to vote for the ordinance, and her expression of the need to show care, were entwined with the framing of the ordinance and anti-gay violence as a civil rights issue. While she did not fully accept the framing of anti-gay violence as a civil rights issue, the testimony about racial violence and oppression, namely, the imprisonment of Japanese Americans in internment camps during World War II, moved her to accept the ordinance; the location of one of these camps in Wyoming is widely remembered as a dark moment in state history, making testimony about the lingering effects of this racial profiling and violence hit particularly close to home. The council had to act in the face of a dominant interpretation of the crime and had to make a decision and a normative statement about feelings and community norms.

The importance of showing care was a way of trying to demonstrate that Laramie joined in mourning Matthew Shepard, to "show the world" the community was not out of whack with the norm. That care came to encompass this norm shows several interesting points about the way that emotional norms in the media coverage projected a particular vision of liberal national identity, as a community or "we" to which the voices cited here hoped the ordinance would allow admission. In these discussions, care is being advanced as a legitimating emotional scenario. Barbara Koziak discusses the emotional scenarios that provide the background for politics, offering paradigmatic examples of how one should participate in politics and the feelings associated with good citizenship. Knowing when to feel anger, whom to grieve for, and who are the proper objects of pity, empathy, and care are important aspects of being political, belonging to a political community, and demonstrating liberalism. She suggests we learn emotional scenarios, or scripts, for the proper emotional responses to situations through drama and narrative but also political rhetoric and institutions, museums, and holidays. Indeed, political rhetoric and institutions are often charged with inculcating basic emotional scenarios, or scripts for the proper emotional responses to situations, that lend legitimacy to a political philosophy or regime.[49] Such legitimating emotional scenarios in turn structure political participation. Classically, within liberalism, the expression of disinterest (or enlightened self-interest) and rationality are considered proper political feelings: they both fit within and legitimize the political philosophy and workings of liberal democracies. These norms in turn structure the emotional norms and processes of political participation. Such scenarios work at both a macro level and a micro level. Regions and communities with their own subpolitical culture have some variations on these legitimating emotional scenarios. Within the broadly libertarian political culture of Wyoming,[50] typically masculine expressions of stoicism, self-care, and enlightened self-interest are often recognized as the most appropriate expressions of political feeling, as they legitimate a libertarian political stance or system. So it is striking that other-oriented expressions of care more associated with femininity became persuasive and widespread among politicians in the passage of the ordinance and afterward. It is striking as well that expressions of feelings marked as such—in contrast to the classic expression of disinterest—were key to performing mainstream (liberal) politics.

The expression of care, in fact, was articulated as proof of the community's "reasonability." This reasonability, in turn, was linked to economic interests or the desire to prove that the community was capable of supporting, and in fact was already involved in, the modern economy. The need to demonstrate reasonability through care came as a response to the way many felt Laramie had been shown as out of synch with the rest of the nation. As Furphy told me, "We felt that the media loved to portray us as, I don't know how to describe it, as a backwards, Western cowboy town, that biases were very prevalent. And that was unfortunate."[51] In a similar vein, Williams explained that Laramie was portrayed as a "wide-open town. Anything and all can happen. Lot of drinking. Fights. Brawling. Just the Laramie of 1868, when the railroad comes through. That'd be the wide-open West. I think it was portrayed that we're not necessarily a modern community with modern people and modern thoughts."[52] Williams in particular linked the representation of Laramie to a deficiency of modernity. This felt deficiency was echoed in other council members' complaints that Laramie had been represented as "backwards," "redneck," or "rundown." In these complaints, issues of economic development, normality, and modernity are interwoven as desirable goals, goals that had been symbolically distanced from Laramie. Shumway echoed these concerns about economic portrayal. His complaints about *The Laramie Project* keyed in on its mise-en-scène. The playwrights focused on the economically depressed Laramie, he noted, not images of prosperity, development, and industry. In general, he said, the media had shown Laramie as backwards and rundown, lacking images or mention of new construction, the university, and the renovated downtown. A similar line of argumentation had been used by UW president Dubois during the council hearings. He had suggested that the murder and its mediation presented an image of Laramie that was scaring away potential students and faculty. Passage of the ordinance would counter this and, in doing so, help grow the local economy.[53]

Community leaders' concerns about appearing modern, reasonable, and caring (all closely intertwined) in the wake of media images of "backwardness" were in part concerns about attracting industry and investment. They feared the murder and its mediation might make the town appear unattractive to "new economy" investment. The ordinance, especially the way it was discussed as representing caring and defining the community as one of "acceptance," was positioned by these council members as a way of presenting Laramie as a feasible site for software, environmental, and other new economy industries.

The linkage between care, or sensitivity, and reasonability and a modern economy is further illustrated by the way council members discussed breaches of sensitivity and reasonability. Several attributed such breaches to Bell, who became the symbol of all that was not quite reasonable or modern in the debates in the recollections of the other council members. Bell, an outspoken libertarian-conservative, was the strongest opponent to the ordinance and was the only council member who continued to heatedly oppose the ordinance in discussions with me, bemoaning the fact that the council had gotten "caught up in the emotion of the case" and had bought what he called the "liberal media line."[54] The other council members discussed Bell less as an opponent in reasonable debate and more as a foil; he stood in for unreasonableness, exemplifying the face that Laramie did not want to put forward to outsiders. The other council members and several of the activists talked about the council's desire to avoid media coverage in terms of Bell. McKracken lamented his lack of empathy, citing it as embarrassing for the council. Similarly, Shumway complained about Bell's insensitivity and "inappropriate comments," remembering,

> "And every time a council meeting was televised, he would speak and people would say, 'What is wrong with this council?' Instead of saying, 'I understand the other side,' he would just say we cannot do this or that or whatever. He was sending a message that a lot of people would just say you are not current on what needs to be done to make our community more tolerant."[55]

An important part of what Shumway laments here is Bell's unreasonableness, marked by his unwillingness to enter into debate and dialogue. It is not merely Bell's position or stridence that comes under attack. It is his refusal to demonstrate sensitivity and care and show that Laramie was "reasonable." Shumway complained that Bell made the council look like "they wanted to stay back in the rough and tumble frontier days of Laramie" rather than move into the modern era of "acceptance." The rough and tumble days of Laramie are marked by a stoic performance of disinterest and what I have described as hard masculinity;

here, masculinity and feeling are linked to unreasonableness and illiberalism, a performance discussed as out of time and place.

Whatever the motivation, the desire to perform reasonability, benchmarked by demonstrating sensitivity and caring, came across clearly in almost all of my interviews with local politicians. All the council members I spoke with save Bell demonstrated their own care (as a normative feeling), either taking credit for passage of the ordinance or qualifying and diminishing their opposition. They remembered the ordinance as a step forward in Laramie politics and remarked that Laramie was somehow a better place than before. This is despite the fact that two of them, not counting Bell, had spoken and voted against the ordinance. The council members took greater credit for the ordinance than they should have, remembering that a council member had drafted and introduced it, when, in reality, it had been forced on the council by the Laramie Coalition and others. No one mentioned the reluctance of the council to consider a hate crime ordinance, that residents had had to "filibuster" to get the issue on the agenda, or the impassioned arguments that many residents felt compelled to present at the council meetings. Meyer remembered the ordinance as having stronger support than it actually had, passing by a wide margin rather than a 5–4 vote. Several rearticulated their opposition in more supportive terms when speaking to me. Williams, who had opposed the ordinance, qualified his opposition in terms of the language and his understanding of bias as interpersonal friction. Perhaps if it had been called a hate crimes ordinance, he said, he would have supported it.

Perhaps tellingly, Shumway, the only person I spoke with who was still on the council at the time of our interview, was the most striking in his performance of care. Whereas he had argued against the ordinance, invoking the Bible and the Constitution against it (saying the Constitution was "divinely inspired"), in our interview he spoke in support of the ordinance.[56] He expressed sympathy for the challenges faced by gay and lesbian residents and lauded the ordinance for showing that Laramie cared about these residents. While he pointed out that the ordinance did little other than give people the "warm fuzzies," he said it was an "appropriate" act, distancing himself from what he termed Bell's "insensitivity." The distance between his words at the time and his words to me invite a reading as an adaptive political performance. He was, after all, an acting city representative at the time we spoke. His words to me were a performance of what he deemed to be the most appropriate face to put forward as such a representative. For Shumway, the ordinance became a way of performing a political, civic identity after the fact. For others, as evidenced above, the ordinance was at the time an important vehicle for performing normalcy: showing a care that would align the community's public image with that of the rest of the nation (and its economy).

Whatever the impact of the ordinance, its actual provisions have likely made little difference in the daily lives of gay and lesbian residents, although changes to police training and culture may mean a greater ability to turn to and trust the police. The categories of administrative knowledge and feeling that were written onto the ordinance through the public deliberation on the ordinance arguably had a bigger impact on broader, implicitly heteronormative local discourse and politics. In passing the ordinance, the council endorsed a new administrative category and procedures for producing a particular form of knowledge. The collection and reporting of data marked altercations that otherwise would have been classified as normal as political violence or altercation; in the first year after the passage of the ordinance, 2001, this meant recording two assaults against men perceived as Arab or Muslim as bias crimes. In passing the ordinance, the council also endorsed caring and sensitivity as ideals. These feelings became legitimating emotional scenarios, officially designated as the proper emotional responses to gay and lesbian (and arguably racial minority) residents in order for the community to live up to its own self-image as a tolerant and safe place. Passing a law became more than just recordkeeping in how it was understood to institutionalize a way of seeing things, of performing political goals and membership. It was, in this sense, a way of inculcating this norm, whether through enforcing police training and standards for police responses to harassment and hate crimes or through the symbolic message and ethical work it did in defining internal and external relationships of proximity and distance.

The outcomes of these emotional or affective politics are perhaps most striking in the public performance of city representatives. The performance of reasonability as care in the way local politicians recounted their involvement in the ordinance and its effects demonstrates a shift in their read on what is a good or desirable political performance. This shift is a structural effect of the media coverage of the murder of Shepard, notably its emotional mediation. In the wake of this mediation, demonstrations of care and inclusion are more palpable in the presentation of Laramie to others. The need to present a face of openness and inclusion, especially to gay and lesbian and racial/ethnic minority residents, is not the same as political ideals of recognition or even cosmopolitan comfort. And even these limited feelings were not expressed or accepted by many. Yet a public norm and expectation of "sensitivity" or "acceptance" as benchmarks of political performance can be a motivator toward more inclusive political behavior and decisions. Against the common disposition that one's true feelings are interior and the unchangeable property of the individual and therefore it is better to know someone's prejudice than for them to hide it, attention to the social elements of affect suggests that behaviors are what is important—that is, the products of affect. Within this perspective, the institutionalization of a set of dispositions and norms for expression concerned not only with Matthew Shepard's death but also with broader issues of sexuality and homophobia is a notable political outcome.

## Conclusion: Law and Legitimate Feelings

To say that the ordinance was a structural outcome of the emotional mediation of the murder of Matthew Shepard is not to say that the law was the most important measure of social change. I did not set out to explore and explain the political and social changes that have taken place since the murder so much as the impacts of the emotional mediation. There were many other important after-effects, both institutional and cultural, better explored by others.[57] For one, the many activisms spurred by the murder and its aftermath constitute key changes. The simple greater visibility of gay and lesbian residents and LGBT politics and organizations and the spaces in which they are visible constitute an important cultural shift. And changes in the university's antidiscrimination policies to include sexuality and sick leave to cover same-sex partners—health benefits for same-sex partners have not been so forthcoming—are also institutional changes.[58] All of these may be among the impacts of the emotional mediation. And, of course, some would say that there has been little meaningful change at all. Several of the activists I spoke with said that the community in many important ways had dropped the ball, with people preferring to put things behind them rather than make the difficult changes required to become a more respectful and just community.

Yet the fact that the bias crimes ordinance came to represent (or stand in for) change to so many is important. In highlighting the law, I mean to emphasize the ability of public expressions of feeling to work their way into the formal institutions of state—or here, city—politics. The symbolism of the law as change points to another important point. Legal change, or the instantiation of a law, is a much more material event than cultural shifts, which can be ephemeral and are certainly difficult to quantify. This is part of the social authority of the law. Legislation has great claim as a democratic institution, mediating claims of the public with the abstract political principles that define the political community. This authority is perhaps why so many people pointed to the ordinance as proof that the community had really "done something." The passage of the law, many of my respondents told me, had made Laramie a more sensitive and tolerant place. The law was the material outcome that proved this to locals and outsiders alike. The passion of the debate surrounding the ordinance certainly had to do with this authority; the fact that it was a law made the statement that the ordinance represented to residents a binding one, an official record.

The fact that these affective politics of the ordinance were expressed via legislation is of further interest. The authority invested in the ordinance—that it had really done something—derives from the ideological and material authority of the law, but also from the very procedures of democratic governance required to pass a law through a legislative body, even a minor one such as a city council. The procedures of hearings, debate, and voting are those upon which the formal legitimacy of democratic governance rests. These procedures provided legitimacy for Laramie's bias crimes ordinance. They also provided legitimacy for the affective norms that the ordinance came to represent. While much of this authority is rhetorically linked to the supposed neutrality and autonomy of law,[59] the public discussions and decision-making process on the part of council members were saturated with affect. The two are difficult to separate. This is an important point, one that parallels Martha Nussbaum's argument that the language of the law is filled with feeling or Barbara Koziak's discussion of emotion within political institutions: the very processes that constitute the ideal norms of democratic governance, from the formation of publics to the decisions made by the governing body, are deeply concerned with feelings and relationships. Discussions of which feelings were legitimate and which relationships were desirable underlay much of the deliberation over the ordinance. In fact, much of what the public debate, official deliberation, and formal decision making (enactment of law) did was to read feelings and relationships into the law and arbitrate which were legitimate and desirable. These processes were not the dry regulations and procedures that procedural theories of governance hold dear, as tools to rein in passion and personal interests and to produce decisions free of these influences. In the political/legal debates traced here, it is difficult to separate process from feeling; passionate feelings animated the process, and the process inscribed particular emotional norms. The debates traced here suggest that affective politics are internal to the procedures of democratic governance and lawmaking and that this is not a corruption so much as a condition of possibility for political action.

The discussion and passage of the law was also an effort to be part of mainstream politics. When affect within politics is not seen as corruption or distraction, it is often attributed to nonnormative politics and publics. These counterpublics, and their political styles, do not have to abide by the more staid discursive norms as mainstream politics and so are free to engage in more embodied and markedly emotional discourse.[60] What I want to suggest is that mainstream politics is just as affective; it is merely a different performance. In this case, the performance of mainstream politics is through self-evidently emotional discourse. This performance was not isolated to advocates of the ordinance. Both sides in this argument were based in attachments, deeply invested in how the law would define the boundaries of community. Politics, here, was motivated simultaneously by attachment to principles and to specific groups of people.

Much media and communication scholarship recognizes the ability of media communication to work on such attachments: to pull us into community and to redefine relationships of proximity and distance, identification and identity. This is the work of mediation. When what is at stake are events and people in the real world, this work of mediation takes on a profound ethical and political charge, and burden. Yet it is difficult to follow the ethics of mediation into the realm of formal political processes and institutions. This difficulty is nicely illustrated by Roger Silverstone's impressive attempt to think through the political impact of the mediation of global events. His focus on the ethics of mediation and the way that appearances in media texts shape our imagined relationships to distant others leads him to focus not on the public sphere but on the mediapolis, which he notes is both more and less than the public sphere.[61] This shift in terminology is indicative of a shift away from the structural focus of the public sphere as much as it is a shift away from a too narrow conception of political communication. Taking up a different democratic paradigm, the polis, allows for a shift toward an analytics focused on membership, hierarchy, performance, and relationships. However, it makes it hard to bring the argument back down to specific political institutions and normative arguments about how media ought to work within a cosmopolitan, or simply just, democratic order.

Emotional discourse in media is a key part of what others have called the ethics of mediation. The "work" performed by emotional discourse in processes of mediation can be traced in sites of formal political processes and institutions and understood within the structures of the public sphere. The affective work of mediation has roots in broad social structures, and it shapes the very political institutions and processes most integral to democracy. This basic argument that the affective work of media impacts formal politics is most visible and easily made in a case of small-scale city politics. The emotional mediation of the murder of James Byrd Jr. and the impact of this mediation on the ongoing debate on hate crimes in Texas complicates the picture, raising questions about how emotional mediation works within more complex democratic politics and about affective politics and questions of distributive justice.

# [ 3 ]

# The Murder of James Byrd Jr.
## *The Political Pedagogy of Melodrama*

> Will the sin against James Byrd be somehow converted into redemption? The Sixteenth
> Street Baptist Church bombing hastened the passage of the Civil Rights Act of 1964.
> More recently, the videotaped police beating of a black motorist named Rodney King
> changed standard operating procedure in Los Angeles.
> —Diane McWhorter, "Texas Killing Recalls Racism's Past,"
> *USA Today,* June 16, 1998
> This isn't *Mississippi Burning,* but it is Jasper having a lot of trouble.
> —Jasper resident quoted in "Jasper, Texas/ Byrd Murder/ Aftermath,"
> *CBS Nightly News,* June 23, 1998

"IN TEXAS TONIGHT, the shocking echoes of a time that many
Americans believed was behind us."[1] With these words Tom Brokaw relayed the
news of the murder of James Byrd Jr. to viewers. Byrd, a 49-year-old black man,
father, and grandfather, had been dragged to death behind a pickup truck by
three white men in the small town of Jasper in rural East Texas. The details of the
murder were both grisly and horribly familiar. The details and location of the
crime seemed to many Americans, especially white Americans, like something
from the past, before the victories of the civil rights movement. Perhaps because
of this, the murder became a flash point for discussing the ability of national
legal and social systems to provide equal protection and inclusion to black and
white Americans. In the weeks that followed the murder, this discussion moved
the focus of the media coverage and public discussion away from the specific
violence visited upon Byrd and what it said about racial equality in the present
and toward the ability of the law to make up for the failures of the past. In this
shift, the story told by the press transmuted from tragedy to triumph.

In order to understand how a black man being dragged to death behind
a pickup truck driven by three white neighbors became a story about national
racial progress, it is necessary to understand the complex of cultural geography
and narrative tradition used to make sense of and contextualize the murder in

mainstream media coverage. The media coverage of Byrd's murder offers an example of how the existing organization of both symbolic power and material resources structure the deployments of feeling via media texts. The narrative forms employed by news convey relationships and messages about who to feel for. In this case, the media coverage was heavily influenced by a preexisting narrative structure and set of feelings surrounding racism, the present, and the past in the United States. This prior narrative structure was melodrama: the form that, as Linda Williams notes, has provided the most common and durable form for telling the history of racial conflict.[2] This chapter analyzes how this narrative form structured relationships and normalized a particular set of feelings in the wake of the murder of James Byrd Jr. These narratives and images mediated the murder, both referencing common emotional scenarios and issuing invitations to feel. In doing so, this media coverage linked feelings about the murder to ways of feeling modern, feeling about the law, and to an image of virtuous whiteness.

In chapter 1, I describe how news texts invited feelings of proximity to Matthew Shepard as a victim of homophobic violence. In that case, the mediation encouraged logics of kinship and substitution: he could have been me, my son, my neighbor. In doing so, the mediation expanded the normative boundaries of inclusion in the mainstream media representations of the nation/national community. In this chapter, I take up another sensational crime in which the role of the media was again crucial. Here, however, the mediation did not construct proximity between viewer and victim but rather distanced the violence and the victim from the audience. Still, the coverage did suggest that the crime was important and relevant to the various media audiences addressed, and a public did form through the mediation of the murder. The mediation, then, did something more complex than merely encourage apathy or construct the event as an isolated moment of personal tragedy.

Taken together, newspaper, magazine, and TV texts circulated invitations to feel pity for the victim, disgust for the killers (and the past), and hope or pride in the nation (as a site of progress).[3] The complicated political outcomes of this deployment are the subjects of this and the following chapter. This chapter focuses on the emotional mediation of the murder. Chapter 4 looks at the politically oriented publics that formed or mobilized through articulation of these feelings. These publics were focused on the institutional politics of the state legislature; analyzing what types of arguments this affective display enabled in the institutional political processes of the legislature allows me to traverse between the cultural politics of affective modes of mediation to the institutional politics of this mediation.

## The Murder and Its Mediation

On Saturday night, June 6, 1998, James Byrd Jr. was walking home from his niece's bridal shower in the small town of Jasper, Texas. Byrd, a former vacuum salesman and father of three, was offered a ride by three white men in a primer-gray pickup truck. Byrd accepted the ride and shared beers and cigarettes with the three men. At some point, they drove down a small logging road and stopped the car. There, they beat Byrd and tied him by his feet to the back of the pickup truck.[4] They then dragged him for 2 ½ miles before leaving his by then decapitated and badly mutilated body on the side of the road, near a black church. According to forensic evidence that would become important to officials seeking capital punishment for his killers, Byrd was alive and conscious for part of this ride. The manner of Byrd's death and the placement of his body in a poor black neighborhood, so near the church, led the police to treat the murder as a hate crime. This allowed local authorities to call on the FBI for additional investigators, expertise, and equipment beyond the capacity/budget of their small-town facilities. Three local white men—Bill King, Russell Brewer, and Shawn Berry—were quickly arrested in connection with the murder, and evidence was compiled for their prosecution. Interactions with the three men, the content of their tattoos, and the white supremacist literature in their possession further convinced the police and public that the motivation was tied to race.

Byrd's body was discovered on the morning of June 7. The news media quickly arrived in Jasper, a town of just over 8,000 people (roughly 48 percent white, 44 percent black) in East Texas, overwhelming the small town.[5] By June 9 his murder was a prominent story on the nightly news on all three major networks, and by the next day it was headline news across the nation. The press stayed in town to report on the progress and tactics in the case. The continuing story largely focused on questions of law and the prosecution of the killers. (One such question was whether the murder could or would be tried under federal hate crimes law. It could not, because the murder had not involved a violation of federally protected activity such as voting.)

In all of this media coverage, a faint portrait of Byrd emerged. His age and race were the primary identifiers. While he had extended family in the Jasper area and was known by many, the details of his life were sketchy; a few stories identified him as an unemployed vacuum salesman, and many referred to an undefined disability. Very few mentioned his three children. One daughter, Renee Mullins, emerged later as an advocate for the James Byrd Jr. Hate Crimes Act, while his son, who became an anti–death penalty activist, was given a less prominent role in the coverage. His younger daughter, Jamie, did not take on a prominent role.

The media and national attention culminated on June 13 with Byrd's funeral, which was paid for by basketball star and Texas native Dennis Rodman, who also reportedly donated $25,000 to Byrd's children (aged 16, 20, and 27 at the time of his death). Although there were no national congregations of mourners or protesters in Washington or elsewhere, as there would be for Matthew Shepard, the Jasper church in which the funeral took place overflowed with both local and visiting mourners. The ceremony was attended by Jesse Jackson, Al Sharpton, NAACP president Kweisi Mfume, California representative and chairwoman of the Congressional Black Caucus Maxine Waters, Texas representative Kay Bailey Hutchinson, and numerous members of the Texas legislature. Bill Clinton, who had made a national conversation on race a cornerstone of his presidency, sent Transportation Secretary Rodney Slater as an administration envoy and called Byrd's mother to offer his personal condolences. Outside the funeral, a small group of black men in paramilitary garb carrying rifles and calling themselves the New Black Panthers marched, in their words, to protect and "wake up" local black residents. Much to locals' dismay, the KKK responded by calling a rally two weeks later. The New Black Panthers (based in Dallas) and the Black Muslims, a paramilitary group from Houston, arranged counterprotests for the same day, all three groups promising to be armed. The media reappeared for the tense turf fight between white supremacist and black militant groups. The rhetoric on all sides rang of claims about who owned Texas or the future and about governmental wrongs.

During this time, there were outbreaks of vitriol clearly tied to the murder in several other states. Few were covered in the national news, and they did not become part of the conversation about the contemporary state of race relations and racism within the national media. In the days after Byrd's death, copycat draggings were reported in Illinois and Louisiana; in each case a black man sustained minor injuries after being dragged for a short distance by several whites in a car. Several months later, shortly after the first of Byrd's attackers was convicted, a morning disk jockey in Washington, D.C., was fired after commenting on a track from Lauryn Hill's Grammy-nominated album *The Miseducation of Lauryn Hill:* "No wonder they drag them behind trucks." He later apologized, but told the TV news magazine *20/20* that he did not deserve to lose his job over the comment. And in New York City, two firefighters and one policeman were fired after entering a float in a Labor Day parade that parodied Byrd's murder in order to protest neighborhood integration. The float consisted of off-duty white policemen and firefighters in blackface and Afro wigs, who mimed eating fried chicken and watermelon on the back of a pickup truck. One of the group inter-mittently mimed being dragged behind the truck.[6] This float would be oddly echoed a few months later in Ft. Collins, Colorado, where a sorority-fraternity float in a homecoming parade mockingly referenced Matthew Shepard's death with a giant scarecrow figure spray-painted with anti-gay epithets.

My analysis here follows the story of Byrd's murder from the immediate newspaper and TV news stories to the later analysis and retelling in magazine articles and dramatizations to examine the patterns of discourse on Byrd's mur-der. As with Matthew Shepard's murder, media attention waned shortly after Byrd's funeral and the attendant protests, to return during the trials. The news initially registered shock that such a crime could still occur in America, with columnists and editorials in some papers engaging in a discussion of the con-temporary character of racism, including some discussions of ongoing structur-al racism (evidenced in housing policy, education funding and opportunities, and bank policy). This focus waned when authorities announced they would seek the death penalty. As the prosecution proceeded, and as militant groups took to the streets in Jasper, the news shifted focus to the killers, the community, and the prosecution. By the end of the month, newspapers and TV news had turned their focus almost entirely to the community and the prosecution, with largely favorable stories on how the community of Jasper was responding to the crime and the racial fault lines it exposed and on the progress of the criminal prosecution.[7] More than was the case with the coverage of Matthew Shepard, news reports followed a strong narrative from crisis to resolution. These reports, borrowing from Hollywood media culture, drew upon a common set of narra-tives about racism and violence in America in order to make sense of the crime.

### Melodrama and the Invitation to Feel

The narratives that emerged in political speeches and news discourse on Byrd's murder revolved heavily around melodrama. News reports spent less time trying to parse the motives of the killers and the rationale of the crime than in the coverage of the murder of Matthew Shepard, perhaps because Byrd's murder was so familiar. Its details echoed a long history of lynching and vio-lence against black men told in history and in fiction. Reporters, locals, and aca-demic commentators all fell back on a familiar set of narratives and references to Hollywood melodramas such as *Mississippi Burning, To Kill a Mockingbird,* and John Grisham stories in order to place and explain Jasper and the murder. These cinematic narratives of the past provided a blueprint for narrating the present in the news coverage. Melodrama offered a familiar structure of understanding for interpreting the murder as well as a familiar structure of feeling, conveying with it a set of complicated affective politics.

The influence of melodrama on the news texts covering the murder can be seen in the narrative structure of the news coverage and in the social logic underlying the presentation of the crime and the problem of racism in general. This narrative structure and social logic is what Linda Williams terms the melodramatic "mode of discourse." Her point is that melodrama is not just a genre but also a deeper structure that limits what we can say and how we understand events.[8] Melodrama as a mode of discourse revolves around the articulation and resolution of moral dilemmas, pitting good against evil, virtue against villainy. This is an issue of both aesthetics and frameworks of understanding. The structure of melodrama revolves around a sympathetic victim and the forces that victimize him or her; the confrontation of the victim with his or her source of suffering (the villainy of the story) demands resolution or redress. This structure as well as the emotive and aesthetic "excesses" that characterize the form are ways in which melodramatic discourse makes abstract and hidden social relations and issues not only visible but "legible." Within melodrama, large-scale, abstract conflicts often play out in the familiar spaces of the domestic sphere and are signaled by bodily distress. While the domesticity and focus on individual pain may seem to predispose melodrama to privatization or the translation of events into personal or psychological terms, this is not the only way to read the politics of melodrama. The very familiarity and individual focus of melodrama have also, historically, worked to make these abstract social relations concrete, present, and pressing.[9] In this way, melodrama uses the language of feeling associated with the feminine, private sphere to make claims in the public sphere, using the language of feeling to make structural social organization and change, even examples of social injustice, available for public discourse. The very focus on emotion and articulations of proximity through sensational depictions of individual suffering (of a hero or victim) is what makes abstract structural issues widely legible as pressing social issues.

The focus of melodrama on making complex social issues and tensions easy to see and understand makes it a particularly pedagogical form. The display of emotions associated with this explication makes melodrama a particularly affective pedagogical form. Melodramas teach us not only to see social and moral tensions but also to recognize and feel for the victims, to desire justice for wronged virtue. In articulating virtue and villainy through feeling, melodramas provide political education through lessons about whom we should pity, love, or revile. In this light, melodramas provide emotional scenarios that act as lessons on proper political feelings. The lessons taught may be reinforcement of existing power structures, arguments for the inclusion of marginalized populations, or demands for justice or recognition. The centering of the plot on deep conflicts and their resolution has made melodrama a popular way of demanding recognition or resolution for the suffering caused by social issues such as the unequal distribution of rights and resources.[10] Indeed, feminist scholars have argued for the importance of melodrama in making women's work and women's issues visible within the public sphere and making these issues legible as ethical and political issues.[11] Similarly, Williams argues, melodrama has provided the most durable, prolific form for articulating the dilemmas of race in the United States, even as it often simplifies these dilemmas. By presenting a complex issue (racial injustice) through portrayals of suffering that everyone can understand and read as unjust, melodrama has worked to make structural inequalities and violence surrounding race visible within the dominant public sphere. This is not simply to align melodrama with racial justice projects; melodrama has also been employed to legitimate some of the worst violence against black Americans, in the popular, journalistic, and cinematic emplottment of lynching narratives as melodrama (in which white women are the victims, black men the villains, and lynching white men the heroes).[12] In its moment of making racial oppression visible, the form has been a major vehicle for making racial oppression legible as an issue of social justice to white audiences, especially in political and social contexts where race and racial conflict are hidden or denied.[13] The price of this visibility is conforming to the mode. Some examples of social antagonism fit the aesthetics and logic of melodrama better than others: violence is more amenable to this form than housing policy or school funding, even though the latter are expressions of deep social antagonisms. The mode of melodrama, as the media coverage and political action that followed Byrd's murder make clear, also imposes a structure for justice claims. If melodramas offer emotional lessons on whom we should value and feel proximity to and distance from, they also teach who may embody civic ideals and who is outside these ideals. Such normative emotional scenarios provide the backdrop against which justice claims are made and the common sense upon which judgments of the legitimacy of those claims are based.

In the mediation of Byrd's murder, the lessons and scenarios were provided through news texts. These texts were narrated as melodrama. This is not a new proposition; others have noted that news, like other nonfictional discourse, is often structured like entertainment.[14] Bill Nichols notes that TV news strikes an uneasy balance between the "discourse of sobriety" of classical documentary and news and the style and spectacles of entertainment media.[15] Others have pointed to a similar melodramatic tendency in print news.[16] In saying that news is often told as melodrama, I am not only suggesting that our understanding of historical, real-world events is structured by the language and tools of fiction, as notably argued by Hayden White, but that these tools bring with them affective structures as well.[17] The aesthetics (or form) of nonfiction discourse not only shapes how we understand events but also how we feel about them. From this perspective, news becomes a sort of docudramatic discourse; it speaks about real events in the real world, but often does so with the same semiotic and poetic (or world-making) tools of fiction and drama. Like dramatic/fictional media texts, news produces a rich picture of the world. Unlike fiction, news produces this as nonfiction discourse on the real. Hence the aesthetic and narrative forms employed in news discourse take on a particularly concrete political relevance.

In the mediation of Byrd's murder, the form of melodrama offered affective political lessons on the nature of racism as a social ill as well as on whom to pity. The articulation of Byrd's murder as melodrama was visible in the recurring portrayals of the event as a conflict between an innocent victim and agents of a social evil (racism) and in attempts to offer a resolution to this conflict. The way in which Byrd was made a mournable victim, Bill King discussed as virulently villainous, and District Attorney Guy James Gray and Sheriff Billy Rowles treated as heroes follow emotional scenarios performed repeatedly in racial melodramas: the need to feel for the victim, though often at a distance, to condemn the villain(s), and to seek resolution to the wrong. Injustice and social conflicts are given concrete form in the presentation of victim and villain, giving form and definition to racism as a social problem.

Because of the focus on the unjust suffering of the innocent victim, and the attendant feelings for the victim, melodrama demands action (either fictional or real) to curtail or redress the suffering.[18] This scenario contains a mobilizing logic. The condemnation of the villain and pity for the victim lend themselves to a demand for action. The way that melodramatic tales present the sources of injustice, the conflicts that bring on the victim's suffering, in turn shape this demand for action. The way that injustice and its source are depicted and defined shapes what type of action is called for.

### STRUCTURES OF LEGIBILITY: THE LESSONS OF JASPER
Melodrama makes social issues legible by making them concrete and articulating them within discourses and aesthetics of injustice. In this case, the issue of racism was made concrete through the embodiment of the killers and the victim as well as through the site of racial violence; both formed the aesthetic presentation of injustice. Most obviously, this aesthetic presentation made racism legible in the present through the graphic violence of the murder, the oppositions

between Byrd and his killers, and the cultural iconography of the setting of the murder. All formed the particular shape and meaning of the injustice and defined the appropriate objects and types of feeling.

The issue of legibility requires some historical, discursive context. The murder took place at the end of a cycle of national conversations and confrontations over the continued impact of racial inequality and racism in American society—most literally, at the end of Clinton's series of national "conversations on race." These conversations, in the form of traveling town-hall meetings, were scheduled to commence with a summative statement about the state of contemporary race relations when Byrd was killed. (There were, in fact, suggestions that this summative meeting should take place in Jasper.) Within this historical context, the murder was far from alone as an articulation of racial conflict, though it was perhaps the most irrefutable. It took place against the backdrop of a number of highly mediated political and legal "spectacles" of black-and-white racial conflicts in the 1990s.[19] Perhaps the most notable of these spectacles was the racial split in perceptions over the O. J. Simpson murder trial and the outcome of the police beating of Rodney King. These highly mediated events staged claims of structural racial injustice against claims that racism was a thing of the past. These events, including the debate over Clarence Thomas and Anita Hill, mounting attacks on affirmative action in college admissions, the media hype over "welfare queens," and the controversies over Clinton appointees Lani Guinier and Joycelyn Elders, became emblematic of a schism in thinking about race. The divisiveness of these events demonstrates the difficulties of making claims on racial justice in the 1990s. Claims that these events were symptomatic of racial injustice were read by many as overzealous "reading into," or imagined. Such refutations were part of a larger contemporaneous idea that American society becomes an equal playing field (and hence that there is no need for programs like affirmative action) and even claims that efforts to redress racism have resulted in reverse racism.[20] This type of claim is among the statements that make up what scholars such as Michael Omi and Howard Winant have termed the "new racism," a set of neoliberal discourses and policies that explain away patterns of social and economic inequality between racialized groups in terms of (private) personal choice rather than (public) history, policy, and structure. The discourses and policies of the new racism obscure structural inequalities, bolstering the idea that racism has already been redressed and is no longer a pressing social or policy issue.[21] Against this backdrop, it was difficult to make events such as jury verdicts, the frameworks used in confirmation hearings, or controversies over Clinton appointees legible as evidence of racism to many Americans. In contrast, the murder of James Byrd Jr. and its mediation offered a clear illustration of the continued hold of an undeniable racism.

Part of the reason that the murder of Byrd was visible as racism was the way the racism was presented as a social problem in the coverage—namely, as direct individual violence. This presentation took shape through the event of the murder itself and through the portrayal of the victim and the killers. The event itself, with its extreme and one-on-one violence and racial motivation, was clearly racism within even the narrowest definition of the term: open physical oppression. It was undeniable. Violence is the most legible form of oppression within the optics of liberalism. While it is only one of the forms of oppression that works to marginalize some groups and maintain the power of others, and not even the most pervasive, it is the most tangible one.[22] As such, it is the most easily acknowledged and addressed within current political and legal systems.

The narration and presentation of the murder, the way Byrd was portrayed as a victim and the killers were portrayed as villains, defined the terms of this visibility as well. The focus on the individuals and the way they came to embody the workings of deep racial conflict presented racism as interpersonal violence. At the same time, a common framing across media outlets of the murder in terms of the past and the South presented the murder as symptomatic of social structures, albeit ones located in the past. In these two frameworks, there was a tension between a recognition of racism as a structural effect and individualist definitions of racism.

The logic by which racism was made visible followed the structure of melodrama in demanding pity for the victim and in the way the killers became villains. Taken together, the distinctions made among these men, the way they were made available for pity, revulsion, attachment, and/or admiration, and the temporal and geographic context within which the murder was placed provided lessons on how to feel not only about the specific men but also about race, racism, and the law. The combination of the heavily melodramatic narrative in the media coverage and the invocation of the complex iconography of race and the South in the United States formed a political pedagogy on race and nation, instructing audiences to feel pity or compassion for Byrd and to feel hope for the law and nation through what was written as the triumph of legal procedure in the rural South.

## REPRESENTING INJUSTICE THROUGH VICTIMIZATION AND VILLAINY

People were invited to feel for Byrd through the narrative and images of media texts. As noted in chapter 1, not all individuals are mourned, much less mourned as national losses or victims. As with the memorialization of Matthew

Shepard, the vast majority of those who were outraged by his killing had never met the man. Instead, this public formed around a mournable victim produced in and through media texts. These texts conveyed the spectacular dimensions of the killing and conveyed the helplessness of Byrd as a victim. They invited people to care, mourn, and feel outrage by describing Byrd the man as well as the spectacular dimensions of his killing, the repeated images (in graphic words as well as the images on the TV screen) of the scene of his death, and the damage done to his body. This terrifying damage became a central point of the discourse surrounding his death, emphasizing both his suffering and the limits of the law and modern social structures to protect actual bodies, especially minoritized bodies, from harm. In print news, the descriptions of the injury done to Byrd's body, while offered in a sober and unsensational voice, offered chilling detail. The television news offered more oblique traces of the violence done to Byrd: the close-ups of orange spray-painted circles on the asphalt, labeled "keys," "dentures," and finally "head," communicated gruesome detail.

In the images and text that publicized and explained the murder in mainstream media, however, Byrd was not fleshed out as a man.[23] He was, rather, depicted only in enough detail to place him as an innocent victim. This lack of resolution is particularly evident, even literal, in the visual representation of Byrd. While a couple of newscasts gave time to family and neighbors to remember and define Byrd as a man, images of him were sparse in both news and print. Television and print media employed the same lone, grainy photo of Byrd. The photo showed him standing, unsmiling, against a wood-paneled interior background, clad in a black baseball cap, blue shirt, and beard and mustache. Its lack of resolution became an issue when the image was to be used to make a case for the passage of the James Byrd Jr. Hate Crimes Act. One of the legislative assistants working on the presentation used Photoshop to enhance Byrd's eyes and make them more visible. He worried, he said, that people could not see Byrd's eyes, and that without being able to see his eyes, they would not be moved by his story.[24] The fuzziness of this image and the lack of others to provide images of the man and his life threatened to leave him distant and unreal, to fail to break through the parade of fictional and entertainment images that crowd the media with the reality of his life and its loss.

This lack of resolution in many ways was repeated in the print descriptions. With fewer constraints on the amount of information conveyed, print news might have been expected to offer more details. A few stories did focus on the family's recollections of Byrd, giving details to his life and allowing them to correct reports that he was hitch-hiking home or "a hitch-hiker," as many initial news reports described him. But the majority of print news stories described

Byrd in vague but racially loaded terms. He was described as affable, happy-go-lucky, joyful, aimless, innocent, defenseless, and an underdog—all terms associated with the tradition of U.S. representations of black men as minstrels and jokesters. However, by far the most common term used in mainstream press was "disabled." Whereas his family described Byrd to television and print reporters in terms of musical talent and good humor, the majority of mainstream news outlets favored descriptions emphasizing his "disability."[25] This description, too, lacked resolution; what this disability was never comes across clearly in the news reports. Some reports said he had a debilitating injury in one hand, while others described him as having a seizure disorder. In most, however, the specifics of his disability are not noted at all. The use of disability as a vague term here suggests that the word is used more to characterize Byrd than to convey journalistic detail. Describing him as disabled highlighted the brutality of the attack with three men ganging up on one defenseless one. It constructed an image of Byrd as a man with reduced agency (similarly to the descriptions of Shepard as childlike). The label ensured Byrd would appear as a clear and compelling victim, one whom people would feel compelled to respond to. It instructed readers to feel pity and compassion for him, drawing upon fraught discourses of black masculinity in order to do so.

As a point of contrast, both Byrd's family and the black-oriented press described him very differently. As noted above, his family's emphasis on personal traits and accomplishments was lost in the dominant media frame of disability. The dominant frame in the black-oriented press also overlooked these traits, although in favor of a less distancing set of descriptors. In a sampling of coverage in black-oriented newspapers, the most common identifications beyond his age, race, and gender were his status as a father and grandfather.[26] Disability was rarely mentioned. His family status was a point of commonality and an invitation for the black reading public to identify with Byrd. This point is underscored by assertions that the crime was a wake-up call "to every African American" or that "[Byrd] could have easily been my own 49-year-old brother."[27] These quotes stand in stark contrast to the distancing rhetoric of the mainstream media, with its invitations to feel pity and compassion. Rather than the horizontal relationships invited in the black press, mainstream news outlets preferred the hierarchical distance of a sympathetic relation, the reification of social distance along lines of race and class. It is important to note that these lines of social distance do not necessarily map to the racial and class identity of actual audiences. Many of the readers addressed by the news were black or working class. Yet these readers were addressed through whiteness and middle- to upper-class position, as presumed points of identification.

The mainstream press's invitation to feel pity for Byrd as a victim was no doubt linked to the presumed demographics of audience as well as an effort to differentiate him from the preponderance of media images of black men as dangerous and criminal.[28] The hypervisibility of black men as criminals in print and television news is coupled with a historical lack of visibility of black victims. Indeed, this coupling goes back to the very inception and definition of crime news; hegemonic ideas of race and gender influence the very definitions of what is considered violent crime.[29] Given the historical coupling of images of black men and violence and crime in news, news portrayals attempted to distance Byrd from these images in order to make him a clear victim. The news emphasis on disability was a way of distancing Byrd from images of threatening black masculinity. This emphasis was key to inviting audiences, in particular, audiences defined through whiteness, to feel sympathy for Byrd. In the way news outlets portrayed Byrd as a victim, they drew upon a broader cultural repertoire of representations of black masculinity. This repertoire is largely dichotomous, limited to polarized stereotypes of either docility (as in the "Uncle Tom" figure) or aggressive, sexualized threat.[30] Disability worked to place Byrd within the tradition of stereotypes of docility. So did the mode of melodrama; melodramas have offered some of the most famous and lasting images of the stereotype of docile black masculinity, including the prototypical narrative of Uncle Tom.[31]

Melodrama and history converge here in the descriptions of Byrd as lacking agency in order to make him a clear object of pity. In de-emphasizing Byrd's agency, the news coverage suggested he was unable to act for himself, implying that others must act for him. In this way, the melodramatic logic present in the news coverage demanded a response from the audience in order to redress the injustice done to Byrd. The discursive effort that went into articulating Byrd as a victim stopped there; that is, he was described as a victim but as little else in most mainstream print and television news. The descriptions of Byrd and the violence done to him had made the effects of racism concrete and compelled condemnation. This contrasts sharply with the ambivalent public response to the racial "spectacles" of the 1990s that had preceded the murder. Compared to these more abstract articulations of the working of racism, Byrd's death was easy to see as racial injustice. The sources of the violence were most clearly the killers, although the geographic setting also presented a set of structures (economy, culture, failures of the law) as potential causes or reasons for the attack, as explored below. The killers presented a particularly concrete embodiment of racism, the source and materialization of the injustice done to Byrd. This embodiment carried with it implicit definitions of what racism looked like, defining racism not only in terms of individual action but also in terms of individuals decidedly distant from the self-image of mainstream media audiences.[32] They became emblematic of what should be condemned and redressed. The "lesson" of this opposition between the victim and the perpetrators was to condemn the individuals as members of white supremacist groups.

These killers, three young white men, were introduced to the public through images and the language of criminality. On television, repeated images of their mug shots and of the "perp walk"—the three men, unshaven and disheveled in their orange prison jumpsuits and handcuffs, being walked up to the Jasper courthouse—introduced them to viewers. In print, they were introduced through their criminal records, with details of their time spent in jail and their ties to white supremacist groups. They were further introduced in print news through descriptors such as twisted, ignorant, monsters, psychopaths, losers, and backwoods felons.

As time wore on, the killers were increasingly differentiated in news as well as dramatic representations. All three were local men. Bill King and Shawn Berry were from Jasper, and Russell Brewer was from the nearby community of Sulphur Springs; he and King met while serving time in prison. Bill King attracted the most attention, being the one who appeared to have led the attack and as the one easiest to see as simply monstrous. Berry emerged as a troubling figure, a man described as well liked and well known by many residents. He was harder for many to see as a monster—or, within an individualist psychological definition of the term, a racist. In the end, all three men were found guilty, but King and Brewer were sentenced to death, while Berry was sentenced to life in prison.

King was, in many ways, the easiest villain and embodiment of racism. Popular narratives of racism not only focus on the Jim Crow era and the struggle for civil rights but also locate racism in examples of pathological whiteness and masculinity. By pathologizing the embodiments of racism, "normal" constructions of whiteness and masculinity are protected from any implications. One common picture of racism in political discourse and popular media is of poor, rural, and Southern (as a place, but also as an indicator of a sort of incomplete whiteness) masculinity.[33] The descriptions and vilification of the killers as poorly educated, unenlightened, and culturally impoverished presumed a readership that shared none of these attributes and furthered the idea that racism is a personal, psychological possession held by some and not by others. The tattoos sported by King and Brewer became the focus of much of this type of attention, as marks of difference and pathology. Both King and Brewer had multiple tattoos on their arms and torsos, collected while in prison and full of racist imagery.

King's tattoos reportedly included the image of a black man hanging from a tree, the words *Aryan Pride*, a pentagram, a baby Jesus with horns (these were the most remarked upon tattoos, listed in news coverage). Television showed the images. Print reports described them. The tattoos were an object of fascination for many, perhaps for how they made the men's racism legible. These tattoos made racism legible in a very literal way, with racist ideologies symbolized and written on the bodies of the killers. Within the historical context of conflicts over what constitutes racial bias that included the trials of O. J. Simpson and the police who beat Rodney King, the tattoos provided evidence of racism that seemed difficult to contest.

The tattoos made racism visible, however, as an individual possession. From the beginning, these tattoos were evidence that the men were what the *New York Times* would later call "real racists," those allied to white supremacists groups.[34] This notion of "real" racists suggests racism is a problem of a few, located on the fringe of society. The designation of "real" sets these racists in opposition to the mainstream institutions and actors (such as the Los Angeles police and Congress) that had been discussed as emblems of racial injustice throughout the public debates on race of the 1990s. These "real" racists were set apart from the broader public through class, geography, and tattoos. This distancing is particularly evident in this *Pittsburgh Post-Gazette* report: "No one in this trio of backwoods felons comes off as particularly enlightened, even by the standards of today's low-rent Ku Klux Klan."[35] Here, the conflation of racism and rural white Southern masculinity and class are made explicit. The *New York Times* elaborated on the theme: "The three men arrested in the killing of Mr. Byrd in east Texas are not university graduates. They are prison graduates—mean, poorly educated, and culturally impoverished."[36] The reference to the KKK here is technically incorrect. King and Brewer had been, or had tried to become, members of the Aryan Brotherhood prison gang (a particularly violent and widespread gang, which uses white supremacist rhetoric as a recruiting tool as well as an intimidation tactic).[37] Even thought this fact was reported, some papers continued to refer to the men's connections to the KKK, which appeared to act as a shortcut for white supremacist organizations (and perhaps "old-fashioned" racism) in general. The two different organizations have origins in very different economies and social organizations. The KKK has its roots in post–Civil War and early twentieth-century economies and politics; it is often represented in popular culture as linked to rural, agricultural social tensions—and the past. The more modern white supremacy of the Aryan Brotherhood is grounded in the economy and social organization of contemporary prisons and the broader racial economy of late capitalism. A deeper discussion of the Aryan Brotherhood in popular discourse around the murder would have required discussing racism in terms of present economic and social structures and undermined the idea that the law adequately redresses racism. Instead, calling the men members of the KKK suggested not only that their racism was aberrant but also that it was a function of geography, education, and personality.

The focus on King's and Brewer's tattoos and ties to white supremacist groups made a comfortable space for most white Americans to vilify them as racist from a distance. The descriptions and vilification of the killers as poorly educated, unenlightened, and culturally impoverished emphasized the men's marginality.[38] (Yet, as reporter Roy Bragg pointed out, this vision of the KKK is not demographically accurate.[39] The Klan in Texas is frequently affluent and suburban, much closer to the target demographic of mainstream news than most of this discussion would suggest.) That these markers of distance were important to the presentation of these men as the source of the injustice is underscored by the treatment of the third man, Berry, in the news coverage. Berry, who did not sport tattoos or an affiliation with any white supremacist group, did not fit so easily within the rhetoric of "real racism" and the image of racial injustice portrayed elsewhere in descriptions of the killers. Jasper residents had a hard time believing that Berry (who drove the truck that dragged Byrd to death) was guilty. His boss suggested that he must have "just got mixed up in the wrong crowd."[40] Residents were perplexed at his involvement, noting that he was not a racist because he had black friends and because he had cried at a black colleague's funeral. A similar logic informed a report in *Salon* magazine, in which reporter Ashley Craddock suggested the trial of Berry was unfair because there was no evidence that he "harbored secret race hatreds."[41] The unfairness of the trial in Craddock's eyes did not rest on a lack of evidence that he had driven the truck that killed Byrd, or any doubt he had attempted to cover up evidence of the crime, but on the point that he did not look and act the part of the "real racist." Dan Rather's report on the investigation for *60 Minutes II* expressed a similar skepticism about the charges against Berry.[42] The reticence to discuss Berry's implication in the attack and his actions that night in terms of racism illustrates the implications of defining racism in terms of fringe groups and ideologies. Anyone who does not express violent racial revulsion or appear socially marginal may not fit within this notion of racism. Discourses and policies that are not expressed within the rhetoric of white supremacy (such as the more pervasive but subtle practices of redlining or school funding) may not be legible as instances or symptoms of racial injustice.

Ellis Cose, writing for *Newsweek,* commented critically on this tendency in the coverage, cautioning against too close an identification of racism with figures of white supremacy as a fringe philosophy:

> Since most Americans cannot imagine being anything like King, and
> cannot imagine their friends being anything like him either, there is a certain
> comfort in castigating him. In condemning him, we celebrate our own relative
> enlightenment, our obvious moral superiority. We celebrate, in short, our own
> innocence. And in the process, we perhaps forget that morally outranking an
> evil lunatic is not a particularly exalted achievement.[43]

The comfort Cose references is telling. Descriptions of King as an "evil lunatic"
reassuringly locate the disruption of the killing—the questions it raised about
contemporary racial injustice—in a geographic and cultural location far from
the liberal, affluent public addressed by the media coverage.[44] In making racism
legible and concrete through the person of King, the media coverage trained
condemnation on King and white supremacists in general. This allows everyone
else to feel comfortable. Comfort here is a feeling that encourages complacency,
even self-congratulation. In this, it hides issues of racial injustice and discour-
ages action.

In addition, the cultivation of condemnation is accomplished through
a focus on King's criminality. This use of criminality as a rhetoric of distance
and condemnation reinforces the idea that racial justice is primarily achievable
via the existing criminal justice system, rather than through structural or legal
change. Within this rhetorical configuration, capturing and punishing the killers is equal to delivering racial justice. In casting redress in terms of criminal
justice, the law is reinscribed as the site of racial justice, rather than as the site
of failures of racial justice or even the agent of racial oppression. It was odd, as
many commentators noted, to see racial justice in the use of the death penalty,
a punitive structure disproportionately used against black men. While the indi-
viduating presentation of racism was prevalent, as suggested here, discussions
of law and the ability of the law to live up to liberal ideals provided another
lens on the murder as racial injustice. References to the geographic setting of
the murder, in the South, brought issues of economy, law, and history into the
discussion.

## THE SITE OF RACIAL VIOLENCE

The focus on the setting of the murder, a geography associated with the failure
of the law to offer equal protection to black and white citizens, presented racial
injustice not so much as individual violence but as an effect of history, even
economy. The community and location of Jasper, Texas, became a focal point
for journalists, just arrived from elsewhere, trying to make sense of the attack
and parse its social implications. In this focus, they spent much discursive effort
locating Jasper in the South. In many ways this placement served to mark or

prove that the murder was racially motivated; that the murder took place in the South ensured it was read as racial violence. Many news sources used geography as a modifier to explain the murder, as when the *Boston Globe* noted that "the slaying of the 49-year-old grandfather revived images of bygone racial violence in the South." Others put more discursive effort into locating Jasper geographically and culturally within an iconic vision of the (old) South. One *New York Times* reporter noted that Jasper, "with its hills and lush vegetation, looks more like the Deep South than the Texas of flat prairies that typify much of the state." *Newsweek* called Jasper "more Deep South than Lone Star"; *Time* followed suit with "East Texas, with its dusty small towns and cotton fields, is more Dixie than Lone Star."[45] The descriptions are striking in the similarity of their prose. The reports stress the hills and pine thickets, more associated with the iconography of the South than that of Texas, separating Jasper from Texas's association with Western imagery. This disassociation was not confined to distant news offices; Texas news outlets also employed the geographical explanation. The Austin paper discussed Jasper's "deep South social mores" as well as emphasizing geographic distance through descriptions of the verdant landscape.[46] This mapping, repeated in the *Houston Chronicle,* serves as well to write the state's history of racial violence in terms of black and white. This obscures another bloody history firmly rooted in Texas: the violent oppressions of Mexicans and other Latinos associated with the Anglocization of Texas.

The discussion of the murder as taking place in the South evoked a set of economic and cultural explanations for racial conflict: an antiquated, agrarian economy, rural life, and a vague idea of Southern culture. The descriptions of geography used to locate Jasper call up a very particular idea of the South that is more iconic than geographic. It is the rural and preindustrial South imagined through movies and the tourism industry. The icons of the South that are traded in media images and tourist traffic are not the auto plants, call centers, interstates, and booming metropolises of the "new South." They are, rather, images of the "Old South": Southern belles, plantation life, the Grand Ole Opry, Mississippi riverboats, and the backwoods. Tara McPherson elaborates the way that such iconic images of the South function to "condense" narratives about place, race, and gender.[47] These images are invested in representing not the actual geographic region, and its more complicated realities, but narratives of race and racism in America as well as nostalgic notions of an agrarian past. The actual town of Jasper is just over 100 miles northeast of Houston, but miles off the major interstates running through East Texas, located in the pine forest known as "the big thicket." The area is, in fact, more industrial than agrarian. In the late nineteenth and early twentieth centuries, the railroad and timber industries attracted settlers and amassed great wealth for a few; John Henry Kirby, a notorious opponent of labor unions and the New Deal, gained his wealth and power in the area.[48] The road along which James Byrd Jr. was dragged was not a country road, as it was so frequently described, but a timber road. Yet in the news coverage there were few clues that Jasper was a postindustrial town in some ways similar to small rust belt towns impacted by the decline in industry, beyond perhaps a few references to the 12 percent local unemployment rate.[49] The visual and verbal images of the news dwelled on the pastoral, positing Jasper as part of the pre- or antimodern South of national imagination: the site of resistance to integration and racial equality projects, acting as contrast to the image of a liberal and racially progressive North/rest of the nation.[50]

These explanations sideline the pervasive racism in the North and West as well as locate racism in the culture and masculinity of the South rather than in the legal institutions at the heart of the national political system that legitimized and legalized Jim Crow segregation.[51] This mapping distances racism from the North in more than miles. The South imagined in this way is always of a different time and mode of production than the (industrial, informational) North. In so firmly anchoring the crime, its motivations, and its implications in a particular (and particularly loaded) time, place, and economy, the media coverage implied a relation of distance between the murder and the reading public, imagined as more urban, more modern, and less "Old South" than this corner of Texas.

The association of Jasper, the South, and the murder with the past was made quite explicit in the language of news reports, which presented the violence and racism of the murder as symptomatic of the past rather than the present. Headlines of editorials and news items in magazines and newspapers ran "Our sad history rears its ugly head," "Texas killing recalls racism's past," "Thought those days had gone," and "List suggests nation is stuck in the '50s."[52] The *New York Times* noted that Byrd's murder was "as stupid, as barbaric as any that horrified the nation more than 30 years ago."[53] An article in the *Atlanta Journal-Constitution* referenced a similar time frame: "Just when we get to the point of thinking it can't happen here, it happens again. We're not that far removed—a mere 30 years—from a time when racism was our way of life, passed along from one generation to another."[54]

In coverage such as this, the murder was a puzzling intrusion of the past into the present. The discussion of the crime in terms of the 1930s and 1960s, figured as the sites of political and legal struggles for racial equality, can be seen as part of a political project of disavowal of contemporary racial injustice. The fact that this chronology reflects a particular set of interests and racial politics is perhaps clearer when this chronology, advanced in mainstream news outlets, is contrasted to the chronology offered by several black Jasper residents. These residents placed the murder in a long and more continuous line of racial violence, noting the similarities between Byrd's death and those of other East Texas black men 5, 10, 20 years ago (all too often, while in police custody).[55] This latter timeline argues a less liberal present, a temporality not punctuated so firmly by the civil rights movement as the end of racism and racial violence, but where such violence is a recurring feature of daily life. These more recent examples of racial violence were erased by the repeated rhetorical trope that the murder was an interruption from the past, a repetition of violence rooted in the political context of the 1960s or 1930s. This temporal framing reflects a particular and interested chronology that places racial violence firmly in the past, undermining contemporary claims for racial justice as unnecessary.

This mapping was perhaps one reason that the law played such a pronounced role in the news coverage and public discourse on Byrd's murder. The setting for the crime was the site of one of the greatest failures of law and liberal institutions in national cultural memory. Jasper was conscripted into popular representations of the South that rely on images and ideas of an agrarian past but that also distance this iconic South from institutions associated with modernity, such as the law. While the law has historically been an instrument of racial oppression as well as liberation, the narratives that place the region of the South (and/or the pathological masculinities that inhabit this region) as the location of racial oppression sidestep this troubling issue. Within contemporary political discourse and optimism about the ability of liberal institutions to facilitate actual democracy, the historic failures of the law to uphold ideals of equality and dignity for black Americans are some of the most shameful points of history. Seeing these failures as a thing of the past allows us to overlook the continuing entanglement of the law in systems of inequity along lines of race/ethnicity, nationality, sexuality, and gender. As one of the headlines quoted above states, the prosecution of Byrd's murderers offered an opportunity to do just this, to place those failures in the past, giving one of America's shameful historical stories a better ending. Framing the murder as a new ending to an old story emphasizes the fact that the news was not merely reporting on an isolated incident but writing another chapter in what is a long cycle of texts on race and racism in America.

The narrative and symbolic frameworks outlined here made racism visible as overt violence, articulated as an outcome of extreme political views and as a symptom of past failures of the law. It also provided an invitation to feel. Perhaps because of the prevalence of melodrama in the cultural repertoire of stories we have in the United States for understanding racial conflict, melodrama provided the framework for feeling. The description of the crime as a restaging of past racial violence, and hence the prosecution of the killers as a restaging of past prosecutions, provided a chance for legal institutions and white lawmakers to, as the district attorney and sheriff suggested, get it right this time around. Getting it right, recuperating the law, is an act of defending the legitimacy of political institutions and existing social relations. It is also a lesson about how to feel about the law and other political institutions.

## Law, Modernity, and Feeling: The Moral of the Story

In a sense, the mediated story of the murder of James Byrd Jr. became less about the specific instance of racism and loss and more about the ability of the law and white enforcers of the law to live up to the promises of liberalism. The positioning of the law as the resolution to the deep social, political, and ethical failings the murder made so visible invited publics to feel good about the law, to feel protected by political and legal institutions whose adequacy had been questioned during the highly visible racial conflicts of the 1990s. The ability of the law to punish the killers was central to the way the news coverage became a hopeful narrative about progressive racial justice. Levying the harshest penalty, death, for two of the killers was posed as resolution not only of the conflicts exposed by the murder but also of a longer history of racial injustice against black men. Sheriff Rowles noted the importance of trying and convicting the men in Jasper as a way of repairing the town's image and proving that the law protected black residents as well as white.[56] Within the melodramatic structure of the narrative, this outcome was posed as resolution to the racism and conflict that the murder made visible.

*Time* reporters, writing on the death penalty outcome of Bill King's trial, captured this sentiment and some of the assumptions upon which it was based:

> It was a more satisfying resolution than many blacks had dared expect. East Texas, with its dusty small towns and cotton fields, is more Dixie than Lone Star. And the South hasn't been a place where blacks always found justice in the courtroom. In towns like Jasper, not long ago, blacks—even black lawyers—were routinely called by their first name in court, often excluded as jurors, their testimony discounted again and again. Black life was so cheap that whites almost never got the death penalty for killing blacks. After Byrd's murder, King gloated to an accomplice that "we have made history." He may just be right. If his death penalty is carried out, he will be the first white Texan executed for killing a black since slavery ended.[57]

The fact that a largely white jury in deep East Texas was willing to put a white man to death for killing a black man was celebrated in various venues as a sign of progress. (Some texts were more critical, and less celebratory, than others.) This quote from *Time* magazine mobilized several stock phrases that mark the influence of melodramas of race and redemption: that Jasper was "more Dixie than Lone Star" to firmly anchor the crime within cultural images of the South and that King was the first white man to be sentenced to death for killing a black man since the Civil War. This latter observation was repeated in various venues (such as the movie *Jasper, Texas;* the magazines *Time* and *Jet*) and given great moral import. While technically true, this statement stretches the truth for melodramatic effect. A white man was sentenced to death for killing a black woman in Texas in 1978, but he died while on death row.[58] The discrepancy in numbers of black and white men on death row—or simply in prison—is shocking enough without embellishment. The overstatement works, however, to create a more dramatic moment of resolution as a counterpoint to the abridgements of equality and justice in the past.

While there is an appealing symmetry in the levying of the death penalty on two white men for the killing of a black man, it is also ethically and politically problematic. Presenting the death penalty as the vehicle by which racial justice is achieved paradoxically offers a punishment disproportionately imposed on black men, and hence deeply entrenched in systematic institutional racism, as the solution to racial injustice. Some commentators, such as Lance Morrow in *Time,* wrestled with this contradiction. Morrow, in the end, tried to explain the appeal of the death penalty in this case as signaling a larger balance—that imposing the death penalty in this case signaled, at long last, equal treatment under the law: "The promising novelty of Jasper is that for a moment, it aligns the black social contract with the white social contract. That is all that racial justice is ultimately about: the equality of the contracts. In the past they have been two different documents, with very different protections under the law."[59] This equalization seemed to offer a resolution to the racial injustice that Byrd's murder so clearly illustrated. That this equalization happened in a locale that had been articulated as the Old South seemed also to make good on, or resolve, past failures of the law; this point is key to the way the narrative ultimately turned into a celebratory one.

What was celebrated was the ability of the law to live up to its promise of equal protection, reinscribing the law as a talisman of progress and modernity. An eagerness to find hope and progress in the law can almost be felt in some of the journalistic prose:

Things have changed—but not completely. Though whites and blacks now monitor their attitudes about race, racial terrorism lives on. Killers who were never charged for their hate crimes roam free. From recent cases one might even be led to surmise that the Klan has given up white uniforms for blue ones. And then there are cases in which there is still time to make good on history. Perhaps this one.[60]

Within this discursive context, the harshest application of the law came to mean much more than punishment for the guilty parties; it also suggested that Americans as a nation could leave the racial injustices ("our racial past") behind us. Whereas the news narrative invited condemnation of the killers as individuals, it invited feelings for, even pride in, the law and national progress.

The ability to invite pride in progress was made possible only by seeing the murder and the prosecution of the killers as a repetition of past racial violence and failures of the law to offer redress. Marita Sturken discusses the way that media culture stages reenactments of moments of the past that are somehow disruptive or traumatic to national narratives of identity. This restaging is an effort to both "strategically forget" and strategically reorganize the past. Such reenactments are often attempts to present the past in ways that support the politics of the present or to attempt to forge closure and healing around moments of traumatic rupture.[61] The discussion of the murder of James Byrd Jr. as a repetition of past racial violence fell into this pattern. Presenting the murder and the official legal response as a repetition allowed commentators to read the prosecution of the three white men as progress—to say that this time, the law and its enforcers were "getting it right."

Such a reading of the murder as a chance to make good on the failures of the past and demonstrate progress was made quite clearly by *Denver Post* columnist Chuck Green: "Two hundred years ago the killing of a black man by three whites would have been cheered in the United States. And 100 years ago it wouldn't have been considered unusual. And 50 years ago it wouldn't have seemed, in Texas at least, newsworthy. And just 30 years ago, in many parts of the United States, it wouldn't have resulted in an immediate arrest and—particularly in Texas—described by a sheriff as a despicable racial crime. That is progress." He adds: "My God, we're making progress—more progress than anywhere else on Earth, where there appears to be no hope that the killing and the hating will stop."[62]

The successful prosecution of three white men for killing a black man seems odd evidence that the United States is a more peaceable and tolerant nation than all others. Green's commentary makes sense only when understood as a celebration of the American legal system, in comparison with that of other nations.[63]

Rather than a sad commentary on the continuing hold of "old-fashioned" racism, he reads the murder and its prosecution as proof of the "civilizing" force of the American legal system, its ability to overcome personal hatred and prejudice.

This message and its appeal were echoed in television images that suggested the prosecution was forging unity and healing. Beginning with an NBC news story featuring Sheriff Rowles's declaration that the prosecution would seek the death penalty, the visuals of television news formed a message of unity and reconciliation. The NBC segment, which began with Rowles's statement, continued to emphasize racial solidarity and unity in Jasper, highlighting images of cross-racial interaction among women and children, ending with the evocative image of two toddlers, one black, one white, playing in a sandbox together. The voice-over emphasized that black and white neighbors were working together; the image conveyed a message of hope that the next generation would overcome racial segregations and prejudices.[64] This thematic was taken up across channels. In the days that followed, the news was filled with images of black and white hands clasped together in mourning; signs declaring that Jasper was "mourning, hurting, crying"; white teens handing out yellow ribbons to passing cars; testimony of local residents that Jasper was not a backwards, racist town; and photos of the many flowers placed on Byrd's marble grave. (Oddly, no mention was made of the fact that the cemetery was still de facto segregated, white and black resting places separated by a chain-link fence.[65]) These news images seemed to hold up Jasper as a symbol of utopian hope, that even a small Southern town could demonstrate racial unity and "healing."

GETTING IT RIGHT THIS TIME

The logic animating the configuration of punitive legal measures as signs of hope and progress becomes apparent in the figures of the two white lawmen who investigated and prosecuted the case. Sheriff Billy Rowles and District Attorney Guy James Gray and their stories embodied the idea that the case had provided the chance to address and make up for past failures, to get it right this time. The "it" that the men promised to get right was the liberal promise of equality.

Within the aesthetic construction of racial injustice in terms of the past and interpersonal violence, Rowles and Gray offered perfect resolution. The framework of interpersonal violence presents injustice in terms of crime—and punishment. The levying of criminal penalties becomes a reasonable response and resolution. With their wide-brimmed hats and Southern drawls that echoed images of real and fictive Southern men who had abrogated the law and racial justice claims in the past, these two white men seemed to restage past conflicts.

The *Washington Post* headline "This Time, Old Story Gets New Ending" made explicit the appeal of viewing the prosecution as a chance to revisit the past.

Rowles and Gray's family histories furthered this narrative. Each man described his father's encounters with racial violence and the abdication of the law, and the sense of guilt and shame each father had for not intervening. They described the deep impressions their fathers' memories left on them. Gray repeated a story his father told him about a lynching in Jasper in the 1920s (or 1930s; the date varies in different accounts), in which a black man was dragged from the back of a truck through the middle of town. The men driving the truck, though seen by a number of people, were never arrested—something for which Gray told the reporter his father had always felt guilt and shame.[66] He cited this memory as his motivation to show "them" (the black community) that "this was not 1920," that the white community and civic institutions would not look the other way this time.[67] In a parallel story, Rowles told of his father's presence at the 1943 riots in Beaumont, where hundreds of white men attacked black residents and pillaged their property in response to a rumor that a black man had raped a white woman in the "good" part of town and that "the blacks were coming to town to take it over."[68] While Rowles describes his father as returning home rather than participating in the riots, he said his father had been haunted by the memory and his own inaction. He references this memory as an important motivator or moral guide in his investigation of the case and his commitment to getting it right this time.

The men described these moments of suspended conscience as haunting presences in their lives that impelled them to do their utmost when confronted with Byrd's murder. This language was explicit in a *U.S. News & World Report* article:

> In one sense, prosecutor Gray represents a bridge between the past and the present in this part of East Texas deep in the piney woods. His family has held office in Jasper County for four generations, and he feels he owes something to blacks here for past injustices. "We never have answered for our history. If we don't face our old ghosts, they'll never go away," says Gray, who has tried only one capital murder case in his career. "If this case turns out all right, we put it behind us a little more. You can't ever erase your history, but the memories won't be as strong."[69]

In these moments, the representatives of the law are quite literally positioned as repeating the past and correcting the sins (discussed as sins of omission or inaction) of their fathers. Performing an airtight and impeccable investigation and prosecution is discursively positioned as a way of revisiting, even rewriting, the past. The title of the article, "Justice Delayed," furthers the point. The investigation promises not only for the sons to embody liberal ideals their fathers failed to fully embody but also to offer some sense of future-oriented reparation to the community—in particular, the black community—for past failures. The structure of getting it right this time both acknowledges a past failure and promises a future free of these failures.

Rowles and Gray were the center of much media coverage, overshadowing the mayor and other black leaders, who received much less journalistic attention. Mayor R. C. Horn, for instance, only appeared once on network TV news in the weeks after the murder. This contrast is made particularly clear when the news is compared to the prominent roles of two black residents in film reconstructions of the events (Showtime's *Jasper, Texas* and PBS' *Two Towns of Jasper*). In these reconstructions Horn and Walter Diggles, the director of the Deep East Texas Council of Governments, take on much more central roles. Somehow these spokesmen did not speak in mainstream print or TV news. In this, the news coverage follows the format of many popular media narratives of the struggle for civil rights, in which the heroes are white avatars of the law rather than black agents: *To Kill a Mockingbird* and *Mississippi Burning* are prime examples of this story structure. Not incidentally, both were referenced by residents and commentators attempting to make sense of the real-life murder of Byrd. The creation of white heroes and black victims in popular tales of the civil rights movement, as Allison Graham suggests in *Framing the South,* performs the cultural work of addressing white audiences and encouraging emotional bonds with black victims of racial injustice. It would seem as well that such stories offer models of virtuous or innocent whiteness for white audiences. They offer double emotional scenarios, telling audiences to feel solidarity with (or pity for) black victims while also feeling admiration for and alignment with the white lawmen.

Whiteness here is closely linked to the functioning and legitimacy of liberal institutions. That is, the failures of the law are failures of whiteness: of the white men and women who make, interpret, and enforce the law but also of the abstract category of whiteness. This category, which defines the racial identity of white, emerged as a category under which to unify the different European Americans into a common racial formation based on abstraction from particularity. The ability to inhabit or perform objectivity (as in the objectivity of the law) is based on the ability to abstract oneself from particular interests—those of national, ethnic, or tribal allegiance as well as those of home and hearth.[70] The ideals of neutrality and disinterest, which provide a common genealogy for both whiteness and legal proceduralism, are implicated in failures of the law. The desire for neutral legal process, and its close relative whiteness, envisioned as the absence of racial particularity or interest, exceeds the impulse to have pride or positive self-esteem in a category of racial identity, to encompass a reassurance that current institutions and policies are fair and that the subjects of white privilege do not need to give anything up to make good on promises of equity and democracy.

Seen in this light, the fascination with the lawmen is even more closely tied to a fascination with the legitimacy of liberal, especially legal, institutions. One of the reasons Jasper, Guy James Gray, and Billy Rowles may have been so compelling for so many chroniclers is that they offered a counterpoint to doubts about law. They seemed to offer hope in the possibility of neutrality or objectivity as affective dispositions central to liberalism—to make good on the claims of neutrality at the heart of both the law and whiteness. Something of this idea can be seen in a June 14 *New York Times* editorial, which lauded the "sheriff bent on color-blind prosecution of this lynching." Considering how important race was in both of the men's presentation of the investigation in media interviews, this characterization has little grounding in the facts of the case. Rather, it is a celebration of the ability of these men to live up to the promises of whiteness and the law. This was particularly evocative given the fact that both men were described initially in terms of the good ole boy image of bad (nonneutral) Southern white masculinity of popular memory and media narratives. With his cowboy hat, Southern drawl, and down-home modes of speech, Rowles seemed to embody the good ole boy villain of real and fictional confrontations during the height of the civil rights movement. His performance made for good TV but set him up as a curiosity, a throwback to an earlier time. Reacting to this, a professor in New York contacted him with tips for appearing more disinterested, more able to represent the law and be taken seriously on TV. The professor told him in effect to play down his particularity (especially the loud ties and colorful speech) in order to better fit within the bounds of legitimate political expression.[71] Fitting within these bounds meant not only losing the tie but also conforming to expectations of abstraction and disinterest associated with the law and modern constructions of white masculinity.[72]

The drift in the focus of the news narratives away from Byrd and his family to two white representatives of the law is, I argue, invested in a deep desire for the narratives of progress, liberalism, and modernity we tell about ourselves to match up to our reality. Rowles and Gray, and the criminal prosecution they led, offered symbols of hope. That even these men, in their wide-brimmed hats and with their Southern drawls and family histories, could represent legal neutrality was figured as a sign of progress—a comforting sign. Each man was, as noted above, haunted by his own familial racial history. The contrasts between these men and their histories offered promise. Along these lines, one journalist juxtaposed DA Gray's aggressive prosecution with the fact that his grandfather had fought for the Confederacy.[73] Look how far we have come, these narratives invited. Even these men. In the end, the mediated stories of the crime offer up Rowles and Gray as images of not only virtuous whiteness but also the ability of the law to live up to the promises of liberal democracy—a "feel good" ending.

## Conclusion:
## Feelings as the Basis for Social Justice

> We need to recognize that it is in ever-modernizing forms of melodrama—not epic drama, not "classical realism"—that American democratic culture has most powerfully articulated the moral structure of feeling animating its goals of social justice.
> Linda Williams, *Playing the Race Card*, 26

Melodramatic texts, and the melodramatic imagination that they further, are for Williams very ambivalent and politically charged. They flatten and offer stereotypes of easy victims and villains. Yet she notes that even though democratic politics trade in abstract articulations of rights, the most powerful claims on rights are often not principled enunciations of how those rights have been denied but melodramatic examples of these denials and the suffering associated with them. The language of melodrama, with its compelling evocation of affect, provides a powerful tool for making abstract social conditions tangible and "educating" political emotions: giving form to ever-shifting notions of what is socially reprehensible and desirable, performing community through invitations to identify with, admire, or revile others. In this, the function of melodrama is not so different from other sites of emotional education such as political rhetoric or the museum.

The questions raised by the melodramatic discourse around the murder of James Byrd Jr. are: What feelings are evoked and what claims on social justice do they enable? What are the avenues and limitations of social justice claims based on invitations to hate racial bigots, pity the victims of racism, and admire the men who made sure the letter of the law was observed? The discursive positioning of the murder, through media representation and historical context, as visible evidence of continuing racial injustice enabled some types of justice claims over others. The focus on the individual killers and their criminality (evidenced both by criminal records and their tattoos) presented injustice within the frame of crime and punishment. In this, the media coverage followed what Carrie Rentschler has identified as a pattern of placing the suffering of others within the frame of military and criminal justice systems, such that the act of mediated witness and the potential avenues for that witness are presented in terms of some of the most repressive state institutions.[74] The particular melodramatic emplottment authorized legal action in the name of social justice, against the individual assailants. In this, it both enabled and limited justice claims. The framing of injustice as (individual) criminality characterized justice in terms of law enforcement. In this framing, the mediation encouraged a limited avenue of response, focused on criminal justice and individual punishment, disabling other types of justice claims (such as economic, social, cultural). In addition, the location of progress and modernity in law and law enforcers directed action toward the legal system. It is no surprise that the law that was enacted in response to the murder was presented as a criminal justice law, although its provisions went beyond criminal prosecution.

In noting that the mediation of the murder directed and limited the social justice claims and political action that followed, I don't want to overlook the outrage and sense of urgency within the public discourse surrounding Byrd's death. The urgency and the explicit discussion of social justice contradicted discourses of color blindness and formal equality so common in the "new racism" arguments prevalent in much public discourse in the 1990s. The demands for social justice, discussion of contemporary social and economic racial disparities, and overall outrage at the murder were notable in a discursive landscape that would soon become all too dominated by the right and language of "reverse racism" and "compassionate conservatism." Within this context, the mobilizations that the mediation produced are remarkable.

Recognizing the continuing relevance of history, especially a racial history that many Americans arguably desire to disavow or overcome, undermines the neoconservative celebratory rhetoric of the level playing field and a color-blind society. While the framing of Byrd's murder in terms of the past upheld the idea that racial violence (and arguably racism) has been overcome, the very violence of the attack exceeded this framing. It made undeniably visible for a moment the continuing economic, social, and physical violence that sustains systems of racial hierarchy and white privilege. Scattered commentary framed the murder within larger contexts in which the forms of black disenfranchisement were less interpersonal: discrimination in housing policies, economics, medical treatment, and education funding.[75] These reports and those that framed the murder in more individualist contexts worked together to suggest certain feelings toward the crime, those involved, and racism in general as the norm of national belonging. This reaction to the killing reiterated a common aversion to overt and especially physical forms of racism. The narrative and discursive context into which the victim, villains, and heroes were written "educated" readers—often, implicitly, readers defined through whiteness—in the proper objects of pity, revulsion, admiration, and identification. These feelings were offered up as the feelings or attachments of a "good" (nonracist) bystander. The following observations on the conviction of Bill King in *Time* magazine offer a relevant example:

> Whatever misgivings arise from the fact of execution itself, the jury's decision declared a happy change in the social organism. One white juror made the argument that King required the death sentence because the community had to show that the murder was "something we cannot accept." If there was encouragement to be taken from Jasper, it lay in her use of the word we.[76]

The author lauds the change in the social organism (or, as he also puts it, the social contract), but notably it is the white community's social contract that is amended. The positive encouragement is in the white juror's comment that the community norms cannot accept white violence against black members. The sentiment educated is that of the white community to recognize a wrong against a black neighbor, to understand black neighbors as full community members. The writer notes that this is encouraging, an important political moment, yet it is important also to note the limitations implicit in this moment. The terms of social, or racial, justice in this moment are defined first through the white social contract. This contract, and the community which it serves, is the gatekeeper determining what counts as a claim on social justice and what does not.

This is perhaps the crux of the issue in melodrama as political pedagogy. Melodrama is a powerful form for training feeling in its ability to arouse sentiment. Melodrama can make visible, even vividly real, abstract social conditions through a sensational and affective rendering of the effects of these conditions on the bodies of individuals. The persistent and troubling issue with so many examples of racial melodrama is that it does this through an address to white audiences and feelings. In this address, the contours of the narrative are determined by the need to capture and move a majority audience. Melodrama may enable the definition, understanding, and pursuit of racial justice, but most do so through a limiting focus on eliciting white sympathy that reinscribes whiteness as the center of the law, justice, and the social contract.

The problematic aspect of the coverage of the murder of James Byrd Jr. is not so much its emplottment as melodrama but the political economy that the most prominent and influential melodramas serve. There is a reason that so many of the heroes of the cinematic racial melodramas are white: the desire to attract the majority, white audience. Several commentators compared the investigation of Byrd's killers to the trial in *To Kill a Mockingbird;* there is much to say about this comparison. Most relevant here are the structure of identification and moral lessons invoked in this comparison. *Mockingbird* is one of the nation's most popular dramatic tales of the injustices of racism and the virtues of tolerance. The story manages to both condemn and defend the U.S. justice system and whiteness; this ambiguity is at the core of the narrative's cultural iconicity. The very structure and lessons of this story are dictated by an address to a white audience. We must enter the scene not through the eyes of the black victim but from the innocent eyes of the young white girl, learning her first lessons in tolerance. The hero is Atticus Finch, both critic and white avatar of the law, an exemplar of liberal principles. And in the end, the lesson is less about the need for racial justice or the demands for equality coming from black communities than about how to be a better, more just and tolerant white person. The white power structure is not only preserved but also presented as the best promise and source of racial justice (however untrue to history this vision is). There is an alternative tradition of black melodrama (there were many examples of this genre in the 1990s), in which resolution to racial injustice is offered through black heroes and communities or in which the very possibility of resolution to racial injustice is troubled. Yet these are not the texts referenced in the news or the primary texts of popular memory.

This political economy translates into a particular mapping of the social, of distance and proximity. In this mapping, James Byrd Jr. was articulated as a distant object of pity, not as an icon of identification. The contours of the mapping, drawn via melodrama, parallel the paradox of evaluating emotions or affect in politics. Melodrama can make visible issues of social injustice and make compelling calls for their redress, but in the very structure of this appeal, it often replicates hierarchies of race (and gender and sexuality). Affect may be an intrinsic part of deliberation and, in particular, the formation of political will and commitment, but it is not distributed evenly, and in this it seems to erode the possibilities of democratic communications. The mediation of Byrd's murder encouraged feelings for Byrd from a distance and feelings for the law—a self-congratulatory identification with the law and other political institutions. How this mediation enabled political actions and arguments at the local level is the subject of the next chapter.

# [ 4 ]

## The Visibility of Suffering, Injustice, and the Law

> There are some people who have got hate in their hearts. That's disturbing, but govern-
> ment can't make people love one another. . . . I think the way to get rid of hate in peo-
> ple's hearts, the best course I know is religion. The truth of the matter is hate and evil
> exist, and something much larger than government will help [heal] the hearts of men.
> —Texas governor George W. Bush, responding to the murder
> of James Byrd Jr. Quoted in the *Houston Chronicle,* April 7, 1999

> It may be true that the law cannot make a man love me, but it can stop him from lynch-
> ing me, and I think that's pretty important.
> —Martin Luther King Jr., *Wall Street Journal,* November 13, 1962

THE DEBATE OVER the James Byrd Jr. Hate Crimes Act in the Texas legislature was couched in terms of justice and mourning, equal protection under the law, and hate. Whereas discussion of the bias crimes reporting ordinance in Laramie showed a concern with eradicating the shame surrounding a single event, the Byrd Act was enmeshed in a longer history of public deliberation over the role of the state in redressing racism. The success of the bill in the 1999 and 2001 legislative sessions hinged upon the media publicity surrounding Byrd's murder and the role of public expressions of grief and vulnerability in victim testimony.

Public testimony focused on the effects of anti-gay and racist violence in terms of affect and liberal ideals of justice. While the act finally passed in 2001, in this chapter I primarily examine the 1999 legislative session. This was when the biggest hurdle was overcome. For years, hate crimes legislation had been defeated by social conservatives in the Texas House of Representatives. Finally, in 1999, the bill gained the momentum, support, and legitimacy it needed to pass relatively smoothly two years later. It was also the year in which the memory of James Byrd Jr. took on the most prominent role and in which victim testimony was most forcefully evoked in public legislative debates. In the 2001 Senate debates, the tone was more technical and the key tension was between the need to "send a message" or use the law to establish a social norm and concerns that the law would restrict freedom of speech and association. Because 1999 was defined as the turning point in my interviews, and because it was the session immediately after Byrd's highly publicized murder, it is the focus of this analysis.

The story of the progression of the bill is pieced together through news reports, the legislative archive, and interviews with lawmakers and lobbyists.[1] Based on these sources, this chapter traces the story of the James Byrd Jr. Hate Crimes Act, beginning with the history and politics of hate crimes legislation in Texas during the decade prior to the act. The moral claims of victim testimony became a powerful tool for making anti-gay discrimination and violence legible as an issue of social justice to lawmakers and journalists during the 1999 legislative session. The concern with visibility here countered conservative doubts about anti-gay discrimination based on the private status of sexuality. The success of victim testimony in making hate crimes legible as injustices to be remedied through law depended on a complicated interplay of the visibility of suffering and discrimination. Ultimately, the fact that the law passed relied on the assimilability of this testimony to different political discourses and the use of personal vulnerability in lawmakers' statements and victim testimony to compel empathetic responses, demonstrated through words and through legislative action.

### The James Byrd Jr. Hate Crimes Act and Its History

The Byrd Act, which added provisions to existing Texas hate crimes law, was first introduced in 1999, shortly after Byrd's murder. The bill was supported in the Texas House of Representatives in 1999, a major victory considering that the House had traditionally been the seat of social conservative opposition to such legislation. When the bill passed to the Texas Senate in 1999, it died in committee there, most likely suppressed due to Governor George W. Bush's presidential aspirations. The bill was reintroduced in the Senate in the next legislative session, in 2001. It passed and was signed into law by Governor Rick Perry. While the bill still had some major hurdles to overcome in 2001, its passage through the Senate was seen as less momentous than its passage through the House, which had been the site of the greatest opposition to hate crimes legislation.

The act that bore Byrd's name capped a decade of struggle over hate crimes legislation in Texas. Texas had passed its first hate crimes legislation in 1993, although the bill was considered largely ineffective. The 1993 bill increased penalties for crimes motivated by bias and explicitly prohibited probation as a sentence for a murder motivated by bias or prejudice. This latter provision was a reaction to the public outcry when one of three young white supremacists who killed Donald Thomas, a black man, at a bus stop in Arlington in 1991 was given probation.[2] However, the law did not define hate crimes or specify which types of discrimination (for example, based on race, religion, or nationality) could be considered to contribute to a hate crime This omission was the result of a compromise between liberal and conservative lawmakers; conservatives agreed to pass the law as long as the language defining hate crimes and naming types of discrimination covered within this definition was stripped out.[3] In political terms, this compromise was a defeat of some of bill's purpose. In practical terms, the omission made the law difficult to use.

The debates over the 1993 law, and subsequent efforts to pass more substantive hate crimes legislation, were deeply enmeshed in the state's racial and sexual politics. While both the support and opposition to the bill were articulated through deeply divided political discourses on racism and "reverse racism," explored below, the common consensus in the legislature was that opposition to hate crimes legislation centered on the inclusion of sexual orientation. In the language of the social conservatives, the objection was that this legislation would "legitimize" homosexuality. By many accounts, this objection was the reason the language defining hate crimes, and hence categories of discrimination, was not included in the 1993 legislation.[4]

Efforts to pass new legislation that would add more specific language defining categories of discrimination (including sexuality) continued throughout the 1990s, led by a small group of politicians and lobby groups, including the Lesbian/Gay Rights Lobby of Texas (LGRL),[5] the American Civil Liberties Union, the Texas Freedom Network, the Texas Civil Rights Project, the NAACP, and the American Jewish Congress.[6] Each effort to pass new legislation was blocked by social conservatives in the legislature, aided by conservative lobbies such as the Texas Eagle Forum (one of the main opponents to the 1999 bill).

The LGRL and Senator Rodney Ellis had been working on pulling together the various pieces of legislation that had been proposed over the previous decade into one larger act in the mid-1990s. With Byrd's murder, the LGRL leadership and politicians saw an opportunity to personalize the bill and tap into the moral outrage. They recognized that the murder had convened a public, and one with a distinct sense of injustice, that they could tap into. With the support of the Byrd family, the LGRL, Senator Ellis, and Representative Senfronia Thompson drew up the bill that would bear Byrd's name.[7] The James Byrd Jr. Hate Crimes Act (HB 938) was introduced to the House in 1999. The version of the bill that was debated on the House floor proposed to

- define hate crimes as those committed against people or property for reasons of bias or prejudice against a person's "race, color, disability, religion, national origin or ancestry, or sexual orientation," and increase penalties for those crimes (with the exception of first degree felonies);
- grant money to small counties prosecuting hate crimes;
- declare a "right to be free from hateful acts" (defined as above);
- create protective orders and other civil remedies for infringement of this right; and
- require police training in recognizing and handling hate crimes.[8]

While the backlash logic of reverse racism that had gained prominence in the 1990s was a major line of opposition to the bill, specifically the idea that the law offered "special protections" to racial minorities, it was widely accepted that sexual orientation was again the main point of objection.[9]

The bill was first considered before the House Committee on Judicial Affairs, which heard over four hours of testimony from interested parties before passing it on for consideration on the floor. The bill was debated in the House on April 27, 1999, for a contentious two and a half hours before passing, in an 83–61 vote. Activists and reporters described the act's passage in the House, where hate crimes legislation had previously been roundly defeated, as an emotional moment. Its supporters had been able to line up some of the heaviest hitters and most respected speakers to present the bill on the floor, and at the last minute, Representative Thompson had been able to persuade Representative Warren Chisum to back the bill and bring several other conservatives with him, in exchange for changing "sexual orientation" to "sexual preference."[10] The bill progressed to the Senate, where it was debated in the Criminal Justice Committee. Senators on the committee heard and responded to another long list of citizen testimony before voting not to let it out of committee. Had it been allowed to pass on to a vote on the House floor, commentators speculated that the bill would have passed in 1999. The press and the bill's supporters speculated that its defeat in committee was due to political pressure to keep it from coming before George W. Bush, forcing him to either sign a law that would alienate social conservatives or refuse to sign it and alienate more moderate voters.

In 2001, Thompson and Ellis reintroduced the bill as HB 587.[11] This time, it passed the Senate and the House and made it to the governor's desk. While most of the legislators remained the same (all but one of the Republicans who had opposed the bill in 1999 returned in 2001), there were several important differences. First, there had been a change in governors, from Bush to Perry. While he had gone on record as opposing the bill in the past, Perry was not running for president. Second, Ellis was chair of the Senate Finance Committee and therefore wielded more clout in 2001.[12] While the act easily passed the House again, Ellis helped get it out of committee and onto the Senate floor. It looked like it might be killed in committee again, but a highly publicized act of vandalism against a prominent black church in Dallas increased pressure to pass the act.[13] It passed in a closely watched 20–10 vote in the Senate, and Perry signed it into law on May 10. The act, as passed, contained a similar set of provisions as the 1999 version, with some additions and amendments. The 2001 version

- increased penalties for hate crimes, defined as crimes committed against a person or property based on the person/owner's "race, color, disability, religion, national origin or ancestry, age, gender, or sexual preference";
- provided monetary aid for small counties prosecuting hate murders;
- declared a "right to be free from hateful acts" (defined as above);[14]
- created avenues for targets of hate crimes to get protective orders and other civil remedies based on interference with this right;
- defined reporting procedures for hate crime convictions;
- provided provisions for community tolerance education as a sentencing option for misdemeanor hate crimes;
- assigned a prosecutor in the attorney general's office to act as a statewide coordinator in hate crimes prosecution;
- provided training to prosecutors in implementing the new law; and
- required the creation of educational curriculum on hate crimes to be created and made available to Texas schools and communities.[15]

While most of the provisions remained the same, there were several changes: crimes based on gender were included in the definition of hate crimes; community education programs were included as a punishment option for misdemeanor hate crimes; and a requirement was added for the creation of educational materials about hate crimes for K–12 schools. In all, the educational and procedural aspects of the bill were increased.

Again, the disputes over the bill were heavily focused on sexuality. The dominant story told by those reporting on and involved in the bill's passage was that on multiple occasions, critics of the bill said they would only pass it if the authors would take out the language on sexual orientation. The extent to which opposition to the bill hinged on the inclusion of sexual orientation was brought home to me when I interviewed Representative Warren Chisum. He remembered the murder of Byrd as motivated by both racism and homophobia—and he incorrectly claimed that before this, hate crimes legislation efforts had only focused on sexual orientation.

What emerges from this history is that, while the bill was debated and framed in terms of racial justice, many of the objections and negotiations centered on the legal recognition of anything that might look like gay and lesbian rights. There was a complicated set of relationships between race and sexuality, with race and debates over the proper role of the state in recognizing and/or redressing racial wrongs often taking the front role in public discussions and sexual orientation often being the explicit or implicit subject of behind-the-scenes discussions and lobbying. In fact, several of those I spoke with said that 2001 was the last year the legislation could have passed. Texas politics shifted rightward through the 1990s and the early years of the 2000s: from the leadership of Democratic governor Ann Richards in the early 1990s to that of Republicans Bush and Perry at the end of the decade. Within this steady shift toward the socially conservative right, increasingly identified with anti-gay politics throughout the 1990s and early 2000s, hate crimes legislation and its implication of some small level of recognition and rights for gay men and lesbians faced increasing opposition.[16]

LGRL leader Dianne Hardy-Garcia described what happened in 1999, and again in 2001, as an example of solidarity between black and Latino lawmakers and gay and lesbian interest groups. The authors and persuasive voices behind the bill were primarily black and Latino lawmakers; when offered the opportunity to compromise and get a bill passed that would recognize racially motivated violence as prejudice, but not violence based on perceived sexuality, they refused. But solidarity alone cannot explain the passage of the bill. The coalition of black, Latino, and gay lawmakers (there was one openly gay representative in the Texas House at this time), along with liberals and moderates sympathetic to the bill, did not make a majority. In order to pass the bill, supporters needed to appeal to moderates on the fence and to convince conservative lawmakers who had opposed similar legislation in the past due to objections over the inclusion of sexual orientation to cross the aisle. The use of victim testimony was one way that this was accomplished. It was difficult for lawmakers to say no to victims and their families; this testimony also provided the grounds for conservative lawmakers to support the legislation without contradicting their political platforms or the values of their conservative political bases.

## Grief and Victim Testimony

The 1993 hate crimes legislation was signed into law by Governor Ann Richards in a symbolic celebration of Juneteenth, the anniversary of the effective emancipation of slaves in Texas. In contrast, the 2001 act was signed into law on Mother's Day. While the signing was not officially aligned with the holiday, Byrd's mother, Stella Byrd, was quoted in multiple news reports as saying the signing was the best Mother's Day present she had ever received. The association was in some ways apt. The grief and pain of the Byrd family and other families of hate crime victims played a very important part in the debate and progress of the act, particularly in obtaining a majority vote in the House. This grief, in testimony before committees and in the press coverage, worked to humanize the bill and put a political and moral pressure on lawmakers to feel and act in ways appropriate to this grief.

The status of victimhood was mobilized in various ways to exert emotional pressure.[17] The workings of this mobilization illustrate the ways in which emotional expectations work. These responses were tied to various levels of social membership, whether it was the broadest (human) or more specific (the civil rights generation). The use of testimonials from "ordinary" people worked to argue for the visibility of discrimination, especially against gay men and lesbians—and to make this victimhood more proximate to the lawmakers. Further, the emotional and moral arguments demanded a response from the state; in less abstract terms, they demanded a response from lawmakers as both political figures and individuals.

## THE MORAL CLAIMS OF VICTIMHOOD

The public testimony in the House and Senate committees was packed with people who had been victims of hate crimes and family members of those killed. This testimony emphasized the families' losses and the injuries suffered. It also conveyed an obligation on the part of listeners. Testifying before a legislative body about personal loss has the potential to publicize an experience and to provide a space for public mourning and for arguments about the value of what, or who, is lost.[18] The logic of public mourning is also a logic of who matters to the polity or who is recognizable as part of the political body. We have publicly defined forms and norms for grieving the deaths of those proximate to us; conferring these forms of public mourning on an individual is a powerful form of political recognition.[19]

The norms of mourning and witness demand respect for the losses of others; this respect bestows on the experiences and feelings of the victims and their families a high level of moral authority and legitimacy. The effectiveness of these norms is evidenced by the fact that both sides of the political debate invoked the wishes of the Byrd family as a way of conferring legitimacy on their political goals. The wishes of the Byrd family became the basis for justification for the bill as well as opposition to it. That Byrd's parents agreed to lend their son's name to the bill gave it a moral and political authority through the link to the politics of the murder and the highly visible suffering of the family.

This moral authority was one that both sides sought to mobilize. Supporters were the first to claim the family's support as a source of legitimacy, placing Byrd's name on the 1999 bill and framing the debate in terms of his murder and its media coverage. This lent supporters a powerful rhetorical, political, and moral authority. Opponents also tried to claim the support of the family in order to attain this authority. Notably, Representative Wayne Christian, whose jurisdiction included Jasper, argued against the bill in the name of the Byrd family. He said that Jasper, and in particular the Byrd family, had done a good job of responding to the crime and that the proposed act suggested otherwise. He added that Jasper had removed fences (referring to the fence in the cemetery that had separated black and white graves) and that the bill would erect new fences, implying it would divide more than unite.[20] The Byrd family had been heroic, he stressed, in trying to discourage public spectacle; they did not want their son's name used to further publicity for the Hate Crimes Act. He justified his opposition to the bill as expressing the wishes of the community and the Byrd family to leave the law, and the murder, alone. Representative Hochberg, who objected that he had personally spoken with the family on three occasions, immediately countered this assertion. "And do you know what they asked me to do? They asked me to pass this bill. To do everything that I can to pass this bill."[21] Byrd's mother Stella, daughter Renee Mullins, and nephew Darrell Varrett had become advocates for the bill. Stella Byrd wrote to the legislators, asking them "to pass the act in the name of our son." Mullins and Varrett testified before the House Committee on Judicial Affairs to ask for passage of the bill and petitioned both President Bill Clinton and Governor George Bush to pass hate crimes legislation. Byrd's son, Ross, remained in the background for these public debates, later becoming an anti–death penalty activist. The support of the Byrd family, especially Stella Byrd, was key to efforts to pass the act. Her support was a sort of badge of legitimacy, emphasized in Representative Thompson's opening and closing statements for the consideration of the bill in the House.

The importance of the ability to claim the support of the Byrd family went beyond the floor debate. Both Thompson and Deece Eckstein, Ellis's chief of staff, volunteered stories about a behind-the-scenes confrontation between Thompson and Christian over claiming the family's support. In response to Christian's claim to be working against the bill on behalf of the family, Thompson called Mrs. Byrd and asked whether she had spoken to Christian. She replied that she didn't even know Christian was her representative. With this response, Thompson and Ellis tracked down Christian and, in a tense confrontation, told him what Mrs. Byrd had told them and got him to backtrack on his claim to have spoken with the immediate family. The immediacy of family ties became a measure of legitimacy. Christian's conversation, Thompson added by way of debunking his claim, was with a distant cousin. When I spoke to Christian, he still claimed to have acted in accordance with the family's wishes. He said the Byrds who had testified in support of the bill were "not the immediate family":

> There was one family member, a niece or something that came to Austin, but the actual family from Jasper mostly, I don't remember them ever being in a press conference or leadership position, or visible places. They just played on the back row. I was not closely involved with them, so I can't testify exactly what they did.[22]

Christian told me this despite the fact that Byrd's mother, daughter, sister, and nephew went on the record to support the bill in testimony before the House and Senate committees. Stella Byrd publicly denounced Bush in 1999 and thanked Perry in 2001. The investment in claiming the support of the "real" family testifies to the pronounced role the family's wishes took on, even conferring a tone of moral authority to those who were able to successfully claim to speak on their behalf.

The ability to claim to be following the wishes of the Byrd family took on a greater persuasive role than strictly made sense. The bill, after all, was crafted to cover a wide range of violence and harassment toward a broad range of people. Yet, because it was cast as a memorial to James Byrd Jr., the role of the family as victims was heightened. In particular, because of the melodramatic narrative within which Byrd's murder had been made public, the role and authority of victim testimony took on a heightened ability to claim and define justice. The logic of melodrama is to render complex social relations associated with industrial and postindustrial capitalism morally and politically legible. Melodrama makes injustice visible and understandable by articulating it through clear examples of victimization and often spectacular suffering. The audience of melodrama knows to feel for the sufferer and to read his or her suffering as an example of either a moral or political wrong. This logic, prevalent in the media narratives surrounding Byrd's murder, transferred into the legislative debates over the Byrd Hate Crimes Act. The moral authority associated with the Byrd family's wishes was tied to the visibility of their pain. The highly mediated and graphic descriptions of Byrd's murder, the way it became a focal point of public concern and confrontations between black militia groups and the KKK, and the desecration of his grave (it was spray-painted with a swastika) highlighted the specificity of the family's suffering. The very spectacular elements of the murder and its aftermath were particularly effective in drawing attention to the crime, as an example of social injustice on a broad scale: as not just a regular crime but a hate crime.

Within this context, victim testimony became a primary form for conveying the underserved suffering of the victims clearly and as social injustice. The clarity of victim testimony was important as a counterpoint to the most prevalent argument against the bill: that it created "special protections" and elevated the rights of some citizens above others. Representative Christian was one of those who relied on this argument in his opposition to the bill. In the speech referenced above, Christian went on to make a claim that the law itself would create racial divisions, by creating "special classes" of victims. He argued that Byrd's murder had been adequately dealt with by the community and by the law. The enactment of the act would only create inequalities that did not currently exist. He explained this by saying:

> Understand that when our Constitution was invented, whenever they came over to this country, the whole purpose [was] that we had lords and ladies that had a different standard of law than did the common peasant. And it started that fight among them that these people had certain rights and privileges that other people did not have.[23]

He suggested that the hate crimes legislation would give special rights and privileges to racial and sexual minorities that the majority would not share, creating "special classes" with "special privileges." These "special classes," racial/ethnic and sexual minorities, would become like "lords and ladies" in the law, with special privileges that those figured as commoners under the law (specifically here, whites) did not have.

The idea that the law would create "special privileges," invoked by many Republicans, was historically situated within a backlash against civil rights legislation that had gained ground in Texas politics in the previous decade. This backlash, at the root of the various anti–affirmative action moves in the Texas legislature in the 1990s, holds that the very provisions aimed at redressing inequality constitute reverse racism and are in fact breaches of the equal protection they sought to enact. Within this backlash logic, legislation such as affirmative action violated constitutional equal protection by conferring "special privileges" on some and not on others.[24] While these arguments have not gained much legal traction, they have accumulated political appeal and power in recent decades. The constitutionality of the provisions in the Byrd Act was never really in doubt; the language was modeled on a Wisconsin hate crimes law that the Supreme Court found constitutional in the 1993 *Wisconsin* v. *Mitchell* decision. Perhaps more than anything else, objections expressed in terms of "equal protection" point not so much to concerns about legality as to battles over structural vs. individualist definitions of racism and over the role of the state in redressing racial wrongs. Arguments that the hate crimes bill would in itself create the conditions of division and racial inequality rely on a refutation of existing structural inequalities in institutions or law. The logic of Christian's speech, and the arguments of many other opponents, was based on the idea that prejudice is in the hearts of men and that structural racial inequalities no longer exist. Within this logic, the attack on Byrd and other violence are interpersonal problems best left to private solutions and the existing criminal code.

In the face of such arguments, victim testimony took on a heightened importance. Family members of murder victims, more than victims (of nonfatal attacks) themselves, brought mourning into the testimony. And with it, they brought the ethical and moral claims of loss. It was difficult for lawmakers to refuse these claims. The presence of victims and the families of victims and the form of their address—testimony—demanded a particular response from those present. Testifying, or bearing witness, to violence carries a heightened claim to truth via proximity and personal experience. It also has a heightened ethical claim. Witnessing asks the listener to become part of the event, demanding attention and even responsibility. As such, testimony conveys a strong pressure to remedy or do justice to the loss or pain described.[25] Given this, it is not surprising that the testimony and grief of the families of murder victims were cited as the most powerful, moving, and persuasive moments in the committee hearings. The bill itself may have been, as many supporters described it, geared more toward stopping intimidation and violence before it became fatal, but the testimony that held center stage was that of families of murder victims. The less spectacular violence of intimidation and harassment does not as frequently coalesce publics as more dramatic and violent cases of murder.

Much of the victim testimony at the hearings was about anti-gay vandalism and violence, seconded by testimony about anti-Semitic violence. Many of those who testified to nonlethal levels of anti-gay violence were women. However, the testimony that several of my interviewees cited as most clearly effective was that of family members of murder victims; these victims were mainly gay men. The testimony of the family of one man in particular was cited by several of those involved as particularly effective: a young Latino gay man killed in Austin. Patrick Johnson, who had been legislative aid to Senfronia Thompson at the time, spoke of how his "macho Hispanic cowboy" persona made him effective, as an "ordinary" (read: heteronormatively masculine) guy testifying for the passage of the act and the inclusion of protection for gay men and lesbians in the act.[26] While this may have to do with the way that straight family members of gay victims could be read as similar to the lawmakers, there are also clearly normative emotions in response to death. That is, certain emotional responses (e.g., sympathy, solemnity, respect) are expected as a "decent" response to death.

My interviewees noted these expectations in discussing how difficult it was to look at the faces of the families and oppose the bill. In discussing his coauthorship of the bill, Representative Pat Haggerty noted that the testimony of the victims, the visibility of Byrd's murder, and the later visibility of Matthew Shepard's murder made it difficult to think of going home (for him, El Paso) to

> face the folks at the Rotary Club or Kiwanis Club and tell them I voted against it, I think it's okay to hang a gay kid on the side of a fence or drag a guy down the street. It got to a point where it became apparent that this is not something that we should be allowing. And that if you are a homophobe or you do have racial feelings, you better overcome it.[27]

The importance is not that the murders persuaded him to support the bill (he had supported similar legislation in the past) but the way that the testimony framed the issue in moral and political terms that were difficult to publicly refuse. Hardy-Garcia noted the import of having "droves" of victims and families of victims testifying:

> I think it made it hard for them to reject the legislation. But, you know, lawmakers hear our sob stories all the time so I think there was another level, that many of these victims went to personally ask [lawmakers to pass the legislation]. . . . I mean, how can you justify not supporting this legislation when you're looking at Ms. Byrd's face or James Byrd's daughter?[28]

Similarly, Reverend Rigby, one of the most active local community organizers supporting the bill, noted that it was difficult to distance oneself from the testimony of families. He said that it was much easier to deal with the issues at stake in the debate over hate crimes legislation when talking at the abstract level, but that "when a kid is sitting there talking or this woman is sitting in a wheelchair talking about her son being drug to death, you know . . . that's when they couldn't push back."[29]

This type of reasoning was behind the naming of the legislation. It originated as a political strategy to personalize the issue; high-profile crimes had been important catalysts for discussions of previous hate crime bill proposals. Adding Byrd's name was intended to put a face on the act and to draw upon public outrage. Byrd was a sympathetic victim. The brutality of the murder and the way it evoked a history of racism for many people spoke to a need to do something. To sit back seemed to accept the crime and the racism it bespoke. Dianne Hardy-Garcia remembered the public response to Byrd's murder as not only anger but also mobilized outrage. In the news, the murder was discussed broadly as a hate crime, which Hardy-Garcia attributed to years of publicity and public education efforts by activist groups.[30] Various activist groups had worked to make anti-gay violence a social issue in the 1990s, to provide language and a structural framework for understanding this violence as political and to articulate anti-gay and racist violence under the label of hate crimes.[31] When Byrd was killed, Hardy-Garcia noted, the public "had a name for it," a name that she hoped would coalesce the public outrage and cries for a response around hate crimes legislation.

There were a number of rhetorical tactics used in the arguments for the bill, but claims that the bill was an attempt to provide justice rested in particular upon the moral claims of victimhood and the ability of this victimization to make injustice visible. This link of visibility and victimization had already been laid in place by the narration of Byrd's murder. The melodramatic logic made injustice visible through the presentation of excesses of undeniable suffering coupled with the stark moral contrast between the victim of suffering and the source of this suffering. This logic transferred from the media coverage into the legislative testimony and debates. Victim testimony before congressional committees was a way of making victimization visible, not only as violence but also as examples of structural injustice, to be addressed through politics and law.

### The Visibility of Victimhood

Victim testimony may have worked to make violence and suffering visible and legible as issues of social justice, but not all testimony was equally visible, and not all violence equally legible, in these debates. Looking at how examples of victimization were deployed within the debates—how visibility was claimed and whose suffering was referenced within the floor debates—shows differences in legibility of racial and sexual discrimination. While much of the actual testimony was geared toward making violence and discrimination against gay men and lesbians visible as political, racial violence took center stage within the floor debates.

As noted above, despite the fact that the act bore Byrd's name, referring to a highly publicized example of racial violence, much of the debate circled around sexual orientation. Conservative lawmakers, while not keen on the bill, could have been persuaded to sign on if the language referring to sexual orientation had been dropped. Given that the coalition of supporters was unwilling to do so, they sought to make anti-gay violence visible as a social issue. The inclusion of sexual orientation meant that the discursive challenge for supporters would be to make anti-gay violence legible as a social injustice. The victim testimony before the House committees did so through an emphasis on personal stories of harassment, intimidation, and violence directed at gay men and lesbians and those thought to be gay. This visibility, however, remained backstage, in committee. The more publicly watched floor debates were framed almost entirely in terms of race and racial violence. The disparity between the focus on sexual orientation in the committee testimony and the focus on race in the floor debate illuminates both the political stakes of visibility and the normative expectations for expressions of feeling that strategically framed the debate. The "visibility" of race, in contrast to the "invisibility" of sexual orientation, was key to convincing lawmakers of the existence of discrimination as injustice.

This difference in "visibility," or legibility, was addressed explicitly in discussions of the "invisibility" of sexual orientation. For those opposed to the bill, the "invisibility" of sexual orientation made it harder to see violence directed at those thought to be gay as a social issue. During the Judicial Affairs committee hearing, one House representative asked Jim Harrington, director of the Texas Civil Rights Project, whether some victims were more visible than others. He went on to inquire how it was possible to tell if someone had been targeted for an "invisible" reason, a thinly veiled reference to sexual orientation. Similarly, Representative Sadler recounted a personal conversation with Governor Bush about the legislation, in which Bush said his main reservation about the act was: "How do you know if they're gay?"[32] For these lawmakers, the fact that sexuality does not carry visible physical markers means it cannot be an axis of discrimination. In both of these examples, the idea that sexuality is invisible works to delegitimize the idea that discrimination based on sexual orientation is a valid public and political concern. The move from the idea that sexual orientation is not visible to the idea that it therefore cannot be the basis of discriminatory actions—or interventions—presumes that the reason for a discriminatory attack inheres in the body and identity of the victim rather than in the social perceptions of those surrounding the victim and/or those doing the attacking. In this presumption, these comments reify identity categories and reinscribe hate crimes within an individualist and interpersonal framework rather than a structural one. Against such inabilities to bridge the "invisibility" of sexual orientation and the articulation of injustice in terms of the visibility of suffering, victim testimony sought to make anti-gay violence visible as public violence through the undeniability of the testimony of victims and their families.

The visibility and moral claim of victimhood here is an important part of the affective economy of victimization. The visibility of suffering acts as a proof of injustice and discrimination and as an argument for the validity of legal remedies. Visibility in general has played an important historical role in creating the conditions of possibility for gay and queer politics, as a tool for both articulating a collective identity and taking a place (and a voice) in the public sphere.[33]

An emphasis on visibility can be seen as well in the mobilization of victim-hood in the testimony examined here. The testimony of both families of victims of anti-gay violence and the gay and lesbian speakers who recounted personal stories of vulnerability emphasized the desire to be recognized and explicitly protected within the law. This was the overt message of one man who got up to testify at the very end of the House committee hearing, to say that the only place that he, as a gay man, was currently recognized in Texas law was in the penal code, where same-sex sexual activity was criminalized. The James Byrd Jr. Hate Crimes Act, he argued, would change this.[34] Others testified to the law's inability to hear or adequately respond to their complaints, due to institutionalized het-eronormativity and the simple inability of the law to see and recognize anti-gay violence as a violation of civil liberties and rights.[35]

This line of argument made it out of the committee hearings into the more public, more visible floor debates. During the debate over the bill, Representative Wolens attempted to make this violence visible as public violence, in terms of social justice, and used a complex play of visibility and proximity to bring the issue closer to home for the lawmakers. Presenting a slide show of pictures of victims, confronting lawmakers with the concrete individuals who had been victims of anti-gay violence, he narrated:

> This is Ernest Saldaña. He was 1 when this picture was taken. And he was killed Nov. 3 of 1994. He was kicked to death by a gang of men. And as they kicked him, they repeatedly called him a faggot. And he was the son of a mother and a father who are sitting up in the gallery here today. And Pablo Zuniga, here at age 5, was stabbed to death in Austin in July of '96. He was 31 years old when he was killed and he is the son of a mother and a father sitting in the gallery today. And he could be just like my son. Grace Latour was 16 years old when she was beaten in her school by a group as they called her a dyke in 1994. Her mother is sitting in the gallery.[36]

Wolens went on to entreat the representatives to each "look into your heart, and think about the rest of us out here who have lived this stuff and its [effects]. Just look around. You can see which of us are black, and you know which of us are brown. It's pretty hard to tell which of us are Jews. And gay." In calling atten-tion to the "invisibility" of sexual identity, he was attempting to remind white, straight lawmakers that someone close to them could potentially be targeted, at-tempting to bring the issue "home" to the individual lawmakers. The speech re-called the details of several incidents of anti-gay violence, asking the representa-tives to attend to the violence and the particular animus that had spurred, mak-ing the violence more present through image and detail. It played on proximity in yet another way, reminding lawmakers that they were deliberating before the eyes of family members of victims and potential targets. Through the repetition of victim testimony and the invocation of the pain—and presence—of the family members, advocates sought to make a particular type of discrimination and injustice visible to politicians loath to see or understand it.

This use of "invisibility," to point out that someone close to any member of the House—most pointedly, children—might in fact be gay or that any member of the House might be mistaken as gay was an effort to ask lawmakers to recognize a danger and a discrimination by making it appear closer to them personally. The advocates I spoke with saw both of these as effective means of convincing some conservative opponents. Several advocates told me that one behind-the-scenes reason some conservatives "crossed the aisle" to vote for the legislation, or absented themselves from the vote in collusion with supporters, was that they had secret or hidden gay relatives.[37] Johnson recounted a story of one conservative lawmaker's conversion to a supporter of the act as a consequence of being read as gay: "One of the reps from East Texas—I'm not going to tell you who—was standing out on the corner, waiting for his driver and somebody yelled "faggot" at him and threw something at him. At that point, he became a supporter."[38] The representative had been waiting outside the Cloak Room, a bar where lawmakers gather informally (and reportedly where many deals and negotiations are made). The Cloak Room happens to be next to a landmark Austin gay bar, Charlie's.

In this story, the fact that anybody can be marked as gay worked to place the lawmaker temporarily in the position of a target of anti-gay violence.[39] The account presented this experience as sufficient to move the representative to vote for the act. In this story, and in the rumors about the hidden sexual orientation of members of lawmakers' families and the effect of this on their thinking and voting on the bill, the "invisibility" of sexual orientation surfaces as a concern and a tactic. If sexual orientation is invisible, designation as gay can accrue to anybody. This was used as a tactic to make anti-gay discrimination more real to lawmakers by making the victimization seem close, a personal possibility. Representative Wolens's speech, stressing that you never know whether your own children might be gay, was one such move. The power of the testimony of the two "traditionally" masculine men about their personal experiences with anti-gay violence was another. Both Rigby and Johnson emphasized that the men were convincing because they were so "ordinary." This ordinariness signaled not only authenticity of the testimony but also the proximity of this violence to lawmakers.

It is telling that, despite the importance of the testimony of victims of anti-gay violence, it was not a gay man's name on the bill. A number of gay men had been killed in Texas in the 1990s (Hardy-Garcia put the number at 30), and high-profile murders such as Paul Broussard's helped galvanize the effort to pass the first state hate crime laws.[40] Yet these murders were not as visible nationally and did not have the same normative call upon the legislators as did Byrd's murder, through both its national publicity and its association with histories of racism. Byrd's murder was particularly visible as a hate crime, and the brutality made racism (under any definition of the term) particularly visible. This visibility helped to put other, less visible violence on the table.

The choice to put Byrd's name on the bill reflected a sense that racial discrimination and violence had greater visibility and legibility within the Texas legislature. Proponents relied on this, especially on the visibility of the violence directed against Byrd. In the most public forums, where reporters and cameras were present and where the public convened in response to Byrd's murder was likely to be watching, the advocates of the bill focused discussions on race. This was a strategic move. Both Hardy-Garcia and Representative Thompson judged that white lawmakers were far more afraid of being called racist than being called homophobic. In this, supporters relied upon a presumption that not only would it be difficult to say no to the families and victims of hate crimes, but that it would be difficult to say no to the existence of racial violence (if not racial discrimination in general), particularly within the wake and framework of Byrd's murder. This is not to say that these lawmakers were particularly sensitive to racial violence, but rather that the combination of the frame of criminal violence and the complex discursive history of race and racism was effective. Supporters were able to convince the same conservative lawmakers who advanced arguments of "reverse racism" to support the bill through a sort of preemptive discursive tactic that highlighted the undeniability of the visibility of racial difference and racial violence, while simultaneously proposing that whites could also be the victims of racist hate crimes.

In the House floor debate, lawmakers of color called upon their own personal experiences, highlighting the difference between their lives and perspectives and those of white lawmakers, calling upon the undeniable "visibility" of racial difference. As Wolens noted, everyone could clearly see who was brown. At another point in the floor debate, Wolens again called on the visibility of minority lawmakers: "For some of us, this is a very serious bill. And it means a lot to many of us, who as children experienced a lot of the hatred. . . . Ask Senfronia Thompson, or ask Glen Maxie, or ask Paul Moreno, or ask Sherry Greenburg, or ask me what it is like."[41] Similarly, in response to Christian's argument that the bill would create special classes and racial divisions (presumably where none existed), Paul Moreno replied with the weight of personal testimony: "One of the things wrong in America is that the white folk that have discriminated against us (for race, sex, disability) deny, deny, deny that it is done." Speaking back to Christian, he noted that racial discrimination was not visible to people like Christian who had no firsthand experience being the targets of discrimination. He countered this argument with his own story of being denied housing in Austin during college because he was Mexican American and being repeatedly stopped by border patrol "even though" he drove an expensive car.[42] Moreno was not the only politician of color to contrast his experiences to those of white politicians. While the testimony had focused on making anti-gay violence visible, in the house debate the personal testimony primarily came from black and Latino lawmakers, emphasizing the visibility of racial markers. This visibility was as key to assertions that discrimination existed as was the personal testimony of experience. These comments both drew on the discursive status of racial markers as indisputable and argued that the experience of racial discrimination was invisible to white lawmakers, seeking to make them visible through personal testimony and experience.

Some lawmakers sought to make these experiences more understandable and proximate to white lawmakers by highlighting whiteness as a racial category, often relying on arguments that whites could potentially be targets of hate crimes, too. For example, Thompson slid into this logic in her opening remarks to the House Committee on Judicial Affairs. She opened the hearing with a speech and a slide show featuring images of victims: James Byrd Jr., and her own legislative aide, bandaged and battered as the target of anti-gay violence. Her remarks concluded with a set of rhetorical questions addressed to the committee members:

> Will your church be targeted because the congregation is primarily black? Will your daughter be called names at school as she is assaulted because [her] skin is brown and she speaks with an accent? Will your house be spray-painted because you do not worship Jesus? Will you be raped, tortured, and stabbed because your skin is white and you stumble across a Latino gang in a field? Will you be enticed for a ride with an anti-immigrant assaultive robber? Will you be chased and pummeled by skinheads with baseball bats because your sexual orientation is different? Will you be beaten by a group of ignorant, macho suburban teenagers waiting outside a bar to use a 2×4 with nails sticking out to beat you to death because your sexual orientation is different? Will you be kidnapped, chained, and dragged to your death by ignorant, hateful racists until your skin rips off, until you are dismembered, just because you are an African American?[43]

Her graphic presentation emphasized the brutality of the attacks and their effects on the victims. The questions referenced the experiences of the victims whose stories would be invoked in testimony before the committee. It also highlighted some of the primary axes of difference between the committee members (primarily, though not exclusively, white, Christian males) and the victims. The interrogative element focuses attention on the relative safety of committee members in their bodies and social positions. The majority of Thompson's questions echoed a common response of supporters to the special protections accusation: that they were only asking for the most basic of human rights. Yet, toward the end of her speech, she veered in a different direction, seeking to close the gap she had opened between the lawmakers and the victims about to testify before them. In an ominous tone, she reminded the predominantly white committee the act would even protect them "if they ever ran out of gas on a lonely street in Oak Lawn, a lonely bayou in the 5th Ward" in Houston.

This rhetoric of white vulnerability undermines many of the structural arguments marshaled elsewhere for hate crimes as symptomatic of social discourse and structural inequalities of access to power and institutions. It was, instead, an effort to make the reasons for the law appear closer to white lawmakers, to close a gap of experience as well as to counter the "special protections" argument. Reverend Rigby, who worked closely with the LGRL and Thompson's office in lobbying for the bill, remembered the argument this way: "All you white people don't think you have race. All you men don't think you have gender. All you straight people think you don't have an orientation. So you think these are special rights."[44] This idea was emphasized in committee hearings, in which legal and civil rights experts testified as to the neutrality of the letter of the law. The language defining hate crimes, or in the language of the debates, defining what groups could be targeted, only mentioned the categories of race, sexuality, religion, etc., not specific races, sexualities, religions. Advocates stressed to white male lawmakers that they had race and gender and so were covered or protected by the bill. In his testimony, Jim Harrington highlighted this category neutrality by noting that the act would penalize a Latino for assaulting a white man based on race. He gave the example of such an attack in the Rio Grande Valley, where whites are a minority.[45] Similarly, Pat Haggerty told me that he had tried to persuade skittish representatives to support the bill using the shift in racial demographics in Texas. He reminded lawmakers, he said, that in the not-too-distant future, whites might be a minority in Texas, and therefore they might want to think differently about who might be the victims of hate crimes.[46] Others emphasized that the Wisconsin law the Byrd Act was modeled on was famous for its use in prosecuting several young black men for attacking a young white man after watching *Mississippi Burning*. All of these tactics can be seen as ways of trying to close the gap between white lawmakers and the subjects the law sought to protect, to heighten their empathetic response as well as to make the injustices at hand appear more visible and immediate, by playing up conservative fantasies of white racial vulnerability.

The circulation of victimhood, as attached to the specific hazards of life as a sexual or racial minority and as attached to the lawmakers, in the repeated argument that everybody in the room was "protected" under the law, rhetorically placed the lawmakers and the victims of hate crimes in proximity to one another. The circulation of victimization in the testimony repeatedly assigned innocence and "ordinariness" to those killed, further pulling them into proximity with the lawmakers, who regularly invoke the rhetoric of ordinariness for themselves and their constituencies. The deployment of the details of loss and victimization brought both bodies (of those killed or endangered, of the families of victims) and feelings into the testimony, relying on the socially expected response of empathy. It became not only difficult to say no to the families and victims of hate crimes but also difficult to say no to the existence of racial violence, if not racial discrimination in general, in particular within the wake and framework of Byrd's murder. Lawmakers were well aware that to do so would appear too unfeeling—as some put it, less than human.

## The Politics and Performance of Feeling

The primacy of victim testimony in the legislative debates was effective in part because of the way the actual testimony and presence of victims and their families demanded a particular set of emotional and ethical responses. Emotional norms required a demonstration of empathy. These norms formed the bounds of legitimate and illegitimate feelings. Within the bounds of legislative debate, the emotional norms regarding responses to the suffering of others included both a proper display of feeling and political (legislative) action. This compulsion was demonstrated in Representative Paul Sadler's comments on the floor. He explained that he did not usually help sponsor bills authored by other representatives, but the James Byrd Jr. Hate Crimes Act was an exception:

> There are defining moments in your legislative career. There are defining moments in every legislative session. There are votes and bills that tell the world who we are, what we value, what we cherish, what we believe. And this bill is one of them. . . . And so I join my friends who say I have been such a victim, I have experienced this lifestyle, I have seen the hatred, I have been ridiculed, I have been the butt of conduct that was inappropriate. We can't end

hatred and violence, but it is our duty to punish conduct. Conduct that we find reprehensible. Conduct that we believe is wrong. And who of you will stand and tell me that conduct based on hatred and bias and prejudice is anything but wrong? I'm proud to support this bill.[47]

His call to support the bill used a strong ethical and moral framing. The obligation to respond is presented not only as a principle but also as a duty to those around him, solidarity with his fellow lawmakers, and empathy for the victims.

Sadler eschewed language of either race or sexuality. Yet overall the debate on the House floor placed discussion of injustice within the frame of racial justice. When the bill moved past the House and on to the Senate, the debate in committee there once again focused on sexuality.[48] While the testimony in committee and strongest objections were about the inclusion of sexuality in the bill, it was largely absent from the public debate. Floor debates, instead, focused on race and racism. This is not to say that the discussion was only *about* race—it was also always centrally about sexuality. It is simply to say that it was expressed in terms of race and the perhaps more established (though still contradictory) public framework or archive of racial injustice. I suggest that this is in part because of the existence of a stronger framework for articulating racism as injustice—and the strong normative injunction not to appear racist (and to display the proper condemnation in word and deed). The idea of discrimination based on sexual orientation was a newer concept and carried less of a normative injunction within the discursive community of the Texas legislature.[49] The focus of floor debates on racial violence also derived from the preexisting melodramatic narrative of the murder circulated in media texts, with the normative requirements of feeling and resolution implied by the form. Framed as a response to racial violence, the law could appear as a resolution to the conflicts highlighted by the murder.

### LEGITIMATE AND ILLEGITIMATE EXPRESSIONS OF FEELING

When expectations for the proper empathy in the face of victim testimony and the presence of the family members of victims were not met, politicians appeared less than human: outside the normal and legitimate range of not only political behavior but also the norms of the social community. The story of George Bush's meeting with the Byrd family was widely circulated at the time and became a minor publicity battle in the run-up to the 2000 presidential election. Byrd's daughter and several other family members wanted to appeal to the governor personally to get the bill passed and, after many attempts, finally got a brief appointment. Reverend Rigby accompanied the Byrd family and recounted the meeting to me with heavy emphasis on Bush's inappropriate affect.

Bush was impatient and told them he hadn't even read the bill, refused to read it when asked, and cursorily dismissed them. Rigby described the family's reaction: "They were just sitting there like they'd been shot. . . . All he had to do was say, 'Thank you very much for coming. You know, I'm on the other side of this, but, you know, I respect you for what you're doing and I'm sorry about your dad.' Or anything human whatsoever."[50] He reacted to Bush's failure to perform the most basic affective cues of belonging. Whatever the reasons, the effect of his words was not only to cast doubt on his membership in the community of decent people but also to call into question his "humanity." In contrast, Rigby remembered Perry more favorably, although he was no more politically sympathetic to the bill or the politics of the groups sponsoring it. Perry demonstrated the proper cues of human feeling, tearing up as he signed the act into law and spoke with Stella Byrd. Despite his politics, he performed proper feeling in the face of the family of a victim and was remembered as more human. The difference between the two did not come down to politics, or interiority, but performance of proper (normative) feeling.

The normative expectations imposed by the presence of victims and the emotional force of their testimony were part of the strategy of the bill's advocates. The impact and normative pull of victim testimony was heightened by the media on several levels. The melodramatic framework of Byrd's murder, which was echoed in the victim testimony and its articulation within the legislative debate, positioned the testimony and victims as not mere sufferers but sufferers of injustice, with a strong normative demand for response on the part of listeners. In addition, the presence of media at the public floor debates put added pressure on lawmakers to respond appropriately, both in terms of political speech and demonstration of feeling.

Because the murder was newsworthy, more media attention was paid to deliberations of the act than to many other legislative matters. Supporters were keenly aware of this, staging media events such as prayer vigils in the House in order to attract and keep media attention on the process and politicians. There was an existing public to attend to the proceedings, motivating press coverage and additional care on the part of politicians about their performance. Lawmakers were careful to perform proper emotions in the face of victims and families of victims and the broader media audience. Hardy-Garcia noted that a lot of "the bad behavior that used to happen" in legislative sessions stopped after the floor debates started being televised on closed-circuit TV and local cable access.[51] The additional publicity afforded by the presence of the media heightened the pressure to meet normative expectations and demonstrate proper feelings for the victims. Much as in Laramie, where the activists and politicians staged the discussion and passage of the city bias crimes ordinance before an imagined national public, the debates and committee hearings in Texas became stages upon which lawmakers felt the need to perform properly.

This desire to perform properly is perhaps best demonstrated in the actions of conservative politicians who moved in 1999 from opposition to support for the bill and those who continued to oppose it. Representative Christian, who remained an opponent of the bill, described the difficulty of navigating this opposition:

> I think people were most careful of what they said and indeed those of us that are Caucasian were most aware that anything that you try to say in opposition was taken as anti-minority. And we had to be very careful to say, "No, that is not the situation here. The situation is that the legislation is not what the people of Texas want."[52]

He was clearly concerned about the danger of appearing racist or insensitive to racism. He noted that he had received hate mail and had been accused of being a Klansman himself. The concern Christian expressed about being very careful with his words and his example of the consequences of his opposition have to do with being affiliated with disavowed communities of white supremacists as much as with principle.[53] The fear of being aligned with the KKK is a fear of being associated with an extreme ideology and those who espouse it. In this way, his concern with not appearing racist was in part a desire to perform belonging in a more desirable political community by showing the expected affective responses.

This desire to disavow racial violence, especially the type of racial violence depicted in media narratives of Byrd's murder, provided the grounds for conservatives to switch sides. The key vote in support of the act came from social conservative Warren Chisum, who had previously opposed similar legislation that included any reference to sexuality. It was in negotiations with Chisum that the language in the bill was changed from "sexual orientation" to "sexual preference." Whatever the reason he agreed to support the bill, the public disavowal of racist violence provided the public rationale. When asked why he changed his vote in 1999, Chisum said (incorrectly) that this was the first time the bill included race and other categories in addition to sexuality. He supported the bill, he said, after he (and the governor's office) persuaded the authors of the bill to include the categories of race, ethnicity, and religion:

> What changed my support for it was myself and Governor Perry's office negotiated that they didn't just have it for homosexuals. We had it for if you could prove hate crime for other reasons like child molesters or people that would batter women, or even religious groups because we had instances where

they've attacked Jewish churches and those kinds of things. . . . Let me tell you, that was after many years of voting against it. I always voted against it because they were just trying to do it for one specific group. They were trying to hold them up as one specific group that you could not do hate crimes against. But if you put it only for the homosexual group, then you're saying it's okay to discriminate against Christians or Jews or child molesters or something like that but you can't do it to this group. I think that laws ought to be equal. That's the U.S. Constitution: equal protection under the law.[54]

He couched his support for the bill in terms of its inclusion of multiple categories of discrimination, sure to address the "special protections" argument by noting that it provided equal protection. His somewhat odd list of groups that might have been discriminated against (in his erroneous articulation of earlier versions of the bill) referenced a number of arguments made by other conservative lawmakers. Inclusion of other forms of discrimination, and especially racial discrimination, provided a rationale to justify his support that was consistent with his political position and base. He said that the visibility and brutality of the crime compelled some sort of legal response. Legislators were compelled to condemn and make a statement about racism, which, he was careful to specify, was a problem in East Texas, not his own panhandle district. In this, he cast his support as tough on crime and "antiracist," and he simultaneously claimed that "racism" existed elsewhere. Supporting a piece of legislation aimed at combating (others') racism was offered up as a more legitimate course of action than giving in to support a bill that includes protection for crimes based on sexual orientation.[55] Of course, the racism that Chisum referenced is only the "old-fashioned" racism characterized by violence and overt physical, psychological, and institutional oppression. The racism Chisum disavowed does not include the more pervasive "new racism" which privatizes issues of structural injustice, casting them as individual or community choice. In this way Chisum's performance of repudiating racism had little to do with the politics or policies of racial justice. Because of the contemporary popular discourses on racism, he (like many politicians) was able to condemn old-fashioned racism while pursuing policies that advance "new," or neoliberal, racism. Lawmakers may strive to avoid appearing racist all the while endorsing the perverse discourse of "special privileges," itself deeply invested in protecting white and other privilege.

This investment in protecting privilege was as well seen in the emphasis on the fact that whites were protected from hate crimes within the language of the law, particularly white men. The references to white victimization were of course persuasive appeals aimed at persuading reluctant lawmakers to support the legislation. The rhetoric of white victimhood can be seen as an effort to meld the melodramatic narrative of racism, suffering, and redemptive progress to the (backlash) neoconservative racial discourse of equal protection. This melodramatic narrative of victimization and redemption was a powerful motivator, but required the recognition of victims of systemic racism. Supporters feared that, within the anti–affirmative action climate and discourse of "special privileges," this recognition might not be forthcoming. Hence they brought up the potential of white victimization, through reference to areas in the state where racial minorities are majorities and the repeated use of statistics detailing the number of anti-white hate crimes.[56]

The greater ability of racial violence to achieve visibility clearly did not mean that the political climate was sympathetic to racial justice projects. The need to perform antiracist feelings and actions did not necessarily translate into advocacy of antiracist political discourse or politics. Nor did the need to show empathy for all the victims of violence who testified before the committee motivate a shift to less anti-gay politics in general. In the words of those who crossed the aisle to support the bill in 1999 and opponents, what emerges is an impression that they felt a greater need to display opposition to racism than to homophobia. Christian was willing to tell me that the main reason that hate crimes legislation had not passed in previous years was that lawmakers felt that the legislation "would allow benefits to the homosexual community that were unwarranted."[57] While he did not say that he agreed, he did not try to distance himself from the statement either. Far from having a sense of needing to show their distance from homophobic policies and statements, many lawmakers simply did not have the words to discuss the inclusion of gay men and lesbians in the law or LGBT issues in general. Hardy-Garcia remembered that at the beginning of the debates in 1999, even supportive lawmakers stumbled with the very words *lesbian, gay,* and *homosexuality,* unsure of what to say or how to say it. She noted that one small victory of the process was that by 2001, lawmakers were more comfortable publicly addressing and discussing the LGBT community and issues.[58]

The testimony of victims and the hypervisibility of Byrd's murder were clearly central to the passage of the act, driving the process and content of the debates. The act would not have passed without them. Yet, at the same time, the passage of the act also depended on the type of legislation. While the act itself offered more than penalty enhancements and punitive language, including public and police education and civil remedies, it was overwhelmingly publicized as a penalty enhancement law. This focus on the bill as criminal law, and hence on violence and interpersonal definitions of discrimination, made it easier for people to define the act within both conservative and liberal political projects— and affective economies. Support for the act was, for some politicians, a way of showing disgust and revulsion for criminals, as those "bad apples" who commit acts of racist, anti-gay, and anti-Semitic violence. For others, it was a way of performing their connection with black, brown, queer, and Jewish communities. Liberal and neoconservative racial projects coincided in the definitions of interpersonal violence as racism and as a proper focus for criminal punishment. While for supporters, the legislation was often described as a foot in the door that might be wedged wider, especially for legislation offering more rights to gay men and lesbians, for conservatives it could easily be a reinforcement of individualist constructions of racism and anti-gay discrimination. That it was not necessarily the first step in a linear progression of recognition of gay rights in the Texas legislature or in Texas in general is all too well illustrated by the 2005 passage of an amendment to the state constitution that effectively banned recognition of same-sex marriage or civil unions (authored by Representative Chisum).

The very legal forms of recognition have their own (internal) limitations. Just as Judith Butler argues that the formal conventions of the obituary limit what lives (and aspects of a life) may be publicly grieved,[59] seeking recognition within the law shapes and limits the ways in which people may be publicly recognized and injustices addressed. In this case, the way in which the institution of the legislature made public space for the recognition of loss speaks both to the politics of public feelings and to the constraints of the institution.[60]

## Conclusion: Shaping Justice Claims

The national visibility of Byrd's murder and the testimony of victims and their families provided evidence of suffering, marshalling norms of feeling that had to be evidenced (performed) in words and in political action. The experiences of discrimination offered by lawmakers, as well as the victim testimony, worked to articulate a sense of injustice through both the power of personal testimony and the strong frameworks for responding to unjust suffering encapsulated in melodrama, as described in chapter 3. In particular, the image of Byrd evoked a long line of images of wronged black men, as victims of (white) power structures. This evidence of suffering made an effective argument for structural change, such as it was in the James Byrd Jr. Hate Crimes Act. As Texas Civil Rights Project director Jim Harrington argued in the committee hearings, Byrd's murder was "an anomaly in a sense, because it was so brutal and violent. But what it did was lay bare so we could all see that racism still exists, hate crime still goes on, that low-level lynching in our society."[61] The violence made evident a moral dilemma that demanded response. The gulf between democratic ideals of equity and the experience of violent discrimination defined a moral conflict that demands resolution (in order to save the democratic ideals). Legislation, in the form of the Byrd Act, was offered as a legitimate and effective response to and resolution of the victims' suffering—and the violation of democratic principles this suffering came to reveal.

The melodramatic narrative and images of minority suffering were effective in producing a broad sentiment of injustice. This sentiment mobilized many of the supporters of the bill and individuals who testified. While in much of the media coverage, the criminal trial was presented as the resolution and restoration of justice, this did not constitute full narrative or political closure. For those who supported the bill, the criminal trials did not offer closure. There was still a broader injustice (within the law) that needed to be addressed. In the discursive positioning of first the murder trials and then the hate crimes legislation as remedy to this injustice and the family's suffering, the law was framed as a remedy. That is, the positioning of legislation as a sufficient and proper response produced the law as *the* site of justice, perhaps even exhausting the possibilities of justice. There are, of course, other sites for articulating justice: for instance, institutional policies, governmental practices, and expressive culture. The heavy emphasis on the law in this case follows a particularly liberal view of justice and politics. In this narration, legislators and activists (including those who testified as victims) take on heroic roles. The passage of the act through the House, even though the act failed to pass that year, became a moment of triumph for both the supporters and liberal legal principles.

This victory was dependent on timing and media publicity. Several of my interviewees asserted that the 1999 and 2001 legislative sessions were the last ones in which such a victory could have happened (the last before religiously tinged social conservatism gained ascendancy in the Texas legislature). In many ways, though, 1999 was the first time the act could have passed. It was the first assembly after the highly publicized murder of James Byrd Jr. The murder and the publicity surrounding it were key in attracting a public and mobilizing feeling. The existence of a public interested in the Byrd murder meant that a law carrying his name would attract at least some of this public's attention, heightening the need for lawmakers to perform properly in front of this public. That this public was one convened through sympathy, albeit distant, for Byrd and longing for social justice (as closure, within the melodramatic presentation of the murder) meant that public sentiment was predisposed toward passage of the law. Opponents had to navigate the presumption of public support as well as the need to respond sympathetically ("humanly") to the victim testimony before them. Often politicians who opposed hate crimes legislation walked a line between these emotional demands and a desire to please their socially conservative base by opposing any legislation that recognized gay men and lesbians. In enough cases to pass the law, the emotional demands won out over the demands of this base—or at least provided political cover for going against it.

Media were vital not only to shaping the legislative debates and actions as organs of publicity but also in the way that texts publicizing the murder provided emotional mediation, defining the narrative and emotional frameworks for understanding Byrd's death. The presence of the media in the capitol heightened the need for politicians to perform properly. But the very understanding of how to perform was also the product of mediation, in the form of the coverage of the murder. The legislative process surrounding the Byrd Act demonstrates the importance of the narrative, semiotic, and historical work of emotional mediation, or the work of the media to define the relationships and feelings between publics and people and events on the page and screen. The contrast between the persuasiveness of the testimony of victims of anti-gay violence and the testimony of experiences of racism and racist violence shows that pain or suffering does not speak for itself. The responses to images of suffering or even the more immediate stories of victims are mediated by the deployment of particular narratives, histories, and images—and the repertoires of social norms conveyed therein. This point goes against arguments that claims for recognition and justice based in suffering and pain universalize that suffering and, in so doing, diminish its ability to stand as political critique, to provide evidence to the specificity and structural underpinnings of that suffering.[62] The evidence of suffering in victim testimony examined here may have used a discourse of universal humanity in demanding a (normative) response, but it did not rely upon the universality of suffering or flatten out the specificity of that suffering and its structural causes. The testimony, in fact, relied on the specificity of that suffering for its effectiveness. In official venues, if not in literature, such testimony demands attention to its specificity. Within this context, the problem with pain is not so much its universality as the opposite. Pain and suffering are in fact conveyed only through highly specific mediations, which determine their legibility and their ability to make claims on our attention and on justice. While pain may be sometimes assumed to make common humanity and demands for rights universally legible, the reasoning here suggests that the very legibility of pain depends upon the political and social contexts within which it is expressed. Here, the pain of some was more readily or predictably legible than that of others.

# [ *Conclusion* ]

## Feeling in the Public Sphere

> Communication sometimes masquerades as the great solution to human ills, yet most
> troubles in human relationships do not come from a failure to match signs and mean-
> ings. . . . Communication, again, is more basically a political and ethical problem than a
> semantic or psychological one. As thinkers such as Hegel and Marx, Dewey and Mead,
> Adorno and Habermas all argue, just communication is an index of the good society. We
> ought to be less worried about how signs arouse divergent meanings than the conditions
> that keep us from attending to our neighbors and other beings different from ourselves.
> —John Durham Peters, *Speaking into the Air*, 269

IN THE FALL OF 2009, several events once again underscored the cultural impact of the murders of Matthew Shepard and James Byrd Jr. On October
12, the Tectonic Theater Project staged *The Laramie Project: 10 Years Later.* The
performance marked the anniversary of Shepard's death, bringing an estimated
50,000 viewers together to remember and once again mourn.[1] Two weeks later,
President Barack Obama signed legislation that overhauled federal hate crimes
law to include crimes based on sexual orientation and gender identity, among
other things. The two events were linked in their reference to the memory of
Shepard as well as in the politics of emotional mediation.

In the staging of an epilogue to *The Laramie Project,* media encouraged
the formation of a dispersed and emotive community. The performance was
coordinated with over 150 simultaneous performances both in the United States
and abroad, united by a live web link broadcasting the prologue and the discussion afterward from New York and by social media throughout. Audiences
used Twitter to post their responses and pose questions to the playwrights and
Shepard's mother, who was in attendance at the New York staging. Once again,
this mourning was directed toward political ends. The performance sought to
reinvigorate public memory of Shepard's death as a hate crime; the question-
and-answer session noted the need for formal legal rights for gays and lesbians,
from same-sex marriage to hate crime prevention.

On October 22, the president signed legislation bearing the men's names. The Matthew Shepard and James Byrd Jr. Hate Crimes Prevention Act changed federal hate crime laws in a number of ways: it included crimes committed based on sexual orientation, gender, gender identity, or disability; it required that the FBI track crimes against transgender people; it gave greater power to federal authorities to investigate alleged hate crimes that local authorities do not investigate; and it broadened federal jurisdiction beyond hate crimes that interfere with protected activities such as voting or attending school. The act and the use of Shepard's name remained controversial; conservatives opposed both. Perhaps most famously, North Carolina representative Virginia Foxx claimed that the labeling of Shepard's murder as a hate crime constituted a "hoax." In the discussion surrounding the act, the men were not memorialized equally. The designation of hate crime in Byrd's case has been less controversial, but he has been less frequently a topic of public discussion at the national level. The bill was popularly discussed as the "Matthew Shepard Hate Crimes Prevention Act," dropping Byrd's name. This is, no doubt, due to the fact that most of the changes to hate crimes law cover sexual orientation and gender identity. Yet the omission of Byrd's name in much media coverage was matched by other inequalities of public presence.

There was, for example, no national ceremony, performance, or mediated coming together to mark the tenth anniversary of Byrd's murder. While many do remember Byrd, this mourning takes place outside of the mediated public sphere. Neither national media outlets nor public institutions have staged memorials or trained public feelings upon his memory. The differential investment of both events in the murders of the two men demonstrates that feelings and attention are unequally distributed via media and cultural texts. This inequality highlights both the role of media as infrastructure for public expressions of feelings and the economics of this infrastructure.

The fact that the act was named after these men illustrates their continuing hold on politics and policy, not only consciousness and culture. Public expressions of feeling were important factors in mobilizing people into political action after each murder, performing not only cultural but also political and legal "work." The cases analyzed in this book demonstrate the institutional impact and relevance of aspects of mediation often understood more as "cultural" than political, in the formal and administrative sense of the term. A divide remains between analyses of cultural politics, in which politics comprises the micro-power relations of everyday life, and of formal politics, or the institutions and procedures of official governance, despite the rapprochement between cultural studies and political economy.[2] Both cultural and institutional politics are, of course, important for understanding the workings of power and politics. Public expressions of feeling, when they are the subject of academic study, are usually analyzed as cultural politics, as the site of micro-power relationships and conflicts. By analyzing both the emotional mediation provided by national news coverage of each murder and the local political responses to this mediation, this book draws a direct line from the "ephemeral" to the material and institutional.

In these cases, the "ephemeral" emotional mediation quite literally became institutionalized in the letter of the law. The way the men's names were attached to different pieces of legislation, as well as the inequalities of this attachment, demonstrate the political nature of this process. Here, the institutional effects examined are all hate crime laws; whether or not these laws are a good starting point for legal redress of structural exclusions and injustices, they do officially recognize and seek to address these structural issues—in and of itself an unusual step in U.S. law. The politics of this recognition are debatable. The publicity garnered by crimes such as the ones examined here runs the risk of reducing public discussions of discrimination to violence alone. And the emphasis on innocence as a reason to feel for the men and attempt to redress the political and social inequalities that authorized the violence against them carries with it a host of problems well explored elsewhere. However, the label and discussion of hate crimes does mark this violence as political. One of the effects of hate crime laws is to define acts of violence premised upon identity categories, especially historically and politically marginalized identities, as public social violence rather than private interpersonal violence. The logic of hate crimes (and indeed the efforts to articulate violence against gay men and lesbians in particular as a social and political problem) follows that of feminists who worked to articulate various forms of violence against women as political violence rather than "crimes of passion," understood as individual crimes, and to transfer the domain of appropriate response away from individual choice and therapy to that of legal rights and social justice. One of the basic premises of hate crime laws is that the violence and the feelings that animate it are products of history and social relations that have marginalized some, making them seem to be easy or logical targets. One of the key aims cited in support of such laws is the need to communicate that hate crimes are not sanctioned and are in fact harms against not only the targeted individual but entire communities. In this logic, the law recognizes feelings as political and social, translating emotion into the dry administrative language of law. This is not the only place where emotion is present in the law, even if masked by language of "disinterest" and administration.[3] Hate crime laws, however, offer a particularly clear recognition of the politics of social emotion; not only of the emotion of the attacker but also the social feelings that paint some as more likely or legitimate targets. They are troubling, in part, because they point to these feelings as public, as political artifacts, an idea that does not sit easily within Anglo-American liberal legal systems.

While the enactment of law is not necessarily the best barometer of social change, it is particularly binding and material change. From the perspective of examining the political efficacy of emotion, this materiality has rhetorical import: these material changes are the outcomes of discourse and politics. The impact of affective discourse and norms, as my analyses show, is concrete and institutional. It has also been my contention that emotion as a political force is not chaotic, random, or purely private but publicly and discursively shaped; in other words, it is an effect of history and power.

In the cases analyzed here, emotional discourse provided frameworks for the construction of different sets of relationships to the murdered men and directed political responses toward political-legal measures. Emotion does not always work in this way. Other scholars have pointed to instances where emotional rhetoric depoliticizes public problems or where the focus on affect is part of neoliberal politics that direct attention and action from the arena of state-oriented politics toward arenas of consumption, lifestyle, and corporate governance.[4] It is true that in some cases feeling may be substituted for action. It is also true that some discourse identified as emotional is particularly well suited to the politics of neoliberalism, particularly that blending of emotive and scientific discourse that constitutes the therapeutic. (Oddly, one of the hallmarks of therapeutic discourse is its very rationalization of emotion and self-identity.) However, the presence of emotion within politics is not simply a symptom of neoliberalism. A simple conflation of affective politics with neoliberalism overlooks the long history of emotion in politics and risks reifying the classical liberal public/private divide. Likewise, to simply assume that feelings and actions exist as dichotomous opposites at best keeps us from seeing and understanding cases where emotion works productively (to produce a variety of types of politics and actions) and at worst reproduces gendered dichotomies and hierarchies that align feelings, passivity, and femininity on one side and argument, action, and masculinity on the other, as opposite and superior.

Opposing emotion to action and conflating it with neoliberal politics both downplay the productivity of emotion. This study has focused on this productivity, looking beyond demobilizing instances of emotion in an effort to broaden the language and tools for thinking about emotion in media communication. Looking beyond the circulation of texts, to the types of political responses enabled (and those disabled) at the local level by emotional mediation, reveals the complexity of the politics of affect in media culture; affect can direct attention away from venues of traditional political action as well as propel people into political allegiances, identities, and political action (both traditional and otherwise). It is too easy to assume simple, unidirectional politics of feeling from an analysis of texts alone. Attention to the circulation of texts and their uptake at specific sites of this circulation, as well as attention to the patterns of distribution of feeling found within the texts themselves, can help to forward a more nuanced, critical analysis of affect in media and politics.

More broadly, the material impact of the more ephemeral and sentimental work of media should be central to discussions of politics. Concerns about how attachments are forged should be as central to our political discourse as concerns about how informed the public is. Questions of who is "lovable" to whom—or who/what bodies can mobilize public compassion and public grief—are key public issues. These are also questions about what types of relationships are imaginable within the polis and what types of publics we will enter into.[5] The distribution of care is closely linked to the distribution of other, more material goods. The link between notions of proximity and community and unjust distribution of material goods is painfully evident in urban development (for example, the uncanny propensity of highways to destroy African American and Latino communities). This linkage is further evidenced in recent political and policy decisions such as the dismissal and abandonment of victims of Hurricane Katrina[6] and the initiatives passed in California and Arizona that would deny basic human services (including access to education and nonemergency medical care) to undocumented immigrants.[7] The recent spate of state initiatives to deny same-sex couples access to marriage can be added to this list as attempts to restrict the distribution of legal rights and the social good of "family" or kinship to heterosexual couples. It is a small step to expand the connection between notions of "us" and "them" and distributive projects to the more general affective work of communication, to note that public expressions of feeling such as outrage, grief, mourning, admiration, pity, fear, and their objects can shape if not determine distribution of material goods and concrete policy decisions. As such, the question of what feelings we express, when, and toward whom are eminently political ones, intimately tied to questions of distributive justice, and should be analyzed in this light. A sort of political economy of feeling can help to highlight the material, institutional stakes of emotional mediation and to provide direction for a supplemented vision of the public sphere.

## The Distribution of Care in the Public Responses to the Murders

The emotional public responses to the murders of Byrd and Shepard were not universal or given, but established through the circulation of media texts and images. The establishment and circulation of proper emotional responses in each case created the discursive grounds of necessity for political action, shaped justice claims, and provided the framework for the actions of politicians (the bounds of reasonability). As such, deployments of feelings in the mediation of events such as these are part of the distribution of social goods and membership and can, as demonstrated here, be tied to the distribution of more material goods such as rights and access to law and institutions.

In Texas, the specific political outcomes of public expressions of mourning, pity, and outrage were new policies and procedures and even the creation of a new political and social right. The response to the murder, cultivated by the narratives and aesthetics of media texts, was key in mobilizing support and providing legitimacy for the new hate crimes law. The use of melodrama in the media coverage directed the form in which these justice claims were made, with a heavy focus on making victimization and suffering visible. The creation of this law was a redistribution of administrative, legal, and monetary resources. The law allocated money for investigation, prosecution, and tracking of hate crimes as well as education. It created new policies and administrative procedures that recognized a subset of violence and harassment as based in histories of structural inequalities including those based on race, sexuality, and gender. Passage of the law recognized continuing histories of racial oppression and attempted to redress this history within the logic of law enforcement. The law not only defined the categories of violence that could be defined as a hate crime (based on race, sexual orientation, gender, disability, religion, national origin, or age) but also created a new apparatus for administering hate crime investigations and recordkeeping, created new civil paths for targets of lower levels of violence or harassment to seek protections (similar to antistalking laws), and created new K–12 curriculum modules teaching about hate crimes and their prevention. In the latter, it allocated time and money as well as a stamp of official approval for educational programs and materials.

In Laramie, the marshaling of feelings of kinship and inclusion at the national level toward Matthew Shepard helped a small, active local public to craft a legal and institutional response to the crime. This response, too, dealt with the distribution of time and money, as well as with the more intangible issue of access to the law and law enforcement. The law required that monetary, administrative, and intellectual resources be turned toward creating administrative policies for defining bias crimes, tracking them, and training officers in investigating them and in interacting with the victims. The law also created what Bern Haggerty called a "tradition" of publicly reporting and publishing statistics on bias crimes in Laramie.[8] In effect, it created a new administrative and procedural category.

It changed the status of all hate crimes, but especially those against racial/ethnic minority and gay and lesbian residents, creating procedures and norms for how victims and the events themselves would be treated by police (and politicians). And the response officially recorded the murder as a hate crime—a definition that was under dispute locally. In terms of institutional effect, both Laramie and Texas measures altered the way that time and money were spent and established new categories and practices of administrative knowledge production. They sought to change how the police respond to allegations of hate crimes, particularly in cases of anti-gay harassment or violence.[9] Both laws recognized that law enforcement officers are often part of the problem, attempting to ensure that police treated these incidents seriously. (In Texas, there was particular concern to ensure that rural police forces were trained and incentivized to comply; in Laramie, there was much discussion of change in police culture and procedure in regard to sexuality.) To varying degrees, they altered the rules of access to law enforcement and legal redress.

Both responses were driven and authorized through notions of legitimate feelings. The emotional tenor of the media coverage of the two murders differed. Media texts circulated different logics of tragedy in each case, inviting diverging expressions of care in response to each man's death and differentially defining the imagined relationships between spectators and the murdered men. Attention to these differences makes clear the historical, political nature of public expressions of feeling and the need to develop a method for evaluating such expressions. The language of distribution is useful here, helping us to think about feelings as resources and social goods, tied to power, access to institutions, and material goods. Seeing emotions, even affect in general, as subject to distribution forces analysis of public articulations of feeling into the frameworks of power and structure.

Analyzing the distribution of feeling further helps to define aspects of media and political culture that seem ephemeral, individual, or otherwise chaotic as subject to the rules and rigor of structural analysis. It is even possible to discuss a political economy of feeling. Political economic analysis usually focuses on the social relations, especially power relations, that structure the distribution and access to resources.[10] This political economy would highlight the structural and discursive foundations that encourage or discourage public expressions of feeling and the often unequal distribution of these feelings as well as the material effects of such public expressions of feeling. The first of these elements is an analysis of structures that can lead us toward some sets of feelings and proximities rather than others. These structures are key to understanding the unequal distribution of feeling. The second of these elements traces what politics the inculcation of feeling enables or how this inculcation has material effects within the social and the political. The case studies elaborated here demonstrate a bit of each, examining the structural reasons for the different emotional tenor of the murders and describing the politics and legislative action sponsored by public expressions of feeling. In each case, prior formations of gender and sexuality, race, class, history, and even geography as well as institutional practices shaped the construction of normal and normative feelings about the murders, the victims, the killers, and their communities. The specific tenor of these emotional mediations authorized different types of political organization; in each case, the expression of feeling underwrote institutional change in the creation of law.

Traditionally, political economy of media is a tool for analyzing the material interests, social processes, and institutional organization that govern the shape of mass culture. It traces back from seemingly effervescent popular culture to the mechanics of production, political arrangements, and administrative norms and policies. The ideologies and social norms circulated in these cultural products become not merely expressions of the popular but also artifacts of the interests of individuals, institutions, and, at the more abstract level, political regimes. Using a similar logic to explore the distribution of feelings, it is possible to see that the way emotion is encouraged and projected in these texts works not only to teach norms that encourage some sets of engagement and political action and discourage others but also to tie these emotional lessons to specific interests, individuals, institutions, and politics. Just as in political economic analyses of popular culture, this analysis shows that public demonstrations of feeling are not merely authentic expressions of sentiment but also products of intense mediation by interested institutions and individuals. It makes clear as well that such demonstrations are constituted by (and constitutive of) relations of power.

The very selection of these murders as events that mattered presumed some interests and identifications to be more important to the public than others. The preceding chapters imply that media producers imagined and spoke to their audiences through assumptions of whiteness, middle- to upper-class status, urban sensibility, normative masculinity, and even arguably heterosexuality. The fact that James Byrd Jr. was killed by three rural white men with ties to white supremacist groups and not, say, while in police custody made him easy to portray as a tragic victim. Likewise, had Matthew Shepard been poor, nonwhite, or less normative in his gender identity (had he appeared more feminine or been transgender), he might not have garnered so much attention, much less the specific emotional mediation as kin that he did.[11] In each case, exclusionary notions of "normal," as well as of who is valuable, animated the media coverage, informing the choice of these men as sympathetic victims. Gender also worked to make the deaths public issues. The intimate tie between masculinity and publicity made the murdered men eligible to become representative, for their status as victims to speak about the nation and its political culture. (Female victims of violence more often become iconic of private pathologies or cultural politics.) The influence of such exclusionary norms is evident as well in the way that media texts imagined the relationships between their audiences and the murdered men. The news media, especially print media targeting affluent and culturally elite audiences, used rhetorics of kinship and similarity to define Shepard, referring to him in the diminutive and stressing his ordinariness, notably in descriptions of his "boy next door" quality and of his interchangeability with readers' family members. In contrast, Byrd was described much less through similarity and much more through pity. His class, his disability, his race, and his rural location made him a proper figure for sympathy, not identification.

The differences in the way that media texts encouraged feelings for and imagined relationships to the two men can be traced back to social organization and hierarchies. The criteria by which media producers attempt to predict what and who their audiences will care about, care for, and how are based on the common cultural archive of stories and images—in this case, stories and images of violence, race, and justice. These criteria are also based on institutional practices and norms (newspaper policies, habits of relying on and trusting public officials, notions of professionalism), generalizations of cultural producers' personal experience and subject positions, and notions of audience based as much in ideologies of value and stereotype as in actual economics. The particular way in which each man was presented as compelling derived from these characteristics. Presumed similarities of masculinity, class, and race between Shepard and news audiences allowed him to become the proper object of close feelings, overcoming resistance to including queer sexualities in the national. The articulation of race and class (again, closely linked) in the coverage of Byrd's murder, in contrast, placed him further from dominant news outlets' imagined audiences and from the center of the national symbolic. Journalists and other gatekeepers found each man and his murder to be compelling and worthy of extended news coverage because of his particular combination of these presumed axes of identification. These axes defined, within the institutional logic of media economics, what lives audiences were willing to pay to read about. In addition to the commonly noted categories of social identification—race, sexuality, gender, and class—both cases show the influence of geography, or cultural notions of place, as a mediator of these identifications. In the way each man was talked about in the media, geography shaped the particular characterization of race, class, sexuality, and gender descriptions, becoming part of the intersectional nexus of subject positioning.

The difference in the types of relationship imagined between the men and their publics and in the logics of tragedy through which each man was mourned was matched by a difference in the visibility and passion of national mourning surrounding each man. While Byrd's funeral was in many ways a much more public and political event than Shepard's, with elected officials from Texas and Washington as well as national political figures such as the Reverend Jesse Jackson, Shepard's death galvanized more public protest in vigils and marches (in D.C. and New York) and public commemoration (the songs and references in television fiction). Shepard was a symbolic first. He was the first openly gay man to be so widely iconic (within discursive spaces that are usually heteronormative by default) as victim of homophobic violence, in a drama of national inclusion. The murder of Byrd, on the other hand, fell in a longer line of black men whose victimizations are deeply interwoven with the national, repeating a well-worn drama. This is seen in the frequent comparisons to the nationally iconic, but temporally distant, victims of Jim Crow (such as Emmett Till) in the mainstream national news. It is usefully contrasted to the more quotidian comparisons offered by black Jasper residents to more recent, more proximate victims from their midst. Yet, locally, within the legislative debates that followed, Byrd was positioned as a more sympathetic victim than many of the other constituents of the Texas hate crimes bill. Within the political body of the Texas legislature, victims of anti-gay violence were not able to guarantee the same demonstrations of care that Byrd could. In the end, the care and sympathy directed toward Byrd (and the normativity of this sympathy) demanded passage of a law that not only recognized continuing histories of racial oppression and attempted to remedy them within the logic of law enforcement, but also recognized the rights of gays and lesbians to redress for homophobic harassment. Sympathy for Byrd marshaled the political will and maneuvering required for this institutional recognition. That the different emotional mediations of each murder authorized changes in local law demonstrates that there is more than one way emotional discourse can help form publics and can become grounds for political action.

The details of each case, however, also exhibit the stakes of unequal distribution of feelings such as care and sympathy. The difficulty of passing what was in some ways a very small law in Laramie, a difficulty that often hinged on how and even whether Shepard should be memorialized, demonstrates the trouble many had with extending care and political kinship to an openly gay young man. And in Texas, the constitutionally cloaked disputes over recognizing racism, sexism, and homophobia show that not all claims on justice or even pain can assume equal legibility. Some pain has more legibility, legitimacy, and claim on the law. Further, the way that the publicity surrounding the murder of Byrd became a venue for legal recognition and protections for gay and lesbian Texans points to inequalities in normative feelings or who legislators felt compelled to display feelings for. At the national level, the disparities are perhaps best crystallized in the discussion of the 2009 federal hate crimes legislation. While both names were attached to the bill, it was Shepard's name more than Byrd's that authorized the bill and anchored it to history. The politics of the selection and projection of Shepard as a more proximate victim, one presented as closer to the lives and families of news outlets' readers, are particularly evident here. The presentation of the bill primarily in reference to Shepard and his murder reflects an assumption that his name would muster a greater national reservoir of emotion, triggering the outrage needed (perhaps in the zip codes needed) to support the bill. The distribution of feeling here clearly links to the distribution of rights and recognition within the law. The public sphere is the space of this distribution. This linkage demands a rethinking of how we treat and talk about, or what we expect from, the public sphere.

## Expanding the Public Sphere

The mediation of the murders of Byrd and Shepard and the impact of this mediation offer important lessons on the politics of commitment and community and the possibility of legitimate democratic communication (a functioning public sphere). This is particularly clear when this coverage is examined within a distributive framework. Within the coverage of the murders, feelings and proximity were not evenly distributed; community was configured differently. Arguably, the commitments within the political responses I trace here differed as well. This points to a basic problem in our ethical and political culture: uneven commitments to others. The failures of law and culture that framed the violence against these men were failures not of information but of connection and commitment. And the responses to these murders were not equal, encouraging distance and pity toward Byrd and proximity and identification with Shepard. Addressing both these failures and the distribution of political feelings requires more than better access to media or better information. It requires attention to the ethics of the media environment, to whether or not media texts and practices encourage us to be more alive to the connections among us (to paraphrase Barbara Koziak).[12]

The most pressing problems facing contemporary democracy and the public sphere do not devolve on better information. More rational content and communication will not counter these problems. Rather than being concerned that drama and spectacle detract from sober discourse, as are many critics of infotainment and proponents of media reform,[13] we should question which commitments, relationships, and practices they pull us into (and which they do not). While compelling, many critiques of the quality of media discourse assume a priori distinctions between public and private, sober and trivial discourse. Yet, as the tradition of feminist scholarship has so successfully argued, these lines are not given but are always under negotiation. This insight prevents easy distinctions between the serious and the trivial, public affairs and entertainment, affective and rational discourse.[14] This is to say that it is not affective or dramatic communication as a form that is to blame for the problems of the pubic sphere, as the logic of much media reform and political discourse would have it, but rather the structures of interest that drive and animate these dramas and expressions.

The traditional-liberal model of the public sphere seeks to hold these interests in check via procedures and norms for inculcating rational and disinterested discourse. Reason and disinterest are treated within liberal models of the public sphere as the most promising tools for reaching consensual politics in the service of the public good. Hence the liberal model of the public sphere presumes that good political institutions, processes, and communicative infrastructures should attempt to inculcate more reasoned thinking and behavior. Procedures aimed at this inculcation become the cornerstone of liberal political theory, the normative ideal of the public sphere, and visions of good politics in general.

Yet, as these cases have shown, procedures are not free from feeling. Procedures themselves may become the sites for adjudicating emotional norms and establishing affective definitions of community. And, within these procedures, claims and performances of disinterest may be denials or effacements of interests and investments. This is perhaps clearest in the legislative debates analyzed here. Law, as an institution, requires discourses of disinterest for its legitimacy. This is despite the very evident interests involved in the creation of law and despite a long tradition of awareness that law is not just a tool for administration but also a way of establishing and enforcing specific communal identities.[15] In each of the debates about hate crimes legislation traced here, some of the arguments against the measures claimed the status of neutral and disinterested. For example, the argument of special privileges in Texas argued that the act would go against legal principles of neutrality and equal protection. In Laramie, opponents claimed that the ordinance would protect gay and lesbian citizens more than white and Christian ones. While expressed differently, both drew on a similar logic. Both arguments were about protecting the interests and freedoms of particular sets of citizens—in these cases, the interests of white and Christian citizens. The arguments about the neutrality of the law were thinly veiled contentions about the preferences and norms of one segment of the community. The debates were, in this sense, about whose interests could be treated as representative of, or aligned with, the public good. The language of disinterest merely served to disguise some of these interests, just as the language of ritual and passion works to mark some events and arguments as too interested or as outside the political.[16]

If the rhetoric and performance of disinterest, even in the formally neutral institution of the law, frequently works not to divest personal interests but to hide them, it becomes particularly important to understand and make these interests visible. Rather than advocate a less passionate politics, we should better understand the passions of our politics. This means seeing the public sphere as, among other things, the place where affiliations, relationships with others, and even interests are formed. Attention to affect can make visible the normally hidden apparatus of political process and discourse. Such a lens will help illuminate what Peter Dahlgren has called the civic culture that gives rise to (or not) democracy.[17] This civic culture provides the building blocks for the formation of political dispositions, identities, and discussions. Ideally, it is the milieu in which a willingness to speak to and listen to the others in the political community and a basic level of affinity toward these others—a willingness to enter into conversation—are formed.

In order to analyze how these more ephemeral actions and relationships are forged and what their consequences are, we need a different descriptive and normative model of the political functions of media (in particular, within democratic politics). We need a supplemented understanding of the public sphere, one that accounts for how media construct relationships and commitments, as well as whose interests are served by these and other affective appeals. This model of the public sphere must, in effect, take into consideration the importance of identification and communion within mediated communication. The liberal-Habermasian model offers some important insights into how egalitarian, democratic communication should look. This model has many strengths, but it does not provide the tools for evaluating whether and how media build the relationships and sentiments required for a more democratic and more committed polis. It has been part of my argument here to show that normative rubrics based on deliberation and reason alone (even the more expansive definition of rationality at the core of Habermas's description of deliberative democracy) are not sufficient to evaluate how media construct relationships and commitments to others or how they create the grounds that shape justice claims. Too much of the work of media, in fact, is rendered invisible or illegitimate within the liberal models of the public sphere and deliberation.

Rather than evaluating democratic communication on the basis of its rationality or adherence to the norms of deliberation alone, we should attend to the ethics embedded in communication: the ethics established in communication, or the establishment of proximities, community, and the related norms of association that are a necessary part of any communicative encounter. This is a small but important shift in focus; attention to ethics does not so much preclude a focus on rationality as precede it. Whatever democratic potential resides in deliberation is in the ethics of the encounter. The norms of give and take, of listening and respect, which demand reasons and rationales for arguments, are based on a particular set of ethical maxims. This is a specific ethical relationship, based on an equitable encounter. Within a hierarchical and differentiated society, not all communication is so equitable.[18] The levels of respect, commitment, and care required for communication are differentiated in part by how we are supposed to feel toward the other and how close or distant they appear to be. These relationships of power and feeling established within a communicative encounter, whether it is mass-mediated or face-to-face, are arguably more fundamental to the prospects of democracy than is the rationality of an exchange. Given this, normative accounts of democratic communication or the public sphere should begin with a deeper description and analysis of the ethics constituted within communication, especially mass-mediated communication.

Such relationships and norms are constructed in large part through media, as one of the main "places" where such community and affinities are formed. Media are central to the public sphere not merely as conduits of distribution but as sites of cultural and political production. The very notion of the "public," and the public sphere, is a consequence of media communication; the ability to see oneself as part of a geographically distributed group in conversation with one another—to see oneself in relationship to distant others—is predicated on the circulation of mass media, from the first newspapers to newer media. This is one of the main functions of media as public sphere. Media texts provide the venues for the formation of imagined relationships with others. These venues, as I have shown here, are not equal. Notions of proximity and distance, as well as directives to feel for others, all ethical norms, are not distributed equally. When these sentiments are understood as foundations for political action and opinion, the material consequences of this distribution become clearer. These notions of proximity and distance shape much more than the level of reciprocity in discourse. They shape our inclination and ability to make justice claims and the legal regimes within which these claims are made. The cases of the mediation of the Byrd and Shepard murders highlight the need to employ critical analyses of the affective work of media in order to better describe and evaluate the contemporary public sphere as well as to explore its potentials. Analyses of the public sphere need to ask not only how equal is access to media and how does the content of media help to inculcate an informed citizenry but also how does the content and circulation of media distribute and define relationships among people? How do media distribute feelings? Does the content and pattern of distribution encourage connection and commitment to the others with whom we share the world? Do the feelings inculcated via media texts encourage justice? On what terms? This is arguably the most important function of the media today. The preceding analysis of the emotional mediation of the murders of Byrd and Shepard offers examples of this type of critical analysis.

The cases examined here demonstrate how media texts not only publicized the murder but also constructed affective frameworks for understanding and reacting to the murders. These frameworks carried over from media texts into the creation of law. The ways and extent to which these losses were made visible in public discourse is a question of whose feelings matter, but it is also a question of how public displays of affect enabled or disabled connections and justice claims. The intense coverage of the murders made moments of violence based in racism and homophobia highly visible. It did so within frameworks of differential feeling and connection. Audiences were encouraged to imagine Shepard as kin and to feel pity and the need for redress in the case of Byrd; these feelings provided the templates for the justice claims and modes of redress in each case. In Laramie, the crux of the response to the murder was defined in terms of political kinship. In Texas, its response was articulated as a redress to suffering, a remedy for legal failures of the past. In this way, the tenor of media texts—the way that they imagined and projected relationships among strangers—determined the availability and shape of political goods such as legal recognition, administrative categories, and rights. The examples of how these men were made available for public care (and forms of legal recognition) in the circulation of media texts show a dimension of political discourse not often analyzed. They are not meant as examples of particularly progressive or promising media practices. Rather, they highlight a type of political discourse that is often not visible as such. The emotional mediation of each man demonstrates the way that media texts construct possibilities for solidarity and commitment as much as they demonstrate that relations of power and existing arrangements of social inequality structure these very possibilities.

# Appendix
## Text and Interview Selection

The murders of Shepard and Byrd generated a huge number and variety of texts. In selecting which texts to include in my analysis, I sought those that were the most widely circulated as well as those that represented the variety of discursive genres used and the way that the murders were narrated and remembered over time. My analysis focuses on print and television news as the most widely circulated media texts describing each murder. I included the magazine stories that continued to spin narratives and solidify the cultural import and memories of the murders. I also included the book and movie dramatizations of each murder that continued to circulate docudramatic discourse on the murders.

I searched the Lexis-Nexis databases for print news and the Vanderbilt Archive for significant stories in the nightly news on the three major television networks. For newspaper and television coverage, I limited this search to the 30 days after each murder. This period reflects the rapid news cycle in television and newspaper production (for each murder, this news coverage was most concentrated in the two weeks after the murder, and fell off afterward). I determined significance by how centrally the news story focused on the murder and by the length of the report; in newspapers, I only considered stories of over 300 words, and in TV news, I included only segments that were longer than a minute. This ruled out mere bulletins and left the longer news reports, in which reporters had the space to make sense of the crimes, weaving basic data into larger cultural and aesthetic frames.

For Shepard's murder, this resulted in 228 newspaper stories and 13 television news segments. Regional newspapers (*Denver Post, Rocky Mountain News, Wyoming Tribune-Eagle,* and the Associated Press State and Local Wire for Wyoming) made up139 of these stories. For Byrd's murder, this resulted in 152 newspaper stories and 14 news segments (these segments were, on average, longer than those covering Shepard). Of the newspaper stories, 73 were in the regional press (the *Austin-American Statesman, Houston Chronicle,* and *San*

*Antonio Express-News*). Part of the discrepancy between the regional newspaper coverage of the two murders is explained by the fact that no Dallas papers were represented in the Lexis-Nexis database, so there were fewer regional sources in my sample of the coverage of Byrd's murder.

In addition, I included articles from major news and general interest magazines in the year following each murder; the time window here reflects the longer production cycle in magazine journalism, also retrieved from the Lexis-Nexis database. There were 24 magazine articles covering Shepard in this period and 22 covering Byrd. I also reference the ongoing docudramatic discourse on each murder elaborated in movie and book dramatizations. These included HBO's *The Laramie Project* (2002) and, in Byrd's case, the Showtime docudrama *Jasper, Texas* (2002), the PBS documentary *Two Towns of Jasper* (2003), and two books written by journalists: *Hate Crime* by Joyce King (2002) and *A Death in Texas* by Dina Temple-Raston (2002).

In the chapters analyzing the legal responses to each murder, I used interviews to piece together the reasons and processes by which people turned to the law as an avenue for response and redress as well as the specific debates, tactics, reasoning, and processes that accompanied the passage of each measure. To do so, I attempted to speak to those most involved in advocating for each law as well as the key decision makers. In Laramie, this meant the activists who lobbied most intently and publicly for the measure as well as those who were on the city council, involved in the debates and in the vote to pass the law. This list of advocates included Jeff Lockwood, Jeanne Hurd, and Bern Haggerty as leaders of the Laramie Coalition, who most vociferously and directly advocated for the city bias crimes ordinance. Haggerty authored the measure, and Lockwood and Hurd were instrumental in organizing and strategizing to pass the measure. Upon the suggestion of several of my interviewees, I also interviewed former police officer Dave O'Malley and the Reverend Sally Palmer. I spoke with six out of the nine members of the Laramie City Council: Dan Furphy, Trudy McCracken, Dave Williams, Joe Shumway, Ed Meyers, and Bob Bell. Of the other three, one councilman had died, one had left town, and one would not agree to be interviewed.

In Texas, I spoke with a number of supporters who played key roles in writing and forwarding the legislation and in the political debates over its passage. This included Diane Hardy-Garcia, head of the Lesbian/Gay Rights Lobby of Texas (LGRL), and the Reverend Jim Rigby, a key lobbyist and religious figure. Within the ranks of the Texas legislature, I spoke with some of those most closely involved in crafting the James Byrd Jr. Hate Crimes Act: Representative Senfronia Thompson, her legislative aides Patrick Johnson and Brete Anderson, and Deece Eckstein, an aide to Senator Rodney Ellis. Representative Pat Haggerty was closely involved in crafting the bill and pushing it onto the docket and was able to speak about Republican opposition. I also spoke with two representatives who "came around" to support the bill in 1999: Paul Sadler, described as a key "moral voice" and moderate supporter, and Warren Chisum, a social conservative and longtime opponent of the bill. Finally, I spoke with Wayne Christian as both the representative of Jasper in the House and as one of the more vocal opponents of the bill.

# Notes

### INTRODUCTION

1. For a comprehensive listing of songs referencing Matthew Shepard and his murder, see www.queermusicheritage.com/matthew.html.

2. For examples of this argument in the public discourse concerning the murders, see Brian Ott and Eric Aoki, "The Politics of Negotiating Public Tragedy: Media Framing of the Matthew Shepard Murder," *Rhetoric and Public Affairs* 5, no. 3 (2002): 483–505; and Larry Williamson, "Racism, Tolerance, and Perfected Redemption: A Rhetorical Critique of the Dragging Trial," *Southern Communication Journal* 67, no. 3 (2002): 245–58.

3. See Judith Halberstam, *In a Queer Time and Place: Transgender Bodies, Subcultural Lives* (New York: NYU Press, 2005); Lisa Duggan, *The Twilight of Equality? Neoliberalism, Cultural Politics, and the Attack on Democracy* (Boston: Beacon Press, 2003); and Ann Cvetkovich, *An Archive of Feelings: Trauma, Sexuality, and Lesbian Public Cultures* (Durham, N.C.: Duke University Press, 2003).

4. For examples of scholars who make strong arguments from different perspectives, see Lauren Berlant, *The Queen of America Goes to Washington City* (Durham, N.C.: Duke University Press, 1997); Dana Cloud, *Control and Consolation in American Culture and Politics: Rhetoric of Therapy* (Thousand Oaks, Calif.: Sage, 1998); Dana Cloud, "Therapy, Silence, and War: Consolation and the End of Deliberation in the 'Affected' Public," *Poroi* 2, no. 1 (2003), http://inpress.lib.uiowa.edu/poroi/papers/cloud030816.html; and Doug Kellner, *Media Spectacle and the Crisis of Democracy: Terrorism, War, and Election Battles* (Boulder, Colo.: Paradigm, 2005).

5. See Cloud, *Control and Consolation,* for examples of emotional rhetoric that have worked to cast structural concerns as private issues.

6. The term *mediation* focuses on the processes behind media texts and, in the process of circulation itself, the many ways in which media shape daily life and institutions. For more on mediation, see Jesús Martin-Barbero, *Communication, Culture, and Hegemony* (London: Sage, 1993); Nick Couldry, "Theorising Media as Practice," *Social Semiotics* 14, no. 2 (2000): 115–32; Lilie Chouliaraki, *The Spectatorship of Suffering* (London: Sage, 2006); and Roger Silverstone, *Media and Morality: On the Rise of the Mediapolis* (Cambridge: Polity Press, 2006).

7. For example, see the classic work, Jürgen Habermas, *The Structural Transformation of the Public Sphere,* trans. Thomas Burger (Cambridge: MIT Press, 1991). Also see James Fishkin, *When the People Speak: Deliberative Democracy and Public Consultation* (Oxford: Oxford University Press, 2009); John Keane, *The Media and Democracy* (Cambridge: Polity Press, 1991); Nicholas Garnham, "The Media and the Public Sphere," in *Habermas and the Public Sphere,* ed. Craig Calhoun (Cambridge, Mass.: MIT Press, 1992), 359–76.

8. George Marcus, *The Sentimental Citizen: Emotion in Democratic Politics* (University Park: Pennsylvania State University Press, 2002).

9. Scholars such as Gamson, Van Zoonen, and Dahlgren have championed such formats as inclusive domains of popular (in the original, noncommercial sense) discourse and discussion. See Joshua Gamson, *Freaks Talk Back: Tabloid Talk Shows and Sexual Nonconformity* (Chicago: University of Chicago Press, 1999); Liesbet Van Zoonen, *Entertaining the Citizen* (Lanham, Md.: Rowman & Littlefield, 2005); and Peter Dahlgren, "Television, Public Spheres, and Civic Cultures," in *A Companion to Television,* ed. Janet Wasko (Malden, Mass.: Blackwell, 2005), 411–32.

10. For an overview and critique of this line of thinking from political philosophy, see Iris Marion Young, "Impartiality and the Civic Public: Some Implications of Feminist Critiques of Moral and Political Theory," in *Feminism, the Public and the Private,* ed. Joan Landes (Oxford: Oxford University Press, 1998), 421–47. For an overview and critique of this approach to emotion and politics from political science, see Marcus, *The Sentimental Citizen.*

11. Young, "Impartiality and the Civic Public"; Cheryl Hall, "Passions and Constraint: The Marginalization of Passion in Liberal Political Theory," *Philosophy & Social Criticism* 28, no. 6 (2002): 727–48.

12. See Peter Lunt and Paul Stenner, "*The Jerry Springer Show* as an Emotional Public Sphere," *Media, Culture & Society* 27, no. 1 (2005): 59–81; Dominique Mehl, "The Public on the Television Screen: Toward a Public Sphere of Exhibition," *Journal of Media Practice* 6, no. 1 (2005): 19–28; and Gamson, *Freaks Talk Back.* In communication and media studies, this concern about affect stems in part from the associations of affect with manipulation in political rhetoric, especially in Nazi Germany, but also with a general stigma of affect being the provenance of manipulative advertising and marketing. See John Durham Peters, "Distrust of Representation: Habermas on the Public Sphere," *Media, Culture, and Society* 15 (1993): 541–71.

13. Habermas, *Structural Transformation of the Public Sphere.*

14. The continuing hold of this Habermasian model is illustrated by its continuing centrality in media studies. The concept of the public sphere, as distilled by Habermas, has been under revision in British and American political theory and media studies (among other disciplines) since its translation into English in 1989. Even after years of critique, it is still the subject of intervention. See, for example, Kevin DeLuca and Jennifer Peeples, "From Public Sphere to Public Screen: Democracy, Activism, and the Lessons of Seattle," *Critical Studies in Mass Communication* 19, no. 2 (2002): 125–51; Van Zoonen, *Entertaining the Citizen;* Mehl, "The Public on the Television Screen"; Lunt and Stenner, "*The Jerry Springer Show* as Emotional Public Sphere"; Dahlgren, "Television, Public Spheres, and Civic Cultures"; Silverstone, *Media and Morality.*

15. This is not a utopian vision of rationality or faith in Enlightenment ideals but rather a set of modest hopes, what Garnham ("The Media and the Public Sphere," 375) characterizes as a "tragic" vision of the fragility of human capabilities and politics.

16. While Habermas's later work, *Between Facts and Norms,* trans. William Rehg (Cambridge, Mass.: MIT Press, 1998), offers a less top-down view of the interactions of publics and media and a more inclusive notion of rationality than many liberal political theorists, he does not fully embrace the aesthetic and affective elements of communication. Rationality remains at the core of his normative conceptualization of communication. And the progressive potentials he so famously finds in communication focus on the instrumental capacities of communication as (rather instrumental) information exchange and coordination.

17. See Hall, "Passions and Constraint," on this rationalist focus in liberal political theory. While most liberal political theory focuses on rationality, influential liberal critics

of liberalism such as Richard Rorty and Martha Nussbaum find space for emotions and identification in their versions of liberal political theory.

18. See Young, "Impartiality and the Civic Public"; Benedict Anderson, *Imagined Communities* (New York: Verso, 1991); Seyla Benhabib, *Situating the Self: Gender, Community, and Postmodernism in Contemporary Ethics* (New York: Routledge, 1992); James Carey, *Communication as Culture: Essays on Media and Society* (Boston: Unwin Hyman, 1989); Peters, "Distrust of Representation"; Benjamin Lee, "Textuality, Mediation, and Public Discourse," in *Habermas and the Public Sphere*, ed. Craig Calhoun (Cambridge, Mass.: MIT Press, 1992), 402-20; Silverstone, *Media and Morality.*

19. For more on the ethics of mediation, see Nick Couldry, "The Ethics of Mediation," *OpenDemocracy,* November 5, 2001, http://www.opendemocracy.net/media-media911/article_247.jsp; Chouliaraki, *Spectatorship of Suffering;* and Silverstone, *Media and Morality.*

20. Michael Warner, *Publics and Counterpublics* (New York: Zone Books, 2005). For more on the reflexive nature of publics, see also Lee, "Textuality, Mediation, and Public Discourse"; Daniel Dayan, "Paying Attention to Attention: Audiences, Publics, Thresholds, and Genealogies," *Journal of Media Practice* 6, no. 1 (2005): 9-18.

21. For a discussion on the limitations of liberal language of tolerance in the face of racial and ethnic injustice, see Enrique Dussel, "Deconstruction of the Concept of 'Tolerance': From Intolerance to Solidarity," *Constellations* 11, no. 3 (2004): 326-33.

22. I do not use Raymond Williams's term *structures of feeling,* from *Marxism and Literature* (Oxford: Oxford University Press, 1977), despite its similar effort to tie affect to structure, because Williams's use is so closely tied to emergence and social change and so rooted in debates over structural Marxism. Here I want to understand the structural role of affect in stasis (in Williams's terms, as part of already precipitated social formations) as well as emergence.

23. I am not denying the libidinal or biological aspects of affective experience. I am just interested in the role of the social, the way affect is used in public, and the way that use shapes personal expression and political action. This discursive approach separates my work from work on feelings that derives from Brian Massumi's interest in the extra-linguistic aspects of affect and sensation, in *Parables of the Virtual: Movement, Affect, Sensation* (Durham, N.C.: Duke University Press, 2002). My own approach owes much to the work on public feelings done by Sara Ahmed, *The Cultural Politics of Emotion* (Edinburgh: Edinburgh University Press, 2004); Cvetkovich, *An Archive of Feelings;* and Barbara Koziak, *Retrieving Political Emotion* (University Park: Pennsylvania State University Press, 2000).

24. Silverstone, *Media and Morality.*

25. Ahmed, *Cultural Politics of Emotion.* For example, Ahmed notes that the ethical disposition of wonder is an affective relationship (and orientation) toward the world; likewise, she suggests that the alienation described by Marx is an affective orientation toward the world (a bodily disposition and a set of feelings that add up to a way of seeing the world).

26. This point follows the insights of feminist ethics articulated by scholars such as Jane Mansbridge, "Reconstructing Democracy," and Nancy Hirschmann, "Rethinking Obligation for Feminism," both in *Revisioning the Political,* ed. Nancy Hirschmann and Christine Di Stefano (Boulder, Colo.: Westview Press, 1996), 117-38, 157-80; Jane Tronto, *Moral Boundaries: A Political Argument for an Ethic of Care* (London: Routledge, 1993); Benhabib, *Situating the Self.*

27. Warner, *Publics and Counterpublics,* 24.

28. Richard Dyer, *White: Essays on Race and Culture* (London: Routledge, 1997).

29. See Warner, *Publics and Counterpublics;* Joan Landes, "The Public and the Private Sphere: A Feminist Reconsideration," in *Feminism, the Public and the Private,* 135–63.

30. Nancy Fraser, "Rethinking the Public Sphere: A Contribution to the Critique of Actually Existing Democracy," in *Habermas and the Public Sphere,* ed. Craig Calhoun (Cambridge, Mass.: MIT Press, 1992), 109–42.

31. See, for example, Robert Solomon, *The Passions: Emotions and the Meaning of Life* (Garden City, N.Y.: Doubleday, 1993), and Martha Nussbaum, *Upheavals of Thought: The Intelligence of Emotions* (Cambridge: Cambridge University Press, 2001) in philosophy; Thomas Scheff, *Microsociology: Discourse, Emotions, and Social Structure* (Chicago: University of Chicago Press, 1990) in sociology; Catherine Lutz and Lila Abu-Lughod, *Language and the Politics of Emotion* (Cambridge: Cambridge University Press, 1990) in anthropology; and Antonio Damasio, *Descartes' Error: Emotion, Reason, and the Human Brain* (New York: Putnam, 1994) in neuroscience.

32. See Koziak, *Retrieving Political Emotion,* on the rise of impartiality as an ideal. See Susan Bordo, *The Flight to Objectivity: Essays on Cartesianism and Culture* (Albany: State University of New York Press, 1987); Daniel Gross, *The Secret History of Emotion: From Aristotle's Rhetoric to Modern Brain Science* (Chicago: University of Chicago Press, 2006) on the relationship between the rise of ideals of objectivity and reason in science and politics and modern notions of masculinity in terms of activity and disinterest. While Gross's history points out there was more than one discursive trend at work, he shares the point that contemporary understandings of political activity and reason have grown out of relatively recent (late modern) discourses on gender and politics.

33. Koziak, *Retrieving Political Emotion.*

34. Judith Butler writes incisively about one example of such questions: the political and ethical stakes of the boundaries of who may be mourned in public in the post-9/11 emotional and political climate. Butler, "Violence, Mourning, Politics," *Studies in Gender and Sexuality* 4, no. 1 (2003): 9–37.

35. For a detailed discussion of the limitations that inhere in analyses of communication based on an understanding of communicative practices as primarily about sharing meaning, see John Durham Peters, *Speaking into the Air: A History of the Idea of Communication* (Chicago: University of Chicago Press, 1999).

36. Lauren Berlant, "Introduction: Compassion (and Withholding)," in *Compassion: The Culture and Politics of an Emotion,* ed. Berlant (New York: Routledge, 2004), 11.

37. For more on the first two critiques, see Wendy Brown, *States of Injury* (Princeton, N.J.: Princeton University Press, 1995); Judith Butler, *Excitable Speech: A Politics of the Performative* (New York: Routledge, 1997); and Barbara Perry, *In the Name of Hate: Understanding Hate Crimes* (New York: Routledge, 2001). For more on how hate crimes campaigns compete with other (queer and gay and lesbian) political campaigns, see Halberstam, *In a Queer Time and Place;* Cvetkovich, *An Archive of Feelings.*

38. This is argued in particular in reference to anti-gay discrimination, where so many aspects of civil law still authorize discrimination in the workplace, military, medicine, and family arrangements In this, hate crimes laws can seem somewhat hypocritical, with the state punishing individuals for actions based on an ideology that is in fact upheld by the state. However, it also seems that hate crimes legislation is important in its effort to enhance basic physical safety and educate law enforcement officers about their duties to queer communities.

39. See Matsuda et al., *Words That Wound: Critical Race Theory, Assaultive Speech, and the First Amendment* (Boulder, Colo.: Westview Press, 1993); Frederick Lawrence, *Punishing Hate: Bias Crimes under American Law* (Cambridge, Mass.: Harvard University

Press, 1999) for support of hate crimes laws from a critical race theory perspective. One reason for supporting hate crimes laws in these approaches is that hate crimes often are not treated as real crimes or are in some way supported by local officials. The mild to supportive response of local officials to recent attacks and murders of Latino immigrants offer examples of this problem. See Jeannine Bell, *Policing Hatred: Law Enforcement, Civil Rights, and Hate Crime* (New York: NYU Press, 2004).

40. Iris Marion Young, *Justice and the Politics of Difference* (Princeton, N.J.: Princeton University Press, 1990). The other four of these five mechanisms are exploitation, marginalization, powerlessness, and cultural imperialism.

41. Bern Haggerty, "Hate Crimes: A View from Laramie, Wyoming's First Bias Crimes Law, the Fight against Discriminatory Crime, and a New Cooperative Federalism," *Howard Law Journal* 45, no. 1 (2001): 1–75, lays out a rationale for hate crime legislation that is focused on providing remedies for victims outside the confines of the criminal court. Likewise, many of those who testified before the criminal justice committee in the Texas Senate focused on these outcomes.

42. This is not to say that the publics were addressed always as white or upper class, but they were often asked to identify in those terms. The articles described the communities of Jasper and Laramie as if they were "lower" class than their readers.

## 1. Mourning Matthew Shepard

1. *USA Today* alone of the national papers examined here did not send a correspondent to Laramie; all of its stories on the attack and aftermath were filed from Denver.

2. Beth Loffreda, *Losing Matt Shepard: Life and Politics in the Aftermath of Anti-Gay Murder* (New York: Columbia University Press, 2001).

3. The majority of my sample is based on the results of a Lexis-Nexis search. I also searched for articles in the archives of West Coast papers not included in the database, such as the *Los Angeles Times, Sacramento Bee, San Francisco Chronicle,* and *Seattle Post-Intelligencer.* For more on text selection, see the appendix.

4. Within the *Los Angeles Times,* Shepard's attack was given greater prominence (earlier in the front section, more front-page space) in the national version than in the local. The paper ran only two news stories of more than 300 words and two editorials on Shepard's attack and death during October.

5. See Daniel Dayan and Elihu Katz, *Media Events: The Live Broadcasting of History* (Cambridge, Mass.: Harvard University Press, 1994); John Gillis, "Memory and Identity: The History of a Relationship," in *Commemorations: The Politics of National Identity,* ed. Gillis (Princeton, N.J.: Princeton University Press, 1994); Marita Sturken, *Tangled Memories: The Vietnam War, the AIDS Epidemic, and the Politics of Remembering* (Berkeley: University of California Press, 1997).

6. For a particularly material example of this dynamic, see Henry Giroux, *Stormy Weather: Katrina and the Biopolitics of Disposability* (Boulder: Paradigm, 2006).

7. Even state-sponsored memorials are hard to dismiss as simple tools of state power; the sites and objects of mourning are also often dictated through internal and external publicity and politics. The establishment of museums commemorating the Holocaust, the Hiroshima bombing, slavery, and Native American genocide all attest to this complicated interplay of state, commemoration, and publicity.

8. For more on such dramas of inclusion and exclusion, see James Carey, "Political Ritual on Television: Episodes in the History of Shame, Degradation, and Excommunication," and Jeffrey Alexander and Ronald Jacobs, "Mass Communication, Ritual, and Civil Society," both in *Media, Ritual, and Identity,* ed. Tamar Liebes and James Curran (London: Routledge, 1998); Barbie Zelizer, "From Home to Public Forum: Media

Events and the Public Sphere," *Journal of Film and Video* 43, no. 1–2 (1991): 69–79; 1994; and Dayan and Katz, *Media Events.*

9. Gay and Lesbian Alliance Against Defamation (GLAAD), "Media Roundup: Matthew Shepard," *GLAAD Alert Archive,* October 22, 1998, http://www.glaad.org/action/al_archive_detail.php?id=1661&.

10. See Chris Bull, "All Eyes Were Watching," *Advocate,* November 24, 1998, 33–37; Justin Gillis and Patricia Gaines, "Pattern of Hate Emerges on a Fence near Laramie; Gay Victim's Killers Say They Saw an Easy Crime Target," *Washington Post,* October 18, 1998.

11. See Butler, "Violence, Mourning, Politics"; GLAAD, "Media Roundup." At the same time, it is unfortunately too often only in the cases of death (namely gay-bashing murders) that the issue of homophobia makes it into public discussion at all.

12. Bill Clinton, "Statement on the Attack on Matthew Shepard," presidential speech, October 10, 1998.

13. See Dayan, "Paying Attention to Attention," for a critique of the linguistic and disciplinary roots of this distinction.

14. See Lee, "Textuality, Mediation, and Public Discourse"; Dayan "Paying Attention to Attention"; Carey, *Communication as Culture;* Peters, "Distrust of Representation"; DeLuca and Peeples, "From Public Sphere to Public Screen"; Warner, *Publics and Counterpublics.*

15. For details on anti-gay murders in 1998, see Gillis and Gaines, "Pattern of Hate"; Jonathan Alter, "Trickle-Down Hate," *Newsweek,* October 26, 1998, 44; Amy Tigner, "*The Laramie Project:* Western Pastoral," *Modern Drama* 45, no. 1 (2002): 138–56.

16. Jon Barrett, "The Lost Brother," *Advocate,* November 24, 1998, 26–30.

17. For example, Rosalind Bentley, "Many Say Shepard Symbolizes Struggle of Gays and Lesbians," *Minneapolis Star-Tribune,* October 14, 1998, A-1; Petula Dvorak, "Slain Student Honored: Vigil Casts Light on Hate Crime," *New Orleans Times-Picayune,* October 16, 1998, B-1.

18. For example, Bentley, "Shepard Symbolizes Struggle"; Melanie Thernstrom, "The Crucifixion of Matthew Shepard," *Vanity Fair,* March 1999, 209–14, 267–75; Moisés Kaufman, introduction to *The Laramie Project,* by Moisés Kaufman and the members of the Tectonic Theater Project (New York: Dramatists Play Service, 2001), v–viii. The politics of naming sexualities is complex. Throughout, the media texts I examine used the terms *gay* and *lesbian* to discuss nonheterosexual sexualities/sexual identities, which is reflected in my use of the term. Transsexual individuals, bisexuality, and the broader concept of queer sexualities do not appear in these media texts.

19. Gillis and Gaines, "Pattern of Hate"; Frank Rich, "Loving Him to Death," *New York Times,* October 24, 1998, A-17; Walt Boulden, quoted in Tom Kenworthy, "Gay Man near Death after Beating, Burning," *Washington Post,* October 10, 1998, A-1.

20. This issue is addressed indirectly in the scholarship on documentary, with its concern with how real people and events are represented and viewed on screen. In particular, Bill Nichols defines the relationship between the camera/viewers and the subjects on screen as one in which aesthetic questions become ethical ones. He suggests the relationship between camera/viewers and the subject of fictional film (which he defines as one of erotics) is replaced with an ethical relationship between camera/viewer and subject in documentary. Bill Nichols, *Representing Reality* (Bloomington: Indiana University Press, 2001). The shift from erotics to ethics is instructive: the relationships of desire associated with fictional film, when transposed into representations of the real, are the ethical questions of who we care for and how and what our obligations are to our neighbors.

21. Luc Boltanski, *Distant Suffering: Morality, Media, and Politics,* trans. Graham Burchell (Cambridge: Cambridge University Press, 1999); Chouliaraki, *Spectatorship of Suffering.*

22. Unfortunately, most media outlets seemed unable to cover the story in terms of both potential drug use and gender/sexuality. The 2004 *20/20* report offered a whole-sale replacement of one motive with another, critiquing the rest of the media (somewhat shamelessly leaving *20/20*'s earlier report out of this critique) for using the wrong frame. Implicit in this critique was the idea that it had to be one or the other explanation.

23. Barbie Zelizer, *Remembering to Forget: Holocaust Memory through the Camera's Eye* (Chicago: University of Chicago Press, 1998). See also Susan Sontag, *Regarding the Pain of Others* (New York: Picador, 2004); Carrie Rentschler, "Witnessing: U.S. Citizenship and the Vicarious Experience of Suffering," *Media Culture & Society* 26, no. 2 (2002): 296–304; and Chouliaraki, *Spectatorship of Suffering,* on the paradoxes of wit-nessing in a visual age.

24. Boltanski, *Distant Suffering;* Chouliaraki, *Spectatorship of Suffering.*

25. One such picture ran in the *New York Times* both in the original coverage and in a 2008 slideshow, "Revisiting Laramie," commemorating the 10-year anniversary of the murder and discussing an epilogue to the famous play, *The Laramie Project.* Similar photos graced *Time, Vanity Fair, U.S. News & World Report,* and *Newsweek.*

26. Richard Slotkin, *Gunfighter Nation: The Myth of the Frontier in Twentieth-Century America* (New York : Atheneum, 1992). This myth continues to underwrite both popular culture and policy; election cycles regularly see its invocation in Western idioms and imagery as signs of this rugged individualism (e.g., the labels "maverick" and "real America").

27. Gail Bederman, *Manliness and Civilization: A Cultural History of Gender and Race in the United States, 1881–1917* (Chicago: University of Chicago Press, 1995). Bederman locates this articulation of manliness as a historical response to the threat that black masculinity posed to "effete" Victorian masculinity in the late nineteenth and early twentieth centuries. It was necessary to forward a new dominant vision of masculinity, in which a physical or "primitive" masculinity was harnessed to the civilizing force of white-ness; this vision is most evident in Teddy Roosevelt's management of his masculinity and in the popular Tarzan stories.

28. Halberstam, *In a Queer Time and Place.*

29. This management of political and ethical failings echoes the geographical dis-tancing that took place after the murder of James Byrd Jr., discussed in chapter 3.

30. James Brooke, "Gay Man Beaten and Left for Dead," *New York Times,* October 9, 1998, A-9.

31. See respectively Gillis and Gaines, "Pattern of Hate"; "Murdered for Who He Was," *New York Times,* October 13, 1998, A-1; Kenworthy, "Gay Man near Death after Beating, Burning"; Debra Saunders, "Murder: The Ultimate Hate Crime," *San Francisco Chronicle,* October 16, 1998, A-27.

32. Joann Wypijewski, "A Boy's Life," *Harper's,* September 1999, 61–74.

33. There were meditations on and controversies over Matthew's decision to leave the bar with his killers and the possibility that the decision was in some part sexual, in alternative publications *The Advocate* and *Z* magazine.

34. While the term *metrosexual* (coined to refer to straight men who dress stylishly and buy grooming products once thought to be the sole provenance of gay men but now a cultural term encompassing a sensibility as much as consumption patterns) was not in circulation at the time of Matthew's death. The "soft" forms of masculinity that the term traces were a reality and subject of debate.

35. Robert Black, Associated Press, "Shepard Case Focus of MTV Film," *Casper Star-Tribune,* January 10, 2001, B-1.

36. Robert W. Connell, *Masculinities* (Cambridge: Polity Press, 1995). See also Robert Hanke, "Redesigning Men: Hegemonic Masculinity in Transition," in *Men, Masculinity, and the Media,* ed. Steve Craig (Newbury Park, Pa.: Sage, 1992).

37. According to the family's memorial website, www.matthewsplace.com/mattslife .htm, these languages were English, German, and Italian, although it was widely reported that he also spoke Arabic.

38. Howard Fineman, with Mark Miller and Andrew Murr, "Echoes of a Murder in Wyoming," *Newsweek,* October 26, 1998, 42.

39. Howard Chua-Eoan, Richard Woodbury, and Maureen Harrington, "That's Not a Scarecrow," *Time,* October 19, 1998, 72.

40. Dyer, *White;* Howard Winant, *The New Politics of Race* (Minneapolis: University of Minnesota Press, 2004).

41. Donna Minkowitz, "Love and Hate in Laramie," *Nation,* July 12, 1999, 18.

42. Several news articles placed great significance on the unpaved streets in West Laramie, the proverbial other side of the tracks. West Laramie has a lower average income than Laramie and a greater Latino population. Social justice activists regularly point to inequalities of infrastructure between the two. Some residents nonetheless suggested that unpaved streets were an urban and inaccurate marker of class; some of the fancier divisions outside of town, they pointed out, also did not have paved streets.

43. James Brooke, "Men Held in Beating Lived on Fringes," *New York Times,* October 15, 1998, A-16.

44. Saunders, "Murder."

45. Ott and Aoki, "Politics of Negotiating Public Tragedy."

46. Jim Hughes and David Olinger, "Beating Wasn't a Hate Crime, Suspect's Family Says," *Denver Post,* October 11, 1998, A-10.

47. Steve Lopez, Maureen Harrington, and Richard Woodbury, "To Be Young and Gay in Wyoming," *Time,* October 26, 1998, 38–40.

48. In particular, the way Matthew Shepard became an icon of gay rights relied upon exclusionary discourses of class, race, and gender.

49. See Dayan, "Paying Attention to Attention," and Landes, "The Public and the Private Sphere," on the gendering of the audience/public divide. See Gross, *The Secret History of Emotion,* on the alignment of political speech with modern notions of manly activity.

50. For example, Berlant, *Queen of America.*

51. For more on definitions of shame and its sociality, see Martha Nussbaum, *Hiding from Humanity: Disgust, Shame, and the Law* (Princeton, N.J.: Princeton University Press, 2004); Ahmed, *Cultural Politics of Emotion;* Elspeth Probyn, *Blush: Faces of Shame* (Minneapolis: University of Minnesota Press, 2005); Robert Solomon, *True to Our Feelings: What Our Emotions Are Really Telling Us* (Oxford: Oxford University Press, 2007); Eve Sedgwick and Adam Frank, eds., *Shame and Its Sisters: A Sylvan Tomkins Reader* (Durham, N.C.: Duke University Press, 1995).

52. Kirk Petersen, letter to the editor, *Wyoming Tribune-Eagle,* October 14, 1998, A-11; R. Hoskins, letter to the editor, *Wyoming Tribune-Eagle,* October 15, 1998, A-11.

53. Gordon and Frances Blakeney, letter to the editor, *Laramie Boomerang,* October 25, 1998, 4.

54. Loffreda, *Losing Matt Shepard.* For more examples of such accounts from gay and lesbian residents, see the excellent documentary *Laramie Inside Out,* VHS, dir. Beverly Seckinger, 2004.

55. For more on the problems of basing law or policy on ideas of what is or should be shameful, see Nussbaum, *Hiding from Humanity*.

56. Ahmed, *Cultural Politics of Emotion*.

57. Thernstrom, "Crucifixion of Matthew Shepard," 212.

58. Hughes and Olinger, "Beating Wasn't a Hate Crime."

59. Kevin McCullen, "Attack on Student Shocks Laramie," *Rocky Mountain News*, October 10, 1998, A-7.

60. The U.S. Department of Justice reported that in 1998, Wyoming youth used more crystal methamphetamine at younger ages than the national average. David Singh, "Wyoming's Methamphetamine Initiative: The Power of Informed Process," *Bulletin from the Field,* May 2001, www.ncjrs.org/pdffiles1/bja/186266.pdf.

61. Loffreda, *Losing Matt Shepard*, 41.

62. Wypijewski, "A Boy's Life."

63. One of the biggest complaints was that the writers had mischaracterized the university as oak- and ivy-lined. This perhaps had to do with a sense that the reporters were reading Ivy League town-gown conflicts onto local university-town economic and cultural divisions, which are less dramatic.

64. Tiffany Edwards, "Students Have Dialogue on Gay Issues, Media Coverage of Shepard's Murder," *Laramie Boomerang*, October 23, 1998, 1. For an example of national stories that discussed the report as anti-gay sentiment, see Tom Kenworthy, "In Wyoming, Homecoming Infused with Hard Lesson on Intolerance," *Washington Post*, October 11, 1998, A-2.

65. Hal Wedel, letter to the editor, *Laramie Boomerang*, October 16, 1998, 4.

66. Henrietta Mueller, letter to the editor, *Laramie Boomerang*, October 18, 1998, 4.

67. Guy Trebay, "Beyond the Fence: Conjuring the Lives of Martyr Matthew Shepard," *Village Voice*, October 28, 1998, http://www.villagevoice.com/news/9844,trebay,951,1.html.

68. Sulk's case has since been the cause for outrage, though not outrage at violence against women. Anti-abortion groups have taken up the cause to argue that Sulk was murdered because she refused to get an abortion. See, for example, http://www.preg nantpause.org/abort/hostet.htm    and    http://www.afterabortion.info/PAR/V8/n1/co ercedabortions.html.

69. See, for example, Elizabeth Pochoda, "The Talk in Laramie" *Nation*, June 19, 2001, 33.

70. Kaufman, introduction.

71. Tiffany Edwards, "Local Reaction Negative," *Casper Star-Tribune*, June 11, 2001, B-1.

72. Student Journalists' Review, *Laramie Boomerang*, March 29, 2000, 9. See also Nate Green, "Priest and Others Like *The Laramie Project*," *Laramie Boomerang*, March 3, 2000.

73. Ahmed, *Cultural Politics of Emotion*.

74. Different performances had different measures of success at negotiating this invitation and the politics of proximity between audiences and Laramie. See Jill Dolan, "*The Laramie Project*: Rehearsing for the Example," in *Utopia in Performance: Finding Hope at the Theater*, ed. Dolan (Ann Arbor: University of Michigan Press, 2005), 113–38; Jay Baglia and Elissa Foster, "Performing the 'Really Real': Bearing Witness in *The Laramie Project*," paper presented at the National Communication Association Conference, New Orleans, 2002.

75. As of the 2000 census, roughly 2 percent of the population were Asian/Pacific Islanders; 8 percent were Latinos, 1 percent were African American, 1 percent were Native American, and 90 percent were white. U.S. Census Bureau, Fact Sheet: Laramie city, Wyoming, 2000, factfinder.census.gov/servlet/SAFFFacts.

76. Special features, *The Laramie Project,* DVD, dir. Moisés Kauffman, HBO Movies, 2002.

77. For a different set of local viewers, the *Project* was not critical enough of local inequalities or the small-town inertia that characterized many local responses.

78. Ahmed, *Cultural Politics of Emotion.*

79. See Russ Castronovo and Dana Nelson, eds., introduction to *Materializing Democracy: Toward a Revitalized Cultural Politics* (Durham, N.C.: Duke University Press, 2002).

80. I focus on the Habermasian strain of deliberative democracy. For a popular example of a deliberative democracy project that revolves around varying degrees of presence, see Fishkin, *When the People Speak.* For examples of theoretical models based on face-to-face exchange, see Habermas, *Between Facts and Norms;* Benhabib, *Situating the Self.*

81. The dialogic basis of Habermasian communicative ethics has been noted and its limits have been discussed by Lee, "Textuality, Mediation, and Public Discourse"; DeLuca and Peeples, "From Public Sphere to Public Screen"; Peters, "Distrust of Representation."

### 2. "Hate Is Not a Laramie Value"
1. Laramie Municipal Code, chapter 9.08.020.

2. For details on the selection of interviewees, see the appendix.

3. The meeting had been announced as a working session to discuss the city's water shortage shortly before it was held. Because it was a special session and not a regular meeting, the session was not telecast on the city's public access TV station. There were numerous angry letters to the local paper protesting the "closed session" and the exclusion of public contributions to the resolution—or discussion on implementing something more than a resolution.

4. Haggerty, "Hate Crimes."

5. Laramie Coalition, "Laramie, Wyo., Council Kills Bias Crimes Law," press release, March 2, 1999.

6. Jeff Lockwood, interview by author, digital recording, Laramie, October 24, 2005.

7. Bern Haggerty, telephone interview by author, digital recording, November 15, 2005.

8. While some locals wanted to understand the crime as simply a "robbery gone wrong," many news outlets offered a simplistic account of the attack (indeed, of hate crimes in general) as an anonymous gay bashing motivated by a prior conscious and murderous homophobia.

9. The campaign followed a similar national print ad campaign over the summer. Both campaigns were sponsored by a consortium of conservative groups including the Alliance for Traditional Marriage–Hawaii, American Family Association, Americans for Truth About Homosexuality, Center for Reclaiming America, Christian Family Network, Christian Coalition, Citizens for Community Values, Colorado for Family Values, Concerned Women for America, Coral Ridge Ministries, Exodus International, Family First, Family Research Council, Focus on the Family, Kerusso Ministries, Liberty Counsel, Mission America, and National Legal Foundation. Ontario Consultants on Religious Tolerance, "'Ex-gay' Advertisements: In Newspapers & on TV," 2002, http://www.religioustolerance.org/ hom_ads.htm.

10. Clinton, "Statement on the Attack on Matthew Shepard."

11. For more on the history of hate crimes legislation at the state level in Wyoming and the conversations about sexuality in relation to the 1999 effort to pass such a law, see Loffreda, *Losing Matt Shepard.*

12. In much of Wyoming, racial projects include a heavy emphasis on the disenfranchisement of Native Americans.

13. Jeanne Hurd, interview by author, tape recording, Laramie, October 25, 2005; Bern Haggerty, interview.

14. As *bias crime* is the term used in the laws and proposed laws discussed here and used by my interviewees, I will use this terminology throughout the chapter to avoid confusion.

15. City Manager's Office, memorandum (to City Council): Regular Agenda Items—Consideration of Resolution no. 99-04 and Ordinance no. 1452, February 25, 1999.

16. Haggerty, interview.

17. Haggerty, interview; Hurd, interview.

18. Haggerty, interview; Lockwood, interview.

19. The Federal Hate Crimes Statistics Act requires the federal government to compile statistics from local data on hate crimes; however, there are no definitions of what a hate crime is or how local law enforcement should go about compiling statistics. Haggerty, "Hate Crimes."

20. The ordinance was discussed briefly on April 18, and a third reading was postponed due to the absence of several council members who represented the swing votes.

21. E. Gerald Meyer, interview by author, digital recording, Laramie, October 25, 2005.

22. In fact, a proposed anti-gay marriage law was defeated in the Wyoming legislature at the same time as the hate crimes ordinance proposed after the murder. Further evidence for a pervasive libertarian streak can be argued in the fact that Wyoming repealed its laws against sodomy (laws which are often used as a way of criminalizing same-sex sexual activity) in 1977.

23. The sign was intended to encourage people to visit the recently revamped historical Territorial Prison, which plays up the Wild West image with exhibits on some of its more famous former residents, such as Butch Cassidy and Calamity Jane, as well as exhibits on everyday life in the prison and in the West during the 1880s. The restoration of the penitentiary was part of an attempt by Laramie to increase the city's share of state tourism funds. (Tourism is one of the top industries in Wyoming, along with mineral and natural gas extraction.)

24. Laramie Coalition, letter to Mayor Dave Williams, January 19, 1999.

25. John Hanks Jr., letter to the editor, *Laramie Boomerang,* May 13, 2000, 4.

26. Judy Coburn, letter to the editor, *Laramie Boomerang,* April 15, 2000, 4.

27. Council meetings were taped for local access TV; Haggerty would take tapes over to the Cheyenne TV station to try to get them to cover it on the nightly news. However, as one of my respondents pointed out, very few people watch the Cheyenne news, those in Laramie at least preferring to get their local news from one of the Denver stations.

28. See Couldry, "Theorising Media as Practice" and Couldry, *Media Rituals: A Critical Approach* (London: Routledge, 2003) for more on the sites and rituals of media power.

29. See Ott and Aoki, "The Politics of Negotiating Public Tragedy," for more on this aspect of the national news coverage of the murder.

30. This analysis of the news coverage was expressed in part or full by many of my interviewees; similar thoughts come through the ethnographic account in Loffreda, *Losing Matt Shepard.*

31. Lockwood, interview.

32. Haggerty, interview.

33. *Black eye* was the term used by E. G. Meyers, but a similar sentiment was expressed by nearly all the former council members I interviewed.

34. Dave Williams, interview by author, digital recording, Laramie, October 25, 2005.

35. Phil Dubois, Speech at the "Gayz into the Millenium" conference at the University of California at Davis, February, 2000, transcript, 3; Joe Shumway, telephone interview by author, digital recording, November 7, 2005; Trudy McKracken, telephone interview by author, digital recording, November 8, 2005.

36. Shumway, interview.

37. Dan Furphy, interview by author, digital recording, Laramie, October 27, 2005.

38. Hurd, interview.

39. Steve Westfahl, letter to the editor, *Laramie Boomerang,* May 5, 2000, 4; Laramie City Council, regular meeting minutes, April 4, 2000, 11.

40. Bob Bell, interview with author, Laramie, October 28, 2005; others hinted at this idea as well.

41. Laramie City Council, regular meeting minutes, April 4, 2000, 11.

42. Laramie City Council, regular meeting minutes, May, 2000, 5.

43. Bell, interview.

44. Laramie City Council, regular meeting minutes, April 4, 2000, 10.

45. Ibid.

46. There may also have been a fear that racial and ethnic minorities might become over-central to the law, although this was not openly expressed.

47. Laramie City Council, minutes, April 4, 2000, 10; Phil Dubois, letter to the editor, *Laramie Boomerang,* April 11, 2000, 3.

48. McKracken, interview. She was referring to Reverend Fred Phelps, from Kansas.

49. Koziak, *Retrieving Political Emotion.*

50. This is, of course, making a generalization that risks obscuring the agonistic plurality of political positions and cultures that exist within any culture.

51. Furphy, interview.

52. Williams, interview.

53. Dubois, letter to the editor. Dubois blamed Shepard's murder for a drop in enrollment at the university, which had a negative impact on local economy. He suggested that passing the ordinance would rectify the situation. Shumway opposed the ordinance on constitutional and religious grounds.

54. Bell, interview.

55. Shumway, interview.

56. Laramie City Council, regular meeting minutes, March 21, 2000, 9.

57. For more detailed accounts of the impacts of the murder and its mediation on local residents, especially gay and lesbian residents, see Loffreda, *Losing Matt Shepard;* Seckinger, *Laramie Inside Out.*

58. As of this writing, 10 years after the murder, the UW Board of Trustees has approved a system that would provide benefits to domestic partners, expanding benefits beyond married partnerships. University of Wyoming, "University of Wyoming Board of Trustees Action," news release, June 2, 2009, http://www.uwyo.edu/news/showrelease.asp?id=31781. Whether this plan will be implemented and whether it will cover same-sex partners remains to be seen.

59. Martha Nussbaum discusses and critiques the notion of law as devoid of emotion, a view she argues is pervasive in common parlance and certain strains of liberal and utilitarian legal thinking. Nussbaum, *Hiding from Humanity.*

60. Warner, *Publics and Counterpublics.*

61. Silverstone, *Media and Morality.*

### 3. The Murder of James Byrd Jr.

1. Tom Brokaw, anchor, *NBC Nightly News,* June 9, 1998.

2. Linda Williams, *Playing the Race Card: Melodramas of Black and White from Uncle Tom to O. J. Simpson* (Princeton, N.J.: Princeton University Press, 2001).

3. The texts that provide the basis for this analysis include 152 print news stories (79 from Texas news sources, which I refer to as regional; 73 from other national news sources); 22 magazine articles; and 14 television news segments (all national news broadcasts). For more on the selection criteria, see the appendix.

4. This much was established through physical evidence. The three attackers' stories about what happened after they picked up Byrd differ and are difficult to piece together. The ringleader of the three, Bill King, did claim, however that he wanted the crime to act as the foundation for a chapter of a white supremacist group centered in Jasper.

5. Other racial identities reported in the 2000 census include: 9 percent Latino, .7 percent Asian and Pacific Islander, and .5 percent Native American. U.S. Census Bureau, Fact Sheet: Jasper city, Texas, 2000, factfinder.census.gov/servlet/SAFFFacts.

6. In 2003, a district court judge found the city had violated the men's First Amendment rights in firing them. See *Locurto v. Giuliani,* 269 F. Supp. 2d 368 (S.D.N.Y. 2003).

7. This coverage included updates on whether the crime would be prosecuted under federal hate crimes law (it was not, although Jasper did receive federal assistance in investigating the case as a hate crime) and whether or not the prosecution would be able to try the case as a capital offense. Within this month, the prosecution announced that they had evidence Byrd was conscious for part of the time he was dragged behind the truck, allowing them to charge kidnapping in addition to murder, making the case a capital one and allowing the prosecution to seek the death penalty.

8. For example, many Westerns are at heart melodramas. Legal debates and even trials are often accomplished through melodramatic discourse. See Williams, *Playing the Race Card.*

9. Melodrama as a form arose within the context of the upheavals of industrialization; scholars have pointed out that the excesses associated with melodrama made the large-scale social upheavals wrought by industrialization easier to see and feel on a human scale. For such historical analyses, see Ben Singer, *Melodrama and Modernity* (New York: Columbia University Press, 2001); Ann Cvetkovich, *Mixed Feelings: Feminism, Mass Culture, and Victorian Sensationalism* (New Brunswick, N.J.: Rutgers University Press, 1992); Christine Gledhill, ed., *Home Is Where the Heart Is: Studies in Melodrama and the Woman's Film* (London: British Film Institute, 1987).

10. See Peters Brooks, *The Melodramatic Imagination: Balzac, Henry James, Melodrama, and the Mode of Excess* (New Haven, Conn.: Yale University Press, 1976); Jane Tompkins, *Sensational Designs: The Cultural Work of American Fiction, 1790–1860* (Oxford: Oxford University Press, 1986); Susan Gilman, *Blood Talk: American Race Melodrama and the Culture of the Occult* (Chicago: University of Chicago Press, 2003); Cvetkovich, *Mixed Feelings.* Cvetkovich eloquently argues that the excesses associated with melodrama worked in both Victorian novels and Marx's *Das Kapital* to embody social and political change and conflicts and to make their effects tangible.

11. See Tompkins, *Sensational Designs;* Cvetkovich, *Mixed Feelings;* and Gledhill, *Home Is Where the Heart Is.*

12. For more on the use of melodrama to legitimate white violence against black Americans, particularly in the practice of lynching, see Williams, *Playing the Race Card*; Amy Louise Wood, *Lynching and Spectacle: Race and Violence in America, 1890–1940* (Chapel Hill: University of North Carolina Press, 2009). For more on how the form has shaped the construction of black men as dangerous within crime reporting, see Carol Stabile, *White Victims, Black Villains: Gender, Race and Crime News in U.S. Culture* (New York: Routledge, 2006).

13. See Williams, *Playing the Race Card*; Gilman, *Blood Talk*. Critics of melodrama point out that it has the propensity to reduce these experiences and justice claims into either universal or personal suffering, in either case flattening out the specific social antagonisms that are the cause of this suffering. See Lauren Berlant, *The Female Complaint: The Unfinished Business of Sentimentality in American Culture* (Durham, N.C.: Duke University Press, 2008) and for more on these critiques.

14. For example, see John Hartley, *Understanding News* (London: Routledge, 1982); Barbie Zelizer, *Taking Journalism Seriously: News and the Academy* (Thousand Oaks, Calif.: Sage, 2004). See also Carey, *Communication as Culture*, on the dramaturgy of news texts.

15. Nichols, *Representing Reality*.

16. See Jostein Gripsrud, "The Aesthetics and Politics of Melodrama," in *Journalism and Popular Culture*, ed. Peter Dahlgren and Colin Sparks (London: Sage, 1992), 84–95; Zelizer, *Taking Journalism Seriously*; Stabile, *White Victims, Black Villains*.

17. Hayden White, *Tropics of Discourse* (Baltimore: Johns Hopkins University Press, 1986).

18. See Williams, *Playing the Race Card*, on melodrama and the demand for justice and Boltanski, *Distant Suffering*, on the politics of denunciation.

19. I borrow the label of spectacle to characterize these highly mediated political and legal conflicts from Eric Lott, "The Wages of Liberalism: An Interview with Eric Lott," *Minnesota Review*, Winter 2005, http://www.theminnesotareview.org/ns63/lott.htm.

20. For more on the pervasiveness of such discourses in the 1990s, see Winant, *New Politics of Race*; Eduardo Bonilla-Silva, *Racism without Racists* (Lanham, Md.: Rowman and Littlefield, 2003).

21. Michael Omi and Howard Winant, *Racial Formation in the United States: from the 1960s to the 1990s* (New York: Routledge, 1994).

22. See Young, *Justice and the Politics of Difference*.

23. Here I use the term *mainstream media* to refer to the press outlets that define themselves as addressing and serving everyone within their circulation. This includes newspapers with local circulation as well as the national editions of the *New York Times, Washington Post, and Los Angeles Times*; the three major national news magazines; and the national network news (all of which claim to address the nation, inclusively, even as they define their readers and viewers in more economically segmented terms to their advertisers). The use of mainstream news here is meant as contrast to the black-oriented press or advocacy news outlets, which identify themselves as addressing a particular community or constituency.

24. Patrick Johnson, telephone interview by author, digital recording, April 17, 2006.

25. One extended piece included more details from his family on his academic success in high school and later "aimlessness." David Firestone, "A Life Marked by Troubles, but Not by Hatred," *New York Times*, June 13, 1998, A-6.

26. This sampling was determined by the newspapers available in the Ethnic NewsWatch database; there were 41 print news stories about Byrd in the database for the month following the murder.

27. Editorial desk, "A Wake-up Call," *Bay State Banner* 33, no. 37 (1998): 4; Joyce King, *Hate Crime: The Story of a Dragging in Jasper, Texas* (New York: Pantheon Books, 2003), 64.

28. For more on racial representation in crime news, see Robert Entman and Andrew Rojecki, *The Black Image in the White Mind: Media and Race in America* (Chicago: University of Chicago Press, 2000).

29. Stabile, *White Victims, Black Villains.* See also Patricia Hill-Collins, "The Tie That Binds: Race, Gender, and U.S. Violence," *Ethnic and Racial Studies* 21, no 5 (1998): 917–38, for a discussion of how race and gender influence definitions of what counts as violence.

30. Donald Bogle, *Toms, Coons, Mulattoes, Mammies, and Bucks: An Interpretive History of Blacks in American Films* (New York: Viking Press, 2002).

31. Williams, *Playing the Race Card.*

32. Initially, this characterization of racism was contested, with several commentators intervening to remark that individual acts of violence were not the best way to envision the shape or harm of racism (cautioning audiences not to overlook the unequal access to education and financial opportunity as evidence of racism).

33. The figure of the "redneck" or "cracker" is that of failed whiteness. Although he has white skin, the label suggests that he does not have the symbolic or discursive trappings of whiteness: he is not able to abstract himself from his body or his particular interests; his physicality and sexuality are marked by excess rather than moderation and control. As the contemporary discursive articulation of whiteness with power, the law, and rationality hinges on these symbolic trappings, the inability to claim them can be discussed as failed whiteness. See Dyer, *White;* Dana Nelson, *National Manhood: Capitalist Citizenship and the Imagined Fraternity of White Men* (Durham: Duke University Press, 1998).

34. "Race, Memory, and Justice," *New York Times,* June 14, 1998, A-14.

35. Tony Norman, "Crying over the Same Spilled Blood," *Pittsburgh Post-Gazette,* June 16, 1998, E-1.

36. "Race, Memory, and Justice."

37. Joyce King's book-length account located the birth of the Aryan Brotherhood in the desegregation of prisons in the 1960s. Prior to desegregation, white, black, and Latino prisoners had been housed separately and treated with distinct sets of rules and privileges. When the prisons were desegregated, white prisoners lost their position of relative privilege and became a minority. The formation of the Aryan Brotherhood was an effort to regain power and position through solidarity, intimidation, and violence. King, *Hate Crime.*

38. The focus on white supremacist groups as illustrations of what racism looks like was carried over into the educational materials PBS produced and distributed along with the documentary *The Two Towns of Jasper.* These K–12 lesson plans, touted as teaching tolerance and raising critical consciousness about racism, repeatedly referenced organized hate groups as examples of, or the source of, racism—and even as examples of white privilege, completely inverting and undermining the concept. Jennifer Petersen, "Media as Sentimental Education: The Political Lessons of HBO's *Laramie Project* and PBS's *Two Towns of Jasper,*" *Critical Studies in Media Communication* 26, no. 3 (2009): 255–74.

39. Roy Bragg, "Racism Alive and Well in America—Just Harder to Spot," *San Antonio Express-News,* June 27, 1998, A-1.

40. Rick Bragg, "Unfathomable Crime, Unlikely Figure," *New York Times,* June 16, 1998, A-12.

41. Ibid.; *Two Towns of Jasper,* dir. Whitney Dow and Marco Williams, DVD, PBS, 2002; Ashley Craddock, "Jasper's Stand," *Salon,* November 18, 1999, http://www.salon.com/news/feature/11/18/jasper.

42. "Killing Time: Shawn Berry Talks about What Happened the Night James Byrd Jr. Was Dragged to His Death in Jasper, Texas," *60 Minutes II,* CBS, September 28, 1999.

43. Ellis Cose, "An Easy Sense of Outrage," *Newsweek,* March 8, 1999, 24.

44. While the murder was covered in numerous small to medium-sized newspapers, in the largest of these (with the broadest circulation) the audience is defined as affluent, educated, and influential. *Time, Newsweek,* and *USA Today,* for example, describe their audiences as professional-managerial, upper middle class, college educated, and with average household incomes of over $65,000. Time Media Kit. Audience Research, Time Inc., 2005, http://www.time.com/time/mediakit/audience/research/index.html; Newsweek Media Kit, MRI: National and Business Plus, Research: Audience Profile, 2005, http://www.newsweekmediakit.com/newsite/us/research/mri.shtml; USA Today Media Kit, MRI Audience Demographic Profiles, Audience, 2004, http://www.usatoday.com/media_kit/usatoday/au_general_demographics.htm.

45. Bob Hohler, "Brutal Slaying Tears at a Texas Town," *Boston Globe,* June 12, 1998, A-1; Carol Marie Cropper, "Town Expresses Sadness and Horror over Slaying," *New York Times,* June 11, 1998, A-16; Sarah Van Boven and Anne Belli Gesalman, "A Fatal Ride in the Night," *Newsweek,* June 22, 1998, 33; Adam Cohen, S. C. Gwynne, and Timothy Roche, "A Life for a Life: As America Watches, a Texas Town Searches for Racial Healing after a Grisly Murder Trial," *Time,* March 8, 1999, 28–33.

46. Courtland Milloy, "This Time, an Old Story Gets a New Ending," *Washington Post,* June 14, 1998, B-1; "Mayor of Jasper Contends Killing Was Not Representative of His City," *Austin American-Statesman,* June 10, 1998, A-8.

47. Tara McPherson, *Reconstructing Dixie: Race, Gender, and Nostalgia in the Imagined South* (Durham, N.C.: Duke University Press, 2003), 18.

48. Diane McWhorter, "Texas Killing Recalls Racism's Past," *USA Today,* June 16, 1998, 15-A.

49. Only 2 out of 73 national news stories mentioned this; none of the Texas sources did.

50. For more on the function of the South in national narratives of racial injustice and civil rights, see Gary Gerstle, "Race and the Myth of the Liberal Consensus," *Journal of American History,* September 1995, 579–86.

51. See McPherson, *Reconstructing Dixie;* Allison Graham, *Framing the South: Hollywood, Television, and Race during the Civil Rights Struggle* (Baltimore: Johns Hopkins University Press, 2001).

52. Joe Murray, "Our Sad History Rears Its Ugly Head," *Atlanta Journal-Constitution,* June 15, 1998, A-11; McWhorter, "Texas Killing Recalls Racism's Past"; "The Jasper Trial: Thought Those Days Had Gone," *Economist,* February 20, 1999, 28; editorial desk, "1998: List Suggests Nation Is Stuck in the '50s," *San Antonio Express-News,* June 13, 1998, B-4.

53. "Race, Memory, and Justice."

54. Murray, "Our Sad History."

55. Roy Bragg, "E. Texas Town Tries to Battle Stigma of Racism," *San Antonio Express-News,* June 14, 1998, A-1; Allan Turner, "Jasper Killing Reopens Old Racial Wounds," *Houston Chronicle* June 14, 1998, A-1.

56. Ricardo Ainslie, *Long, Dark Road: Bill King and Murder in Jasper, Texas* (Austin: University of Texas Press, 2004).

57. Cohen et al., "A Life for a Life," 28.

58. Ashraf Rushdy, "Reflections on Jasper: Resisting History," *Humanist* 60, no. 2 (2000): 24-28.

59. Lance Morrow, "Something We Cannot Accept," *Time,* March 8, 1999, 92.

60. Bebe Moore Campbell, "The Boy in the River," *Time,* March 8, 1999, 35.

61. See Sturken, *Tangled Memories.*

62. Chuck Green, "Progress in Race Relations," *Denver Post,* June 10, 1998, B-1.

63. This comment also takes on a "clash of civilizations" tone when placed against the backdrop of the international conflicts that dominated the news of the 1990s; namely, the disintegration of former Yugoslavia and the international attention to and intervention in the Somali civil war. Seen in this light, Green manages to turn an example of racial violence into an argument about the "civilized" nature of the United States and the "barbarity" of other nations.

64. Tom Brokaw, anchor, *NBC Nightly News,* June 11, 1998.

65. In the months after Byrd's murder, the fence segregating the cemetery was taken down. The removal of the fence was one of the symbolic efforts to redress continuing segregations and racial divides in Jasper in the wake of the murder and its mediation.

66. Dan McGraw, "Justice Delayed," *U.S. News & World Report* 126, no. 8 (1999), 28.

67. Ainslie, *Long, Dark Road,* 118.

68. Dina Temple-Raston, *A Death in Texas: A Story of Race, Murder, and a Small Town's Struggle for Redemption* (New York: Holt, 2002), 92.

69. McGraw, "Justice Delayed."

70. See Nelson, *National Manhood;* Dyer, *White;* Colette Guillaumin, *Racism, Sexism, and Ideology* (New York: Routledge, 1995).

71. Richard Stewart, "Loud Tie Appropriate for Sheriff; Professor's Critique Doesn't Faze Rowles," *Houston Chronicle,* June 14, 1998, 2.

72. On whiteness, masculinity, and disinterest, see Nelson, *National Manhood;* Bederman, *Manliness and Civilization;* Warner, *Publics and Counterpublics.*

73. McGraw, "Justice Delayed," 28.

74. Rentschler, "Witnessing."

75. See "Battling a Chronic Problem," *St. Louis Post-Dispatch,* June 11, 1998, B-6; McWhorter, "Texas Killing Recalls Racism's Past"; Cose, "Easy Sense of Outrage"; Jack E. White, "Prejudice? Perish the Thought," *Time,* March 8, 1999, 36.

76. Morrow, "Something We Cannot Accept," 92.

### 4. The Visibility of Suffering, Injustice, and the Law

1. This includes the 24 articles found in a Lexis-Nexis search of Texas newspapers in 1999 and 2001, the interim report published by the House Committee on Judicial Affairs containing a summary of consideration of the James Byrd Jr. Hate Crimes Act, and the focus report and bill analysis published by the House Research Organization. These texts offered me background information on the content, legal issues, and procedural issues surrounding the act. The actual text of the floor debates and committee hearings was transcribed from the Texas legislature's audio archives. See the appendix for more details on text and interview selection.

2. Diane Hardy-Garcia, telephone interview by author, digital recording, April 3, 2006. Hardy-Garcia also cited the 1991 murder of young, gay Houstonian Paul Broussard as background for the 1993 bill; Broussard died after a group of 10 young men beat him and his friends in a gay district of Houston. The crime, and the fact that 5 of his assailants received probation (albeit for 10 years), outraged many people and was instrumental in instigating police training and aggressive "sting" operations aimed at would-be gay-bashers.

3. Some commentators linked this compromise to the simultaneous consideration of the state sodomy law (being reviewed at the same time as part of an overhaul of the penal code). Conservatives agreed to support the hate crimes law, minus the language defining categories of discrimination, and liberals agreed not to remove the sodomy laws from the penal code. See Clay Robison and Ross Ramsey, "The 73rd Legislature; Senate, House at an Impasse over Sodomy Laws; Progress Made in Proposal on Hate Crimes, Parole Reforms," *Houston Chronicle,* May 24, 1993, A-9. An amusing insight into the debates surrounding the review of the sodomy laws can be seen in the documentary *The Dildo Diaries,* dir. Laura Barton and Judy Wilder, VHS, IA Films, Inc., and Roadtrip Productions, 2002.

4. This was the narrative expressly cited by several senators in hearings. See Texas Senate Committee on Criminal Justice, *938 Public Hearing,* 76th legislature, regular session, May 6, 1999, audiocassette, tape 1.

5. LGRL became a formal lobbying body in 1989; it represented the joining of the Lesbian/Gay Democrats of Texas and the Texas Gay Taskforce, which had both worked to represent lesbian and gay interests in the Texas legislature during the 1980s. Hate crimes legislation had been one of the group's priorities from its beginning. The LGRL has since become Equality Texas.

6. Representatives for the NAACP testified for the bill in 2001, but not in 1999.

7. Hardy-Garcia, interview.

8. HB 938, engrossed version, 76th legislature, regular session, 1999; House Research Organization, *HB 938 Bill Analysis* (Austin: Texas House of Representatives), April 26, 1999.

9. Deece Eckstein, interview by the author, digital recording, Austin, April 13, 2006. Going on in the background of this debate, whether lawmakers were aware of it or not, was the beginnings of *Lawrence v. Texas,* the Supreme Court case that would strike down Texas sodomy laws. John Lawrence and Tyron Garner were arrested on sodomy charges in 1998. Their challenge to the constitutionality of the Texas law (on grounds that it violated due process) was heard by the Texas Fourteenth Court of Appeals on November 4, 1999. See Steve Brewer, "Conduct Law Unfair to Gays, Attorney Says," *Houston Chronicle,* November 4, 1999, A-29.

10. Hardy-Garcia, interview; Senfronia Thompson, interview by author, digital recording, Austin, April 17, 2006; Brete Anderson, telephone interview by author, digital recording, April 6, 2006. During the same legislative session, Chisum introduced HB 838, a bill prohibiting the recognition of same-sex marriages performed in other states. The bill died in committee in the 1999 session (it did not make it to a floor debate).

11. It was concurrently introduced as SB 87 in the Senate; the Senate Committee on Criminal Justice substituted the House version for the Senate version. It was the text of HB 587 (the same text as HB 938, passed in 1999) that passed into law, with minor amendments, in 2001.

12. Anderson, interview.

13. Eckstein, interview.

14. The text of HB 587 later states explicitly that the law does "not create any legal status or right not already existent in statute or common law" for any of the groups listed.

15. HB 587, enrolled version, 77th legislature, regular session, 2001; House Research Organization, *HB 587 Bill Analysis,* April 19, 2001.

16. Hardy-Garcia, interview; Pat Haggerty, interview by author, digital recording, Austin, April 19, 2006.

17. I use the term *victim* to refer to the targets of hate crimes. This is not to insist that victimhood is a primary social identity for those who testified, but to highlight the rhetorical and political use of victim status.

18. For an analysis of the use of testimony as therapy and the dangers this poses within the courtroom, see Jennifer Wood, "Justice as Therapy: The Victim Rights Clarification Act," *Communication Quarterly* 51, no. 3 (2003): 296–311.

19. See Koziak, *Retrieving Political Emotion;* Butler, "Violence, Mourning, Politics."

20. Representative Chisum explained the murders with a similar logic. He argued that King and the others had killed Byrd because they were angry because laws such as this one treated black and white citizens differently. The argument references the idea that affirmative action and other reparative laws conferred "special privileges" on African Americans (a very similar rhetoric to that used by the KKK when they visited Jasper). His use of this argument to explain the murder comes off a bit like the "gay panic" defense, in its suggestion that they were angry as an explanatory, if not mitigating, factor.

21. Texas House, floor debate, 76th legislature, April 27, 1999, audiocassette tape 80.

22. Wayne Christian, telephone interview by author, digital recording, April 6, 2006.

23. Texas House, floor debate, tape 80.

24. Eckstein, interview. This backlash logic was at the heart of the famous Hopwood decision that made affirmative action illegal in admissions to the University of Texas at Austin law school, as well as an attempt to amend the state constitution to ban affirmative action in 1995.

25. For more on witnessing, see John Ellis, *Seeing Things: Television in the Age of Uncertainty* (London: I. B. Tauris, 2000); John Durham Peters, "Witnessing," *Media, Culture, and Society* 23, no. 6 (2001): 707–24.

26. Johnson, interview.

27. Haggerty, interview.

28. Hardy-Garcia, interview.

29. Jim Rigby, interview by author, digital recording, Austin, April 5, 2006.

30. Hardy-Garcia, interview.

31. Valerie Jenness and Kendal Broad, *Hate Crimes: New Social Movements and the Politics of Violence* (New York: Aldine de Gruyter, 1997).

32. Paul Sadler, telephone interview by author, digital recording, April 17, 2006.

33. See Larry Gross, *Up from Invisibility: Lesbians, Gay Men, and the Media in America* (New York: Columbia University Press, 2001).

34. Texas House Committee on Judicial Affairs, *HB 938 Public Hearing,* 76th legislature, March 11, 1999, audiocassette tape 3.

35. More examples of these arguments can be found in the House Committee hearing, *HB 938,* tapes 1–2.

36. Texas House, floor debate, tape 80.

37. Thompson, interview; Eckstein, interview.

38. Johnson, interview.

39. Houston City Council member and gay activist Annise Parker told a similar story about the Houston Police Department in her testimony before the committee. After the murder of Paul Broussard, the police organized a sting operation to try to catch Broussard's assailants. When police went undercover as gay men, they were shocked at the magnitude of harassment and violence they faced; several police officers were injured in the first week. The experience made evident a problem the police had not taken seriously before, leading them to perform specialized training, outreach to gay and lesbian communities, and create a special hate crimes unit. See House Committee, *HB 938,* tape 1.

40. Patrick Johnson told me that previous attempts to pass the hate crimes legislation had used gay victims less successfully to personalize the bill. When I asked him why Byrd was more successful in terms of putting a face on the bill, he responded simply that Byrd wasn't gay.

41. Texas House, floor debate, tape 80.

42. Ibid.

43. House Committee, *HB 938,* tape 1.

44. Rigby, interview.

45. House Committee, *HB 938,* tape 1.

46. Haggerty, interview.

47. Texas House, floor debate, HB 938, 76th legislature, April 27, 1999, tape 81.

48. Senate Committee, *938 Public Hearing,* tapes 1–4.

49. Thompson, interview; Hardy-Garcia, interview.

50. Rigby, interview.

51. Hardy-Garcia, interview.

52. Christian, interview.

53. The actual content of the KKK speech in Jasper was not all that far from mainstream Republican positions: the protesters expressed resentment over affirmative action and anti-immigration arguments similar to those heard in the Texas legislature and U.S. Congress.

54. Chisum, interview.

55. Several supporters of the bill had in fact offered sympathetic readings of Chisum's change of heart: that the mounting number of murdered gay men was beginning to get to him and that he supported the bill out of a humanitarian impulse. However, this is not how he represented himself to me. The divergences here are telling. That supporters ascribed a sympathetic rationale through humanitarian feeling and that Chisum presented a politic justification to me in terms of taking care of the problem of racism (in some other parts of Texas, not Austin and not his own panhandle district) offers insight into the ways in which the different speakers defined proper or just feelings in this case.

56. Some of those who showed up to testify did express fear that whites (and particularly white men) would be excluded from the law. See Senate Committee, *938 Public Hearing,* tape 2.

57. Christian, interview.

58. Hardy-Garcia, interview.

59. Butler, "Violence, Mourning, Politics."

60. This limitation was evident, among other places, in how the discussion framed different axes of identity in either/or terms: race or sexual orientation or gender. The one exception was the representative of the National Organization of Women: when asked whether she supported the bill even though it did not protect women, she responded that the bill in fact protected women of color and lesbian women. House Committee, *HB 938,* tape 2.

61. Ibid.

62. See, for example, Berlant, *The Female Complaint.*

### CONCLUSION

1. This audience estimate comes from Patrick Healy, "*The Laramie Project: 10 Years Later* Draws 50,000 Theatergoers," ArtsBeat Blog, *New York Times,* October 15, 2009.

2. This divide often splits along the lines of scholarship defined as humanities and as social science. Jodi Dean nicely lays out the history and problems of this divide. See Jodi Dean, ed., introduction to *Cultural Studies and Political Theory* (Ithaca, N.Y.: Cornell University Press, 2000), 1–22.

3. See Susan Bandes, ed., *The Passions of Law* (New York: New York University Press, 2000); Nussbaum, *Hiding from Humanity.*

4. See Cloud, *Control and Consolation;* Berlant, *Queen of America;* and Laurie Ouellette and James Hay, *Better Living through Reality TV: Television and Post-Welfare Citizenship* (Malden, Mass.: Blackwell, 2008).

5. For an evaluation of love as an ethical category of inclusion and exclusion, see Diane Davis, "Addicted to Love; or, Toward an Inessential Solidarity," *JAC: A Journal of Composition Theory* 19, no. 4 (1999): 633–56.

6. See Giroux, *Stormy Weather.*

7. This initiative, Proposition 187, passed overwhelmingly in California but was quickly found unconstitutional in court.

8. Haggerty, interview.

9. Much of the conversation about hate crimes legislation focuses on the penalty enhancement elements of such laws or the ways in which they increase the powers of potentially repressive law enforcement agencies. Yet one key element of many hate crime proposals is the education of local police or other efforts to intervene in local law enforcement, understood as part of the problem. Education, training, funding for investigations, and the creation of alternative (civil) venues for dealing with lower-level harassment all seek to address social relations and problems not currently addressed by law (for example, extending provisions of antistalking law to cover harassment based on gender identity or sexual orientation).

10. Vincent Mosco, *The Political Economy of Communication* (London: Sage, 1996).

11. One need only contrast the media and public response to Shepard's murder with that of Brandon Teena. Even after a major Hollywood movie and a popular documentary publicizing Teena's death, Teena does not hold the same place in cultural memory and is not used as widely to compel political attention and action.

12. Koziak, *Retrieving Political Emotion,* 178.

13. For an example of this type of critique, see Robert McChesney, *Rich Media, Poor Democracy: Communication Politics in Dubious Times* (New York: New Press, 1999). For an overview of these discussions and their focus on better information as the central tenet of constructing a better public sphere in both political science and media reform efforts, see Marcus, *The Sentimental Citizen.*

14. In fact, regulatory recognition that entertainment programming as well as news might be considered under the purview of the Fairness Doctrine was one of the contributions of the women's rights movement to media policy debates. See Allison Perlman, "Feminists in the Wasteland: The National Organization of Women and Television Reform," *Feminist Media Studies* 7, no. 4 (2007): 413–31.

15. See the influential discussions of the ritual elements of law in Emile Durkheim, *The Division of Labor in Society,* trans. W. D. Halls (New York: Free Press, 1984).

16. For more on how the political work of spectacular events is often obscured by the language of ritual and commemoration, which marks them as outside of the political, see Rentschler, "Witnessing." The language of disinterest works in an analogous, opposing manner: removing markers of the interests, passion, and ritual that inhere in legislative processes.

17. Dahlgren, "Television, Public Spheres, and Civic Cultures."

18. That communication can never be fully equitable (or rational, in Habermas's terms) in a society that is materially stratified is a key point of Nancy Fraser's critique of the public sphere as an ideal. Fraser, "Rethinking the Public Sphere."

# Bibliography

Ahmed, Sara. *The Cultural Politics of Emotion*. Edinburgh: Edinburgh University Press, 2004.

———. *Queer Phenomenology: Orientations, Objects, Others*. Durham, N.C.: Duke University Press, 2006.

Ainslie, Ricardo. *Long, Dark Road: Bill King and Murder in Jasper, Texas*. Austin: University of Texas Press, 2004.

Alexander, Jeffrey, and Ronald Jacobs. "Mass Communication, Ritual, and Civil Society." In *Media, Ritual, and Identity*, ed. Tamar Liebes and James Curran. London: Routledge. 1998.

Anderson, Benedict. *Imagined Communities*. 2nd ed. New York: Verso, 1991.

Appadurai, Arjun. *Modernity at Large: Cultural Dimensions of Globalization*. Minneapolis: University of Minnesota Press, 1996.

Arendt, Hannah. *The Human Condition*. Chicago: University of Chicago Press, 1958.

Artz, Lee. "Hegemony in Black and White: Interracial Buddy Films and the New Racism." In *Cultural Diversity and the U.S. Media*, ed. Yahya R. Kamalipour and Teresa Carilli. New York: State University of New York Press, 1998.

Baglia, Jay, and Elissa Foster. "Performing the 'Really Real': Bearing Witness in *The Laramie Project*." Paper presented at the National Communication Association Conference, New Orleans, 2002.

Baker, Houston A., Jr. "Critical Memory and the Black Public Sphere." In *The Black Public Sphere*, ed. Black Public Sphere Collective. Chicago: University of Chicago Press, 1995.

Bandes, Susan, ed. *The Passions of Law*. New York: New York University Press, 2000.

Barber, Benjamin. *Strong Democracy*. Berkeley: University of California Press, 1984.

Bederman, Gail. *Manliness and Civilization: A Cultural History of Gender and Race in the United States, 1881–1917*. Chicago: University of Chicago Press, 1995.

Bell, Jeannine. *Policing Hatred: Law Enforcement, Civil Rights, and Hate Crime*. New York: New York University Press, 2004.

Benhabib, Seyla. *Situating the Self: Gender, Community, and Postmodernism in Contemporary Ethics*. New York: Routledge, 1992.

———, ed. *Democracy and Difference: Contesting the Boundaries of the Political*. Princeton, N.J. Princeton University Press, 1996.

Berlant, Lauren. *The Queen of America Goes to Washington City*. Durham, N.C.: Duke University Press, 1997.

———. "The Subject of True Feeling: Pain, Privacy, and Citizenship." In *Left Legalism/ Left Critique*, ed. Wendy Brown and Janet Halley. Durham, N.C.: Duke University Press, 2002.

———. "Introduction: Compassion (and Withholding)." In *Compassion: The Culture and Politics of an Emotion*, ed. Lauren Berlant. New York: Routledge, 2004.

———. *The Female Complaint: The Unfinished Business of Sentimentality in American Culture*. Durham, N.C.: Duke University Press, 2008.

Bobbit, David. *The Rhetoric of Redemption: Kenneth Burke's Redemption Drama and Martin Luther King, Jr.'s "I Have a Dream" Speech*. Lanham, Md.: Rowman and Littlefield, 2004.

Bogle, Donald. *Toms, Coons, Mulattoes, Mammies, and Bucks: An Interpretive History of Blacks in American Films*. New York: Viking Press, 1973.

Boltanski, Luc. *Distant Suffering: Morality, Media, and Politics*. Translated by Graham Burchell. Cambridge: Cambridge University Press, 1999.

Bonilla-Silva, Eduardo. *Racism without Racists*. Lanham, Md.: Rowman and Littlefield, 2003.

Bordo, Susan. *The Flight to Objectivity: Essays on Cartesianism and Culture*. Albany: State University of New York Press, 1987.

Brooks, Peter. *The Melodramatic Imagination: Balzac, Henry James, Melodrama, and the Mode of Excess*. New Haven, Conn.: Yale University Press, 1976.

Brown, Wendy. *States of Injury: Power and Freedom in Late Modernity*. Princeton, N.J.: Princeton University Press, 1995.

———. *Regulating Aversion: Tolerance in the Age of Identity and Empire*. Princeton, N.J.: Princeton University Press, 2006.

Burke, Kenneth. *A Rhetoric of Motives*. New York: Prentice-Hall, 1950.

Butler, Judith. "Violence, Mourning, Politics." *Studies in Gender and Sexuality* 4, no. 1 (2003): 9–37.

Caldwell, John. *Televisuality: Style, Crisis, and Authority in American Television*. New Brunswick, N.J.: Rutgers, 1995.

Calhoun, Craig, ed. Introduction to *Habermas and the Public Sphere*. Cambridge, Mass.: MIT Press, 1992.

———. "Plurality, Promises, and Public Spaces." In *Hannah Arendt and the Meaning of Politics*, ed. Craig Calhoun and John McGowan. Minneapolis: University of Minnesota Press, 1997.

Carey, James. *Communication as Culture: Essays on Media and Society*. Boston: Unwin Hyman, 1989.

———. "Political Ritual on Television: Episodes in the History of Shame, Degradation, and Excommunication." In *Media, Ritual, and Identity*, ed. Tamar Liebes and James Curran. London: Routledge, 1998.

Cartwright, Lisa. *Moral Spectatorship: Technologies of Voice and Affect in Postwar Representations of the Child*. Durham, N.C.: Duke University Press, 2008.

Castronovo, Russ, and Dana Nelson, eds. Introduction to In *Materializing Democracy: Toward a Revitalized Cultural Politics*. Durham, N.C.: Duke University Press, 2002.

Chouliaraki, Lilie. *The Spectatorship of Suffering*. London: Sage, 2006.

Clinton, Bill. *Statement on the Attack on Matthew Shepard*. Presidential speech. Washington, D.C.: Government Printing Office, 1998.

Cloud, Dana. *Control and Consolation in American Culture and Politics: Rhetoric of Therapy*. Thousand Oaks, Calif.: Sage, 1998.

———. "Therapy, Silence, and War: Consolation and the End of Deliberation in the 'Affected' Public." *Poroi* 2, no. 1 (2003), http://inpress.lib.uiowa.edu/poroi/papers/cloud030816.html.

Connell, R. W. *Masculinities*. Cambridge: Polity Press, 1995.

Couldry, Nick. "Theorising Media as Practice." *Social Semiotics* 14, no. 2 (2000): 115–32.

——. "The Ethics of Mediation." *openDemocracy,* (November 5, 2001), http://www.opendemocracy.net/media-media911/article_247.jsp.

——. *Media Rituals: A Critical Approach.* London: Routledge, 2003.

Curran, James. "Rethinking the Media as a Public Sphere." In *Communication and Citizenship: Journalism and the Public Sphere in the New Media Age,* ed. Peter Dahlgren and Colin Sparks. London: Routledge, 1991.

——. *Mixed Feelings: Feminism, Mass Culture, and Victorian Sensationalism.* New Brunswick, N.J.: Rutgers University Press, 1992.

Cvetkovich, Ann. *An Archive of Feelings: Trauma, Sexuality, and Lesbian Public Cultures.* Durham, N.C.: Duke University Press, 2003.

Dahlgren, Peter. *Television and the Public Sphere.* London: Sage, 1995.

——. "Television, Public Spheres, and Civic Cultures." In *A Companion to Television,* ed. Janet Wasko. Malden, Mass.: Blackwell, 2005.

Damasio, Antonio. *Descartes' Error: Emotion, Reason, and the Human Brain.* New York: Putnam, 1994.

Davis, Diane. "Addicted to Love; or, Toward an Inessential Solidarity." *JAC: A Journal of Composition Theory* 19, no. 4 (1999): 633–56.

Dayan, Daniel. "Paying Attention to Attention: Audiences, Publics, Thresholds, and Genealogies." *Journal of Media Practice* 6, no. 1 (2005): 9–18.

Dayan, Daniel, and Elihu Katz. *Media Events: The Live Broadcasting of History.* Cambridge, Mass.: Harvard University Press, 1992.

Dean, Jodi, ed. *Cultural Studies and Political Theory.* Ithaca, N.Y.: Cornell University Press, 2000.

DeLuca, Kevin, and Jennifer Peeples. "From Public Sphere to Public Screen: Democracy, Activism, and the Lessons of Seattle." *Critical Studies in Mass Communication* 19, no. 2 (2002): 125–51.

de Souza, Ronald. *The Rationality of Emotion.* Cambridge, Mass.: MIT Press, 1990.

*The Dildo Diaries.* Directed by Laura Barton and Judy Wilder. 63 min. IA Films, Inc. and Roadtrip Productions, 2002.Videocasette.

Dolan, Jill. *Utopia in Performance: Finding Hope at the Theater.* Ann Arbor: University of Michigan Press, 2005.

Downing, John. *Internationalizing Media Theory.* London: Sage, 1996.

Dubois, Phil. Speech at "Gayz into the Millennium" conference at the University of California at Davis, February, 2000. Transcript. Matthew Shepard Collection. American Heritage Center, Laramie, Wyo.

Duggan, Lisa. *The Twilight of Equality? Neoliberalism, Cultural Politics, and the Attack on Democracy.* Boston: Beacon Press, 2003.

Durkheim, Emile. *The Division of Labor in Society.* Translated by W. D. Halls. New York: Free Press, 1984.

Dussel, Enrique. "Deconstruction of the Concept of 'Tolerance': From Intolerance to Solidarity." *Constellations* 11, no. 3 (2004): 326–33.

Dyer, Richard. *White.* London: Routledge, 1997.

Dyson, Michael Eric. *Come Hell or High Water: Hurricane Katrina and the Color of Disaster.* Cambridge, Mass.: Basic Civitas Books, 2006.

Edgar, David. "Theater of Fact: A Dramatist's Viewpoint." In *Why Docudrama? Fact-Fiction on Film and TV,* ed. Alan Rosenthal. Carbondale: Southern Illinois University Press, 1999.

Edkins, Jenny. *Trauma and the Memory of Politics.* Cambridge: Cambridge University Press, 2003.

Eley, Geoff. "Nations, Publics, and Political Cultures: Placing Habermas in the Nineteenth Century." In *Habermas and the Public Sphere,* ed. Craig Calhoun. Cambridge, Mass.: MIT Press, 1992.

Ellis, John. *Seeing Things: Television in the Age of Uncertainty.* London: I. B. Tauris, 2000.

Entman, Robert, and Andrew Rojecki. *The Black Image in the White Mind: Media and Race in America.* Chicago: University of Chicago Press, 2000.

Felman, Shoshana, and Dori Laub. *Testimony: Crises of Witnessing in Literature, Psychoanalysis, and History.* New York: Routledge, 1992.

Fishkin, James. *When the People Speak: Deliberative Democracy and Public Consultation.* Oxford: Oxford University Press, 2009.

Fone, Byrne. *Homophobia: A History.* New York: Picador, 2000.

Foucault, Michel. *The History of Sexuality, Volume I.* Translated by Robert Hurley. New York: Vintage Books, 1978.

Fraser, Nancy. "Rethinking the Public Sphere: A Contribution to the Critique of Actually Existing Democracy." In *Habermas and the Public Sphere,* ed. Craig Calhoun. Cambridge, Mass.: MIT Press, 1992.

Freud, Sigmund. "Mourning and Melancholia." In *The Standard Edition of the Complete Works of Sigmund Freud,* vol. 14. Trans: James Strachey. London: Hogarth Press, 1953.

Fuller, Jennifer. "Recovering the Past: Race, Nation, and Civil Rights Drama in the Nineties." PhD diss., University of Wisconsin, 2004.

Gamson, Joshua. *Freaks Talk Back: Tabloid Talk Shows and Sexual Nonconformity.* Chicago: University of Chicago Press, 1999.

Garnham, Nicholas. "The Media and the Public Sphere." In *Habermas and the Public Sphere,* ed. Craig Calhoun. Cambridge, Mass.: MIT Press, 1992.

Gay and Lesbian Alliance Against Defamation (GLAAD). Media Roundup: Matthew Shepard. GLAAD Alert Archive, October 22, 1998, http://www.glaad.org/action/al_archive_detail.php?id=1661&.

———. Covering Hate Crimes. Media Center: Resource Kits (October 1, 2003), http://www.glaad.org/media/resource_kit_detail.php?id=3495&.

Gerstle, Gary. "Race and the Myth of the Liberal Consensus." *Journal of American History* 82 (September 1995): 579–86.

Gilligan, Carol. *In a Different Voice: Psychological Theory and Women's Development.* Cambridge, Mass.: Harvard University Press, 1982.

Gillis, John. "Memory and Identity: The History of Relationship." In *Commemorations: The Politics of National Identity,* ed. John Gillis. Princeton, N.J.: Princeton University Press, 1994.

Gilman, Susan. *Blood Talk: American Race Melodrama and the Culture of the Occult.* Chicago: University of Chicago Press, 2003.

Giroux, Henry. *Stormy Weather: Katrina and the Biopolitics of Disposability.* Boulder, Colo.: Paradigm, 2006.

Gilroy, Paul. "After the Love Has Gone: Bio-Politics and Bio-Ethics in the Black Public Sphere." In *The Black Public Sphere,* ed. Black Public Sphere Collective. Chicago: University of Chicago Press, 1995.

Glascock, Jack. "The Jasper Dragging Death: Crisis Communication and the Community Newspaper." *Communication Studies* 55, no. 1 (2004): 29–47.

Gledhill, Christine, ed. *Home Is Where the Heart Is: Studies in Melodrama and the Woman's Film.* London: British Film Institute, 1987.

Graham, Allison. *Framing the South: Hollywood, Television, and Race during the Civil Rights Struggle.* Baltimore: Johns Hopkins University Press, 2001.

Gregory, Steven. "Race, Identity, and Political Activism: The Shifting Contours of the African American Public Sphere." In *The Black Public Sphere,* ed. Black Public Sphere Collective. Chicago: University of Chicago Press, 1995.

Gripsrud, Jostein. "The Aesthetics and Politics of Melodrama." In *Journalism and Popular Culture,* ed. Peter Dahlgren and Colin Sparks. London: Sage, 1992.

Gross, Daniel. *The Secret History of Emotion: From Aristotle's Rhetoric to Modern Brain Science.* Chicago: University of Chicago Press, 2006.

Gross, Larry. "Out of the Mainstream: Sexual Minorities and the Mass Media." *Journal of Homosexuality* 21, no. 1–2 (1991): 19–46.

———. *Up from Invisibility: Lesbians, Gay Men, and the Media in America.* New York: Columbia University Press, 2001.

Guillaumin, Colette. *Racism, Sexism, and Ideology.* New York: Routledge, 1995.

Habermas, Jürgen. *The Structural Transformation of the Public Sphere.* Translated by Thomas Burger. Cambridge, Mass.: MIT Press, 1992.

———. *Between Facts and Norms.* Translated by William Rehg. Cambridge, Mass.: MIT Press, 1996.

Haggerty, Bern. "Hate Crimes: A View from Laramie, Wyoming's First Bias Crimes Law, the Fight against Discriminatory Crime, and a New Cooperative Federalism." *Howard Law Journal* 45, no. 1 (2001): 1–75.

Halberstam, Judith. *In a Queer Time and Place: Transgender Bodies, Subcultural Lives.* New York: New York University Press, 2005.

Hall, Cheryl. "Passions and Constraint: The Marginalization of Passion in Liberal Political Theory." *Philosophy & Social Criticism* 28, no. 6 (2002): 727–48.

Halley, Janet. "'Like Race' Arguments." In *What's Left of Theory? New Work on the Politics of Literary Theory,* ed. Judith Butler, John Guillory, and Thomas Kendall. New York: Routledge, 2000.

Hanke, Robert. "Redesigning Men: Hegemonic Masculinity in Transition." In *Men, Masculinity, and the Media,* ed. Steve Craig. Newbury Park, Pa.: Sage, 1992.

Haraway, Donna. "Situated Knowledges: The Science Question in Feminism and the Privilege of Partial Knowledge." In *Simians, Cyborgs, and Women: The Reinvention of Nature.* New York: Methuen, 1991.

Hardt, Michael. "Foreword: What Affects Are Good For." In *The Affective Turn: Theorizing the Social,* ed. Patricia Ticineto Clough and Jean Halley. Durham, N.C.: Duke University Press, 2007.

Held, Virginia. *The Ethics of Care: Personal, Political, Global.* Oxford: Oxford University Press, 2006.

Hill-Collins, Patricia. "The Tie That Binds: Race, Gender, and U.S. Violence." *Ethnic and Racial Studies* 21, no. 5 (1998): 917–38.

Hirschmann, Nancy. "Rethinking Obligation for Feminism." In *Revisioning the Political,* ed. Nancy Hirschmann and Christine Di Stefano. Boulder, Colo.: Westview Press, 1996.

Honig, Bonnie. *Democracy and the Foreigner.* Princeton, N.J.: Princeton University Press, 2003.

hooks, bell. *All About Love: New Visions.* New York: William Morrow, 2000.

House Research Organization. *HB 938 Bill Analysis.* Texas House of Representatives. 26 April, 1999.

———. *Focus Report: Major Issues of the 76th Legislature Regular Session.* Texas House of Representatives, June 30, 1999.

Husselbee, Paul L., and Larry Elliott. "Looking beyond Hate: How National and Regional Newspapers Framed Hate Crimes in Jasper, Texas, and Laramie, Wyoming." *Journalism & Mass Communication Quarterly* 79, no. 4 (2002): 833–52.

*Jasper, Texas.* Directed by Jeffrey W. Byrd. Showtime Networks, 2003. DVD.

Jenness, Valerie, and Kendal Broad. *Hate Crimes: New Social Movements and the Politics of Violence.* New York: Aldine de Gruyter, 1997.

Kaufman, Moisés, and the members of the Tectonic Theater Project. *The Laramie Project.* New York: Dramatists Play Service, 2001.

Keane, John. *The Media and Democracy.* Cambridge: Polity Press, 1991.

Kellner, Douglas. *Media Spectacle and the Crisis of Democracy: Terrorism, War, and Election Battles.* Boulder, Colo.: Paradigm, 2005.

King, Desmond. *Making Americans: Immigration, Race, and the Origins of the Diverse Democracy.* Cambridge, Mass.: Harvard University Press, 2000.

King, Joyce. *Hate Crime: The Story of a Dragging in Jasper, Texas.* New York: Pantheon Books, 2002.

Klinger, Barbara. *Melodrama and Meaning: History, Culture, and the Films of Douglas Sirk.* Bloomington: Indiana University Press, 1994.

Koziak, Barbara. *Retrieving Political Emotion.* University Park: Pennsylvania State University Press, 2000.

La Capra, Dominick. *Representing the Holocaust: History, Theory, Trauma.* Ithaca, N.Y.: Cornell University Press, 1994.

Landes, Joan. "The Public and the Private Sphere: A Feminist Reconsideration." In *Feminism, the Public and the Private,* ed. Joan Landes. Oxford: Oxford University Press, 1998.

———, ed. *Feminism, the Public and the Private.* Oxford: Oxford University Press, 1998.

Laramie City Council. Council Agendas and Minutes Archive, http://www.ci.laramie.wy.us/cityhall/council/agendasminutes/.

Laramie Coalition. *Laramie, WY, Council Kills Bias Crimes Law.* Press release, March 2, 1999.

Laramie City Manager's Office. Memorandum (to City Council): Regular Agenda Items—Consideration of Resolution No. 99–04 and Ordinance No. 1452, February 25, 1999.

*The Laramie Project.* Directed by Moisés Kauffman. HBO Movies, 2002. DVD.

Lawrence, Frederick. *Punishing Hate: Bias Crimes under American Law.* Cambridge, Mass.: Harvard University Press, 1999.

Lee, Benjamin. "Textuality, Mediation, and Public Discourse." In *Habermas and the Public Sphere,* ed. Craig Calhoun. Cambridge, Mass.: MIT Press, 1992.

———. "Publics and Peoples." *Public Culture* 10, no. 2 (1998): 371–94.

Levinas, Emmanuel. *Ethics and Infinity.* Translated by Richard A. Cohen. Pittsburgh, Penn.: Duquesne University Press, 1985.

Lipkin, Steve. *Real Emotional Logic: Film and Television Docudrama as Persuasive Practice.* Carbondale: Southern Illinois University Press, 2002.

*Locurto v. Giuliani,* 269 F. Supp. 2d 368 (S.D.N.Y. 2003).

Loffreda, Beth. *Losing Matt Shepard: Life and Politics in the Aftermath of Anti-Gay Murder.* New York: Columbia University Press, 2001.

Lott, Eric. "The Wages of Liberalism: An Interview with Eric Lott." *Minnesota Review,* Winter 2005, http://www.theminnesotareview.org/ns63/lott.htm.

Lunt, Peter, and Paul Stenner. "*The Jerry Springer Show* as an Emotional Public Sphere." *Media, Culture & Society* 27, no. 1 (2005): 59–81.

Lutz, Catherine, and Lila Abu-Lughod, eds. *Language and the Politics of Emotion.* Cambridge: Cambridge University Press, 1990.

Mansbridge, Jane. "Reconstructing Democracy." In *Revisioning the Political,* ed. Nancy Hirschmann and Christine Di Stefano. Boulder, Colo.: Westview Press, 1996.

Marcus, George. *The Sentimental Citizen: Emotion in Democratic Politics.* University Park: Pennsylvania State University Press, 2002.

Martin-Barbero, Jesús. *Communication, Culture, and Hegemony.* London: Sage, 1993.

Massumi, Brian. *Parables of the Virtual: Movement, Affect, Sensation.* Durham, N.C.: Duke University Press, 2002.

Matsuda, Mari J., Charles R. Lawrence III, Richard Delgado, and Kimberle Crenshaw. *Words That Wound: Critical Race Theory, Assaultive Speech, and the First Amendment.* Boulder, Colo.: Westview Press, 1993.

McChesney, Robert. "The Problem of Journalism: A Political Economic Contribution to an Explanation of the Crisis in Contemporary U.S. Journalism." *Journalism Studies* 4, no. 3 (2003): 299–329.

———. *Rich Media, Poor Democracy: Communication Politics in Dubious Times.* New York: New Press, 1999.

McPherson, Tara. *Reconstructing Dixie: Race, Gender, and Nostalgia in the Imagined South.* Durham, N.C.: Duke University Press, 2003.

Mehl, Dominique. "The Public on the Television Screen: Toward a Public Sphere of Exhibition." *Journal of Media Practice* 6, no. 1 (2005): 19–28.

Minow, Martha. *Breaking the Cycles of Hatred: Memory, Law, and Repair.* Princeton, N.J.: Princeton University Press, 2002.

Morrison, Toni. *Playing in the Dark: Whiteness and the Literary Imagination.* Cambridge, Mass.: Harvard University Press, 1992.

Mouffe, Chantal. *The Democratic Paradox.* London: Verso, 2000.

Nelson, Dana. *National Manhood: Capitalist Citizenship and the Imagined Fraternity of White Men.* Durham, N.C.: Duke University Press, 1998.

Newcomb, Horace, and Paul M. Hirsch. "Television as a Cultural Forum." In *Television: The Critical View,* ed. Horace Newcomb. 5th ed. New York: Oxford University Press, 1994.

Nichols, Bill. *Representing Reality.* Bloomington: Indiana University Press, 1991.

Nussbaum, Martha. *Upheavals of Thought: The Intelligence of Emotions.* Cambridge: Cambridge University Press, 2001.

———. *Hiding from Humanity: Disgust, Shame, and the Law.* Princeton, N.J.: Princeton University Press, 2004.

Okin, Susan Moller. "Reason and Feeling in Thinking about Justice." *Ethics* 99, no. 2 (1989), 229–49.

Omi, Michael, and Howard Winant. *Racial Formation in the United States: From the 1960s to the 1990s.* 2nd ed. New York: Routledge, 1994.

Ontario Consultants on Religious Tolerance. "'Ex-gay' Advertisements: In Newspapers & on TV." Religious Tolerance.org, 2002, http://www.religioustolerance.org/ hom_ads.htm.

Osiel, Mark. *Mass Atrocity, Collective Memory, and the Law.* New Brunswick, N.J.: Transaction, 1997.

Ott, Brian, and Eric Aoki. "The Politics of Negotiating Public Tragedy: Media Framing of the Matthew Shepard Murder." *Rhetoric & Public Affairs* 5, no. 3 (2002): 483–505.

Ouellette, Laurie, and James Hay. *Better Living through Reality TV: Television and Post-Welfare Citizenship.* Malden, Mass.: Blackwell, 2008.

Paget, Derek. *No Other Way to Tell It: Dramadoc/Docudrama on Television.* Manchester: Manchester University Press, 1998.

Parker, Ian, ed. *Social Constructionism, Discourse, and Realism.* London: Sage, 1998.

Perry, Barbara. *In the Name of Hate: Understanding Hate Crimes.* New York: Routledge, 2001.

Perlman, Allison. "Feminists in the Wasteland: The National Organization of Women and Television Reform." *Feminist Media Studies* 7, no. 4 (2007): 413–31.

Peters, John Durham. "Distrust of Representation: Habermas on the Public Sphere." *Media, Culture & Society* 15 (1993): 541–71.

———. *Speaking into the Air: A History of the Idea of Communication.* Chicago: University of Chicago Press. 1999.

———. "Witnessing." *Media, Culture, & Society* 23, no. 6 (2001): 707–24.

Petersen, Jennifer. "Media as Sentimental Education: The Political Lessons of HBO's *Laramie Project* and PBS's *Two Towns of Jasper.*" *Critical Studies in Media Communication* 26, no. 3 (2009): 255–74.

Probyn, Elspeth. *Blush: Faces of Shame.* Minneapolis: University of Minnesota Press, 2005.

Reeves, Jimmie. "Re-Covering Racism: Crack Mothers, Reaganism, and the Network News." In *Living Color: Race and Television in the United States,* ed. Sasha Torres. Durham, N.C.: Duke University Press, 1998.

Rentschler, Carrie. "Witnessing: U.S. Citizenship and the Vicarious Experience of Suffering." *Media, Culture & Society* 26, no. 2 (2004): 296–304.

Rothenbuhler, Eric. *Ritual Communication: From Everyday Conversation to Mediated Ceremony.* London: Sage, 1998.

Rushdy, Ashraf. "Reflections on Jasper: Resisting History." *Humanist* 60, no. 2 (2000).

Sarat, Austin, and Thomas Kearns, eds. Introduction to *History, Memory, and the Law.* Amherst Series in Law, Jurisprudence, and Social Thought. Ann Arbor: University of Michigan Press, 1999.

Scheff, Thomas J. *Microsociology: Discourse, Emotions, and Social Structure.* Chicago: University of Chicago Press, 1990.

Schudson, Michael. "Why Conversation Is Not the Soul of Democracy." *Critical Studies in Mass Communication* 14, no. 4 (1997): 297–309.

Sedgwick, Eve Kosofsky. *Touching Feeling: Affect, Pedagogy, Performativity.* Durham, N.C.: Duke University Press, 2003.

Sedgwick, Eve, and Adam Frank, eds. *Shame and Its Sisters: A Sylvan Tomkins Reader.* Durham, N.C.: Duke University Press, 1995.

Sherwin, Richard. *When Law Goes Pop: The Vanishing Line between Law and Popular Culture.* Chicago: University of Chicago Press, 2000.

Silverstone, Roger. *Media and Morality: On the Rise of the Mediapolis.* Cambridge: Polity Press, 2006.

Singer, Ben. *Melodrama and Modernity.* New York: Columbia University Press, 2001.

Slotkin, Richard. *Gunfighter Nation: The Myth of the Frontier in Twentieth-Century America.* New York : Atheneum, 1992.

Solomon, Robert. *The Passions.* Garden City, N.Y.: Doubleday, 1993.

———. *True to Our Feelings: What Our Emotions Are Really Telling Us.* Oxford: Oxford University Press, 2007.

Sontag, Susan. *Regarding the Pain of Others.* New York: Picador, 2004.

Stabile, Carol. *White Victims, Black Villains: Gender, Race, and Crime News in U.S. Culture.* New York: Routledge, 2006.

Stein, Laura Lynn. *Speech Rights in America: The First Amendment, Democracy, and the Media.* Champaign: University of Illinois Press, 2006.

Sturken, Marita. *Tangled Memories: The Vietnam War, the AIDS Epidemic, and the Politics of Remembering.* Berkeley: University of California Press, 1997.

Temple-Raston, Dina. *A Death in Texas: A Story of Race, Murder, and a Small Town's Struggle for Redemption.* New York: Holt, 2002.

Texas House Committee on Judicial Affairs. *HB 938 Public Hearing*, 76th Legislature, March 11, 1999. Audiocasettes.

Texas House. Floor Debate. *HB 938*, 76th Legislature, April 27, 1999. Audiocassettes.

Texas House. *Interim Report to the 77th Texas Legislature*. Committee on Judicial Affairs, December, 2000.

Texas Legislature. *HB 938*, engrossed version. 76th Legislature, 1999.

———. *HB 587*, enrolled version. 77th Legislature, 2001.

Texas Senate Committee on Criminal Justice. *938 Public Hearing*. 76th Legislature, May 6 and 13,1999. Audiocassettes.

Tigner, Amy. "*The Laramie Project*: Western Pastoral." *Modern Drama* 45, no. 1 (2002): 138–56.

Tompkins, Jane. *Sensational Designs. The Cultural Work of American Fiction, 1790–1860*. Oxford: Oxford University Press, 1986.

———. *West of Everything: The Inner Life of Westerns*. New York: Oxford University Press, 1992.

Tronto, Jane. *Moral Boundaries: A Political Argument for an Ethic of Care*. London: Routledge, 1993.

*Two Towns of Jasper.* Produced and directed by Whitney Dow and Marco Williams. PBS, 2002. DVD.

U.S. Census Bureau, Fact Finder, Census 2000, http://factfinder.census.gov/home/saff/main.html?_lang=en.

U.S. Department of Justice, Bureau of Justice Assistance (BJA). Wyoming's Methamphetamine Initiative: The Power of Informed Process, May 2001, http://www.ncjrs.org/pdffiles1/bja/186266.pdf.

Van Zoonen, Liesbet. *Entertaining the Citizen*. Lanham, Md.: Rowman and Littlefield, 2005.

Warner, Michael. "The Mass Public and the Mass Subject." In *Habermas and the Public Sphere*, ed. Craig Calhoun. Cambridge, Mass.: MIT Press, 1992.

———. *Publics and Counterpublics*. New York: Zone Books, 2005.

West, Cornel. "The Role of Law in Progressive Politics." In *The Politics of Law: A Progressive Critique*, ed. David Kairys. 2nd ed. New York: Pantheon Books, 1990.

———. "Christian Love and Heterosexism." In *The Cornel West Reader*, ed. Cornel West. New York: Basic Civitas Books, 1999.

White, Hayden. *Tropics of Discourse*. Baltimore: Johns Hopkins University Press, 1986.

Williams, Linda. *Playing the Race Card: Melodramas of Black and White from Uncle Tom to O. J. Simpson*. Princeton, N.J.: Princeton University Press, 2001.

Williams, Patricia J. *The Alchemy of Race and Rights*. Cambridge, Mass.: Harvard University Press, 1991.

Williams, Raymond. *Marxism and Literature*. Oxford: Oxford University Press, 1977.

Williamson, Larry. "Racism, Tolerance, and Perfected Redemption: A Rhetorical Critique of the Dragging Trial." *Southern Communication Journal* 67, no. 3 (2002): 245–58.

Winant, Howard. *The New Politics of Race*. Minneapolis: University of Minnesota Press, 2004.

*Wisconsin v. Mitchell,* 508 U.S. 476 (1993).

Wood, Amy Louise, *Lynching and Spectacle: Race and Violence in America, 1890–1940*. Chapel Hill, N.C.: University of North Carolina Press, 2009.

Wood, Jennifer. "Justice as Therapy: The Victim Rights Clarification Act." *Communication Quarterly* 51, no. 3 (2003): 296–311.

Woodward, Gary. *The Idea of Identification*. Albany: State University of New York Press, 2003.

Yaeger, Patricia. "Consuming Trauma; or, The Pleasures of Merely Circulating." In *Extremities: Trauma, Testimony, and Community*, ed. Nancy K. Miller and Jason Tougaw. Champaign: University of Illinois Press, 2002.

Young, Iris Marion. *Justice and the Politics of Difference*. Princeton, N.J.: Princeton University Press, 1990.

———."Asymmetrical Reciprocity: On Moral Respect, Wonder, and Enlarged Thought." *Constellations* 3, no. 3 (1997): 340–63.

———. "Impartiality and the Civic Public: Some Implications of Feminist Critiques of Moral and Political Theory." In *Feminism, the Public and the Private*, ed. Joan Landes. Oxford: Oxford University Press, 1998.

———. *Inclusion and Democracy*. Oxford: Oxford University Press, 2000.

Zelizer, Barbie. "From Home to Public Forum: Media Events and the Public Sphere." *Journal of Film and Video* 43, no. 1–2 (1991): 69–79.

———. *Remembering to Forget: Holocaust Memory through the Camera's Eye*. Chicago: University of Chicago Press, 1998.

———. *Taking Journalism Seriously: News and the Academy*. Thousand Oaks, Calif.: Sage, 2004.

Žižek, Slavoj. *The Fragile Absolute; or, Why Is the Christian Legacy Worth Fighting For?* London: Verso, 2000.

# Index

affect: affective media theory, 10; affective orientations, 11, 14; biological aspects of, 173n23; defined, 11; formation of publics and, 58; justice claims and, 15, 119–21, 148–50; legislation as "affective work," 62–64, 83–85, 90, 153–54; melodrama as medium for, 119, 131–33, 149; politics of affective discourse, 70–77, 82–83; structures of feeling and, 173n22; as technology of belonging, 27, 144. *See also* emotional discourse; feeling

affiliation (with victims): as Byrd/Shepard media component, 7–8, 20, 57–58; emotion as fundamental to, 10, 58; local vs. national affiliation, 65–66; logic of mourning and, 18, 160; melodrama and, 97–98; as political discourse component, 155; public sphere communication and, 13; qualities of sympathetic victims, 158–59; Shepard link to anti-gay violence, 30–31; tolerance rhetoric and, 43–44, 57–58, 77–82; victim distancing and, 44–45, 51–52, 103. *See also* class; gender; inclusion/exclusion; proximity/distance; race; sexuality; victimhood discourse

Ahmed, Sara, 11, 48, 173n25

American Civil Liberties Union (ACLU), 125

American Jewish Congress, 125

Anderson, Brete, 168

anti-gay sentiment: anti-gay Shepard protests, 25; Byrd Act anti-gay vandalism testimony, 133; conservative politics and, 67; "gay panic" discourse, 31–32, 189n20; as hate crime, 24; Laramie anti-gay graffiti, 71–72; libertarianism and, 70; lobbying/education efforts against, 135; media discussion of, 30–31; scapegoating and, 3, 42–44, 46; "special classes" political argument and, 77–84, 174n38. *See also* sexuality

Aoki, Eric, 42

Arendt, Hannah, 8

Armey, Dick, 67

Aryan Brotherhood, 106–107, 185n37

atrocity. *See* suffering

attachment. *See* affiliation

Austin (Texas), 21, 47, 109, 140

Bederman, Gail, 177n27

Bell, Bob, 78, 79, 86–87, 168

Berlant, Lauren, 15

Berry, Shawn, 94, 105–107

Black Muslims, 95

Brewer, Russell, 94, 105–107

Broussard, Paul, 139, 187n2, 189n39

Bush, George W., 3, 124, 126–28, 130–31, 136, 143–44

Butler, Judith, 148

Byrd family, 3, 129–31, 143–44

Byrd Foundation for Racial Healing, 15

Byrd, James, Jr.: designation as hate crime, 94, 132, 134–35, 183n7; funeral of, 95, 160; melodrama as narrative response, 19, 93, 96–99, 104–105, 119; murder of, 1, 92, 94, 110, 183n4; as symbolic figure, 20, 102–103; tributes to, 3, 152; visual imagery of, 102

Byrd, Jamie, 95

Byrd, Ross, 130

Byrd, Stella, 129–31, 144

care: ethics of care, 155; expressions of care, 82–89, 157; as political value, 159–61, 165

Casper (Wyoming), 36, 39, 68–69

Castor, Robert, 49–50

Cheyenne (Wyoming), 47, 68–69

Chisum, Warren, 126, 145–46, 148, 169, 189n20, 190n55

Christian, Wayne, 130–33, 139–40, 145, 147, 169

civil rights discourse, 27, 72, 84, 92, 132–33

class: Byrd killers and, 107; class prejudice of the 1990s, 100; Laramie class depiction, 40–41, 50–51; media audiences and, 55–56; rationality as class-free functionality, 9; Shepard victimhood and, 3–4, 39–42; Sulk

feminism: affective media theory and, 10; crimes against women and, 153; melodrama and, 98; rationality/emotionality dichotomy and, 12–13

Foxx, Virginia, 152

Fraser, Nancy, 13, 191n18

Furphy, Dan, 85, 168

Gaddis, Tom, 69

"gay panic" discourse, 31–32, 189n20

gender: crimes against women and, 153; hegemonic masculinity, 38; melodrama and, 97; metrosexual gender identity, 38, 177n34; mythology of the American West and, 34–35, 86–87, 177n27; public/private dichotomy and, 45; rationality/emotionality dichotomy and, 12–13, 85, 174n32; Shepard masculinity, 36–40. *See also* affiliation; sexuality

graffiti, 71–72

Graham, Allison, 117

Gray, Guy James, 99, 115–19

Greenburg, Sherry, 139

Gross, Daniel, 174n32

Guinier, Lani, 100

Habermas, Jürgen, 8, 9, 59, 163, 172n14

Haggerty, Bern, 65–66, 68, 74, 156, 168

Haggerty, Pat, 134, 141, 169

Halberstam, Judith, 35

Hale, Tim, 79–80

Hardy-Garcia, Dianne, 134–35, 139, 144, 147, 168

Harrington, Jim, 136, 141, 148

hate crime legislation: Byrd/Shepard as symbols for, 3, 24, 152; civil remedies as component of, 17, 147; civil rights discourse and, 27, 72, 84; constitutional tests of, 132–33; critical scholarship on, 16–17; emotional discourse in, 5, 15; equal protection principles in, 61, 77–82, 108–109, 112–14, 132–33, 145–46; "hate crime" media coverage as precursor, 16, 24; law enforcement training as component of, 17, 61–62, 88, 147, 157, 189n39; penalty enhancement focus of, 147–48, 191n9; physical violence as scope of, 17; political efficacy of, 153–56; religious support for, 80; reporting of hate crimes as component of, 49–50, 61–62; "special classes" political argument, 77–82, 125–26, 132–33, 139–41, 145–47, 162–63, 174n38. *See also* James Byrd Jr. Hate Crimes Act; law; Matthew Shepard and James Byrd, Jr. Hate Crimes Prevention Act; political action

hate crimes: anti-gay violence as, 24; marginalized groups as fundamental component,

153–54; as news frame, 16, 67, 167–68; visible affiliation and, 6, 135–42

hate groups: Aryan Brotherhood, 106–107, 185n37; Byrd killers identified with, 94–95, 183n4; homophobia attributed to, 31–32; white supremacist groups, 105–108, 125, 145, 158, 183n4. *See also* Ku Klux Klan; racism

hegemony: circulation of shame and, 48–49; hate crime legislation and, 16–17; hegemonic masculinity, 38; national loss as official discourse, 26–27

Henderson, Russell: class depiction of, 41–42; explanations for Shepard killing, 43–44; as Shepard killer, 1, 24, 31; trial of, 69, 74, 76; Western motif and, 36

Hochberg, Scott, 130

homophobia: anti-homophobia initiatives, 44; Byrd mourning effect on, 134; distancing of, 46, 51–52, 87; libertarianism and, 70; media depiction of, 31–32; response to Shepard mourning, 25; scapegoating and, 3, 42–44, 46

homosexuality. *See* sexuality

Horn, R. C., 117

Hurd, Jeanne, 65, 68, 74, 168

Hutchinson, Kay Bailey, 95

identification (of hate crimes), *See* reporting

identification (with crime victims), *See* affiliation

imagined community, 10–12, *See also* publics

inclusion/exclusion: exclusionary discourses, 3–5, 58, 158–59; local vs. national affiliation, 65–66; mourning as occasion for, 27–28; Shepard hate-crime narratives and, 32–33; Shepard masculinity and, 36–39. *See also* affiliation

infotainment, 7

intimidation, 17

Jackson, Jesse, 95

James Byrd Jr. Hate Crimes Act: Byrd photo used for, 102; cultural mapping and, 21; hate crime bill of 1993, 124–25, 128; inclusion of sexuality in, 67–68, 125–28, 135–36, 142–43, 145–46; melodramatic narrative as influence in, 19; passage of, 18, 124–28, 148–49, 188n3, 190n55; as redistribution of political resources, 156; terms of debate of, 123. *See also* hate crime legislation; Texas

James Byrd Jr. Racism Oral History Project, 15

Japanese Americans, 84

Jasper (Texas): Byrd funeral and burial, 115, 140, 187n65; history and economy of, 108–109; Laramie distancing from, 73; minority

population, 94, 183n5; "Old South" geographical positioning, 109–119; reconciliatory projects in, 16; response to Byrd murder, 1–2, 18; segregated cemetery in, 130, 187n65; views of Berry as killer, 106–107. *See also* cultural geography
*Jasper, Texas* (movie), 113, 117, 168
Jensen, Carol, 80–81
Johnson, Patrick, 133, 138, 168
journalism: crime news, 104; depiction of Laramie/Wyoming, 49–51; depiction of Shepard, 39; documentary film, 176n20; geographical distribution of Byrd coverage, 103–112; geographical distribution of Shepard coverage, 25–26, 65; *Laramie Project* television airing, 54–55; letters to national vs. local newspapers, 46–47; local specificity of print news, 26, 40–41; mainstream Byrd murder coverage, 2–3, 92–96; "mainstream media," 184n23; mainstream Shepard murder coverage, 2–3, 24, 27–28, 32–33, 36–37, 40–44; media reform strategies, 7; melodramatic narrative structure in, 19, 93, 96–99, 104–105, 119; network television Shepard murder dramatizations, 25–26, 38; news audiences, 4, 25, 28, 45, 73–74, 103–105, 117, 121–22; as public sphere component, 8–9; "show the world" local-to-national relationship, 73–77, 84–85; television vs. print, 102–106

Kaufman, Moisés, 54–56
King, Bill, 94, 99, 105–107, 112–13, 121
King, Joyce, 168, 185n37
King, Rodney, 71–72, 100, 106
kinship, 30, 44, 45, 57, 60, 159
Koziak, Barbara, 84–85, 90, 161
Ku Klux Klan, 2, 106–107, 131, 145, 189n20, 190n53

Lamb, Christin, 53
Laramie Bias Crimes Ordinance: affect as impetus for, 61–64, 70–71, 75–77, 82–83; debate/discussion of, 69–70, 73–75; equal rights principles in, 61, 77–82; history of passage of, 64–71, 82, 87; impact on residents, 88, 156–57; Laramie Coalition arguments for, 71–72; Laramie demographic recognition in, 56; local agency in, 74; political community important for, 58; text/substance of, 62, 68–69, 76; Wyoming state-level hate crime legislation, 67–68
Laramie Coalition, 64–65, 68–69, 71, 76, 87
Laramie (Wyoming): author's association with, 21; circulation of shame in, 46–47; class depiction of, 40–41, 50–51, 53, 55,

178n42; cultural geography of, 35–36, 45–46; mythology of the American West and, 34–36, 39, 44, 46, 49, 65, 82–83, 85–87; reconciliatory projects in, 16; "Resolution of Sympathy" passage, 64; response to Shepard murder, 2, 18, 47–54, 61, 66–67. *See also* cultural geography; Laramie Bias Crimes Ordinance; Laramie Coalition
law: emotion in the law, 5, 13, 15–16, 129, 153–54, 182n59; emotional mediation and, 70–71, 89–91, 153, 160; as form of recognition, 17, 148; legislation as "affective work," 62–64, 83–85, 90, 153–54; as a limitation on political action, 148–49; neutrality and, 117–19, 141, 162–63; political action and, 90, 149; social role of, 16–17, 89, 156; "special classes" political argument, 77–82, 125–26, 132–33, 139–41, 145–47, 162–63, 174n38; whiteness and, 117–19, 121. *See also* criminal justice system; hate crime legislation
Lee, Benjamin, 28
Lesbian/Gay Rights Lobby of Texas (LGRL), 125, 128, 188n5
LGBT movement: anti-gay violence as public education issue, 135; hate crime legislation effect on, 89; Laramie Coalition contact with, 65, 68; Laramie protest by, 24–25; lawmakers' discomfort with LGBT issues, 147; same-sex marriage initiatives, 70, 89, 148, 155, 181n22; "special classes" political argument and, 77–79; support for Texas hate crime legislation, 125, 128. *See also* gender; queer theory; sexuality
liberalism: Byrd murder as equal protection failure, 108–109, 112–14, 132–33, 145–46; defined, 32; Laramie Bias Ordinance debate and, 70, 73, 77–82; *Laramie Project* role, 56–57; liberal tolerance as Shepard framework, 32, 43–44, 46–47, 57–58, 82–83, 89–90; public feelings and, 45–46; rationality associated with, 7–9, 58–59, 154, 162, 172n17, 174n32; sexuality issues as component of, 65–66; "special classes" political argument and, 77–82
libertarianism, 70, 86
local publics: circulation of shame in, 46–47; formation of, 65–66; local newspapers as media filters, 26; "show the world" local-to-national relationship, 73–77, 84–85; as site for emotional mediation, 5–6, 75, 88–89. *See also* community
Lockwood, Jeff, 65–66, 68, 74, 168
Loffreda, Beth, 47, 181n30
*Losing Matt Shepard* (Loffreda), 47
Lott, Trent, 67
lynching, 15, 33, 96, 98

**Jennifer Petersen** is Assistant Professor of Media Studies at the University of Virginia, where she researches and teaches on the role of media in the public sphere, the philosophy of communication, and the mediation of public trauma. Her work has appeared in a number of scholarly journals, including *Media Culture and Society* and *Critical Studies in Media Communication*.